*f*P

Shut Up,
I'm Talking

And Other Diplomacy Lessons
I Learned in the Israeli Government

A MEMOIR

Gregory Levey

Free Press
New York London Toronto Sydney

Free Press
A Division of Simon & Schuster, Inc.
1230 Avenue of the Americas
New York, NY 10020

This work is a memoir. It reflects the author's present recollections of
his experiences over a period of years. Certain names and identifying
characteristics have been changed.

First Free Press hardcover edition April 2008

FREE PRESS and colophon are trademarks of Simon & Schuster, Inc.

For information about special discounts for bulk purchases,
please contact Simon & Schuster Special Sales at 1-800-456-6798 or
business@simonandschuster.com

Manufactured in the United States of America

1   3   5   7   9   10   8   6   4   2

Library of Congress Cataloging-in-Publication Data

Levey, Gregory.
Shut up, i'm talking: and other diplomacy lessons I learned in the Israeli
government, a memoir / Gregory Levey.
p. cm
1. Levey, Gregory. 2. Jews—Canada—Toronto—Biography. 3. Jews,
Canadian—Israel—Biography. 4. Speechwriters—Biography. I. Title.
F1059.7.J5L485 2008
327.56940092—dc22
[B]
2007039783

ISBN-13: 978-1-4165-5613-8
ISBN-10:   1-4165-5613-3

For Abigail, of course.

Contents

If you're going to tell people the truth, you'd better make them laugh. Otherwise, they'll kill you.

—George Bernard Shaw

Author's Note

As I write this note, things don't look good in the Middle East. I'm not sure when you're reading this, but I assume that things still don't look good in the Middle East, because they never really do. If things looked good in the Middle East, it wouldn't look like the Middle East. It might look like, say, Canada, with camels.

But things are always *interesting* in the Middle East. And relevant. Like it or not, the Israeli-Palestinian situation—along with the situation in the wider region, of course—is intricately tied to the credibility of the United States and to worldwide security. There are countless vantage points from which to look at the region, but my hope is that providing an account of my own bizarre experience—which I have tried to set out as faithfully as the significant limitations of memory allow—will bring some measure of clarity to one aspect of the situation.

Or at least show that, along with the tragedy, there are moments of comedy. Israelis frequently deal with their difficult situation by laughing about the absurdity that surrounds them. There is no reason outsiders should not do the same. Sometimes it is the comic details that best reflect the gravity of the larger picture.

G. L.
Paris, 2007

Shut Up,
I'm Talking

Foreword

I was twenty-five years old and not even an Israeli citizen, but as a result of a bizarre series of events, I was sitting alone at the State of Israel's seat at the United Nations General Assembly, minutes before a vote on a U.N. resolution.

Worse still: I had no idea how Israel wanted to vote, and very little concept of what the vote was even about.

How on earth had I ended up in this situation?

I looked at the Irish representative on my left and the Italian one on my right. Each of them was much older than me and had several assistants sitting with him. More importantly, they both clearly knew how their governments wanted them to vote. At very least, unlike me, they were citizens of the countries that they were representing.

For something like the tenth time, I called the office of the Israeli ambassador on my cell phone and asked to speak to someone who could give me instructions, but the terrible phone reception at the United Nations meant that I got cut off before I could get any help. Again. I looked across the room at the diplomat representing the United States and thought that maybe I should just vote however he did, since Israel often followed the lead of its closest ally.

Then I looked at the door leading out of the large hall, and thought that maybe a wiser option would be to run and not look back. I thought of that famous story from the middle of the Cold

War when Nikita Khrushchev took off his shoe and angrily banged it on the table at the United Nations. I considered doing the same, for no reason other than delaying the vote.

I could see that the voting was about to begin, and I quickly tried my cell phone again. This time, miraculously, I got through to someone with authority at the Israeli Mission.

"They're going to vote," I whispered urgently, trying to keep my voice down so that the Irish and Italian representatives wouldn't recognize the fact that I was an idiot.

"Who is this?" the voice on the other end of the phone said.

At this point, I came perilously close to throwing my cell phone across the room. *Or maybe,* I thought, *I should slam my phone down on the table instead of my shoe.*

"It's Greg," I answered. "I'm at the General Assembly, and there's going to be a vote."

"A vote? A vote on what?"

"On resolution number"—and I told him the specific resolution at hand.

"What is that?" he asked.

"I don't really know," I answered. "I was hoping that maybe someone there had some idea of what it was, and could tell me how I should vote."

"I'll look into it, and call you back," he said, and immediately hung up.

The chairman presiding over the meeting called it to order, and began the prevoting procedure. I waited anxiously for the cell phone gripped tightly in my right hand to ring, the fingers of my left hand hovering uncertainly over the voting buttons before me.

1

There Must Be Something Wrong with You

When people ask me how I wound up writing speeches for the Prime Minister of Israel during one of the Middle East's most turbulent times, my usual answer is, "Just bad luck, I guess." This is mostly a joke. Although the two and a half years I spent as a speechwriter for the Israeli government were a sometimes rocky—and always very strange—ride, I feel privileged to have contributed to Middle Eastern diplomacy in some small way. This is the story of a typical twentysomething New Yorker who accidentally stumbled into the nerve center of the Israeli government—and an account of all that I saw along the way before realizing that I really had no business being there.

My story begins, to put it bluntly, with an overwhelming sense of boredom: I was in law school.

By the outset of my second year of law school, I had decided that I needed a break. At the end of the school year I would take some time off, leave New York, and volunteer to serve in the Israeli army. My reasons for this were somewhat complicated, but anyone who's ever gone to law school will understand when I say that, at the time, the risk of being shot at or blown up by Islamic Jihad, or perhaps kidnapped by the Hezbollah and taken to Iran to be tortured and murdered, seemed almost preferable to the notion of continuing to suffer through another semester of classes.

In a way I blame my parents. Their decision to enroll me in Jewish day school two decades earlier had set me on a path that would, almost inevitably, lead me either to law school or to the Israel Defense Forces. That said, I'm pretty sure they were hoping I'd stick with the former.

A few years before I was born, my parents—South African Jews with no real connection to Israel—had decided that Johannesburg was not the place they wanted to raise children, and began looking at other options. One of these was Israel, and in the mid-1970s, they spent a few weeks exploring the country, with an eye to relocating. As a place to live, it was not to their liking. They roamed around, desperately looking for a place where they could see themselves setting up a home, and found that there wasn't any. Also, my mother later told me, they "couldn't stand the rudeness of the people." Finally, instead of a desert land of ill-mannered people who had opinions about everything, they settled in a snow-covered land of cloyingly polite people who had opinions about nothing. Canada.

But the school my parents eventually sent me to in Toronto, Bialik Hebrew Day School, harked back to their abortive Zionist experiment. It was somewhat anomalous as far as Jewish elementary schools go in that it focused almost entirely on Zionism and Israel, instead of on religion. Every day, we would dutifully rise to sing the Israeli national anthem, unaware of the incongruity of singing the song against the snowy Canadian backdrop outside. Along with our regular studies in math and English, we would then spend about half the day studying Modern Hebrew, Israeli history, and even Zionist literature. Since we didn't know anything different, this all seemed normal to us, even if, when the school day ended, we went off to watch American television or play hockey with our friends from public school, the day's Zionism forgotten until the next morning, when we would again rise for the national anthem of a foreign country.

Every year we would spend a few days putting together little gift packages for Israeli soldiers, and writing cards to them to express our gratitude—for exactly *what* I don't think was ever made quite clear to us—and once a year an entertainment troupe from the Israeli military would visit our school to perform for us, just as they did for the troops back at home.

For some reason—probably because at six years old I was extremely excited about the idea of seeing honest-to-god soldiers—I still remember the first time this group came to visit us. We were ushered into the hall and given the impossible instruction to stay quiet until the show began. Beside me sat a boy named David, who, like me, was very eager to see the soldiers we had heard so much about: fearsome, proud, and strong Jewish soldiers who had come from so far away to showcase their skills for us. As we sat there, waiting for the older children—who seemed in no rush to see the performance—to file in behind us and be seated, we chatted quietly about what we were about to witness.

"No," he told me, continuing the discussion we had been having since much earlier that morning, "there is no way that they will have guns."

"But then how can they be soldiers?" I pressed.

"They have guns at home, but you can't bring them on a plane with you!"

"You can," I insisted, almost lecturing him, "if you are a soldier."

This argument persisted until it was announced that the show was about to start, at which time we quieted down, gripping the seats of our rickety metal chairs and leaning forward in breathless anticipation.

The curtains parted—which is to say that a teacher pulled them aside—and standing on the makeshift stage was a group of men and women in army uniforms. I was disappointed to see that they were not only unarmed, but weren't even wearing helmets.

"They're not even wearing helmets!" I whispered to David, who didn't respond.

And then, instead of gunfire or explosions, or whatever it was that we were expecting, music—of all things, music—started to play. Even worse, the soldiers started to dance around the stage, singing the same inane Hebrew folk songs that our teachers had been trying to shove down our throats for some time already. They pranced and jumped around, shaking tambourines in a manner that infuriated me.

What kind of soldiers were these?

This was my first experience with the Israeli army and at the time it seemed, well, just a little bit fruity.

Beyond the somewhat flamboyant soldiers, my only other childhood experiences with Israelis were with the teachers at my school, who seemed far more dangerous, and far less merry, than the visiting soldiers. I don't know if the school actually chose its faculty from those Israeli women who were deemed too cruel to serve as jailers for Palestinian prisoners, but it certainly seemed like it.

My parents and the parents of my friends would sometimes tell us that in the future we would look back fondly at these Israeli teachers and the way they treated us, grateful to them for making us tougher and more studious. It's now been over twenty years, and I'm still waiting for those warm feelings to set in. These teachers would berate us, insult us, even put down our families in front of our friends, and in doing so, they provided me, and many of my peers, with our first impressions of Israelis. It didn't produce particularly robust feelings of ethnic solidarity.

The worst of these teachers, whom we referred to—in timid, hushed tones—simply by her appropriately sinister last name, Witchler, had apparently been in some kind of hard-core combat unit of the Israeli military. Or so the stories floating around suggested. Once, though, some of my schoolmates supposedly saw some confirmation that the rumors might actually have been true.

They were on a class trip to New York City, and had stopped at a pay phone near Times Square so that Witchler could call back to the school. Suddenly, in front of the group of frightened thirteen-year-old Canadians, a large man ran at her and grabbed her purse. Witchler would have none of that, though, and angrily ripped the purse back from him so forcefully—she was a big woman—that the would-be purse snatcher fell to the sidewalk in front of her. As the story was repeated to me several times afterward, she then began to beat the unlucky man with her purse while she waited for the police to arrive. Another teacher who saw this incident apparently later said that he actually "felt sorry for the poor man."

Although I had plenty of contact with Israelis—or at least with this particular type of Israeli—I don't think I ever met an Arab during my childhood. At least I don't remember meeting any. They didn't make up a big part of the student body at Bialik Hebrew Day School.

The *idea* of Arabs, though, was ever present in our classrooms, although we were really not accustomed to thinking of them as three-dimensional people. To us they were more or less just the villains of the Zionist stories told to us—not real humans so much as cartoonish "bad guys," similar to the biblical enemies of Israel we were taught about, or even to the Nazis, whose presence seemed to hover above all the lessons we received.

The first time I remember the Palestinians being mentioned at all was in the third grade, when a teacher—second only to Witchler in notoriety, and later actually forced to resign because of allegations of misconduct—brought up the Palestinians in a discussion about Israel. After she had told us a little about some acts of terrorism perpetrated against Israel, one of my classmates asked about the Palestinians' motivations.

"They don't want us to have a country of our own," she told us. "They want our land for themselves."

We were silent for a few seconds, struggling to digest what seemed to us like an obvious absurdity in Palestinian psychology.

"What do you think of that?" the teacher asked, but no hands went up.

She surveyed the room and suddenly, for some reason, she looked straight at me. Staring up at her as she leaned threateningly above me, I thought, *Good God, no!*

"Greg," she said. "What do you think about this?"

I really didn't know what I thought about this. In fact, I didn't actually think about this at all. Nervously, I tried to decide what to say. I was immediately close to tears, which was the state I always seemed to be in during my encounters with these Israeli teachers.

"Well," I began slowly, "do they have their *own* country?"

On my part, this was an honest question. I had absolutely no idea what a Palestinian even looked like, let alone the status of their national sovereignty. But the teacher obviously didn't see it that way. Her face darkened, her brow furrowed, and she walked quickly across the classroom toward me. I had clearly not said the right thing. My first thought was that she was going to strike me in some way, and I leaned back in my chair to avoid the blow.

There was a dangerous silence that seemed to last forever. The teacher appeared to be considering how she would most enjoy hurting me.

"They have twenty other countries!" she shouted angrily, her voice echoing through the room and out into the hallway, while I cowered in front of her. "They have twenty other countries! We have just one!"

With this, she regained her composure and backed away from my little desk. It is not as if I had any idea that she might be conflating Palestinians with other Middle Eastern Arabs, and implicitly denying the existence of a separate Palestinian nation. I was just glad that

I had not been smacked by her, and was more than happy to accept whatever she told us.

That incident more or less summed up the rest of my time at Bialik Hebrew Day School.

When I attended public high school afterward, Israel faded far into the background and didn't really cross my mind for months at a time. During college, it stayed mostly off my radar as well, and only after I had moved to New York in my early twenties, during the Second Intifada, did I really start to pay attention to it again.

In those days, Palestinian suicide bombers were blowing up Israeli buses and cafés on a frighteningly regular basis, and Ariel Sharon's military was retaliating hard. It was difficult *not* to pay attention to it, especially living in the politically charged climate of post-9/11 New York City. I started to spend a fair amount of time following events in the region, reading up on it, even visiting Israel for the first times on a couple of short organized trips. I recognized that there was deep complexity in the situation, but perhaps partly because my school lessons were so ingrained in me, I almost instinctively took the Israeli side of the conflict.

I bore no grudge against the Palestinians whatsoever, and earnestly believed that the solution to the conflict was for them to have a real state of their own. I thought that the Jewish settlers were not helping the issue at all, but not having yet examined the situation fully, I didn't really think that they were the root of the problem either. I did, however, have serious misgivings about their religious take on Zionism. Although I had grown up in a family that was vaguely observant of the most basic of Jewish customs, by the time I had begun high school, I was a declared agnostic, and by the time I had reached college, I was very firmly an atheist. And when Israel came back into focus for me during the Second Intifada, and I began to root for the country from the sidelines, my distaste for religion didn't diminish at all. For me, Zionism was based on simple, secular Jewish nationalism, the idea that the Jewish people should have a national home like any other people, that that home should be in the land that was, at least in part, historically theirs, and that they should be allowed to fight to defend it. I didn't trust anyone who put a religious spin on it, but I also didn't trust anyone who denied that basic claim.

But by the end of my first year of law school, boredom—a much more powerful force than mere ideology—had me in its grasp. Studying literature in college, I had hoped to become the next Ernest Hemingway or James Joyce. Instead, I now found myself studying corporate tax law; the tedium was driving me crazy, and, still following the news from the Middle East daily, I gradually decided that my ticket out was the Israeli army. I would volunteer for one year of service, and by doing so not only get a break from torts and contracts, but also have my first real adventure—certainly Hemingway would approve of that.

So, in October of that year I signed up online for an army program especially designed for foreign volunteers. The website told me that I was required to be in Israel in May to study Hebrew before undergoing basic training and then being posted in the field for a year's worth of combat duty.

Just a few clicks of the mouse, and it was all settled. I leaned back in my chair, looked at the screen in front of me, and suddenly my textbooks on corporate law seemed a lot less important than they had before—which, to be perfectly honest, wasn't all that important.

In the meantime, I knew that I still had many months ahead of me filled with the monotony of law school, and with Israel on my mind, and hearing about my classmates all doing various internships and externships to gain practical experience, I decided to apply for an internship at the Israeli Mission to the United Nations. I had a master's degree and was almost halfway through a law degree, so I thought I had a reasonable chance of getting a part-time internship at the Mission to help pass the time until my departure date.

I went to the Mission's website, and emailed the general address listed there. After a week I had received no response, so I called the number on the site. Reaching the secretary's answering machine, I politely listed my name and number and stated that I was interested in an internship. Again I waited a week and got no response. But if law school had taught me anything, it was that no ocean is crossed without a bridge of paperwork, so I faxed a letter to the number listed on the site, waited another week, and got no response. This went on for a few months, and I became convinced that they didn't need or want interns, but I stubbornly refused to give up until I was informed of this fact directly.

Finally, during one of my phone calls, I spoke to an operator at the Israeli consulate who didn't really understand English at all, and seemed to think I was a journalist. After a minute or two—probably mostly just to get rid of me—she transferred me to a woman at the U.N. Mission who dealt with the media. Her name was Maya and she was later to become a colleague of mine, but at this point she was just confused as to why I was calling her.

"I don't really know why they transferred me to you," I told her. "I think they thought I was a journalist, but—"

"Yes," she said. "I'm the one who deals with journalists."

"Well, I'm not a journalist," I told her.

"Then why are you calling me?"

"Look," I said, "I'm trying to apply for an internship at the U.N. Mission. I've been trying to apply for about two months now."

Perhaps sensing the irritation in my voice, she assured me that if I faxed my résumé directly to her, she would pass it on to the right people. It had taken me a long time to reach anyone there, much less to get any information, so I was grateful just to speak to her.

Of course, even after faxing my résumé to Maya, I still didn't hear from anyone. So I decided to give up the whole idea, and left for Christmas break.

But shortly after I returned to New York in January, I was sitting on the couch in my apartment, with the latest dreary law school readings on my lap, when my cell phone rang.

"Hello?" I answered.

"George Levey?" asked a man with a thick accent that I did not immediately recognize.

I hesitated.

"Do you mean *Gregory* Levey?"

"No, eh, it says *here* George Levey."

"Well, my name is Gregory Levey."

"Eh, hold on," he said, and disappeared. I waited for what seemed like a very long time and was debating hanging up the phone when he came back.

"Eh, Gregory," he said, with no apology. "This is Yaron, from Israeli security."

"Hello."

"I, eh, need to ask you some questions."

There was no explanation, no information, not even really a request—just, more or less, a demand. But I had nothing to hide.

"Okay," I said, and when he asked me his first question, it sounded like he was shuffling documents, probably my CV.

"You live on the Thirteenth Street?"

"Yes."

"What number?"

"Two twenty-four."

"What side of the street is that?"

"What?"

"Is that on the north or south side of the street?"

I had no idea what the point of this question was, unless he was planning to visit me, but I answered nonetheless, "South."

"It's on the south side?"

"Yes."

"Gregory, eh, you are sure?"

"Yes."

"Okay."

And it proceeded like this. The questions on this first call were basically just confirming some of the details on the résumé, but Yaron informed me that he would probably be calling back with more questions in the near future, which he did—*almost every day for the next two weeks.*

I also got a call from the deputy ambassador's secretary informing me that I would have a meeting with him after this security check was finished, which made Yaron's calls more understandable, if no less maddening. At least once a day, sometimes more, Yaron's calls came in, increasingly intrusive and weird. It got to the point where I would be in a cab or walking down the street, and when my cell phone would ring, I would answer it, "Hey, Yaron. What's up?"

"Hi, George," he would respond. "How are you?"

Then he would ask me about the Jewish summer camp I attended as a child, or the classes I had taken in college, or even, again, what side of the street my apartment was on. The reasoning behind a few of the questions was clear, but a lot more of them didn't seem relevant at all and I could not see their connection to any security risk I might pose.

Sometimes, in response to a question that seemed particularly frivolous, I wanted to ask, *Yaron, does that really matter, or are you just being nosy?*

I imagined him answering, *No, you're right. I didn't really need to ask that. I was just curious.*

But I answered the questions fully and patiently, and eventually this security check was completed and I was invited to the Mission to meet the deputy ambassador.

I dressed in a conservative suit, took the subway to Grand Central station, and walked a few blocks to the address they had given me. The Mission, along with several other Israeli offices, was housed in the New York consulate. It was a large square building with no real indication that it belonged to Israel unless you strained your neck upward to see the Israeli flag waving atop it. Also, if you looked carefully at the plant boxes arrayed in front of the building, you could tell that they were actually cement blocks to protect against car bombings—not the kind of thing sported by the typical New York office building.

Inside, quite obviously guarding the elevators, was an enormous man with a totally shaven head. Israeli security. At first I thought that he must have been at least three times my size, but as I got closer to him, I decided that was probably an underestimate. He wore a dark suit and tie, and the way he held himself—feet apart, his gigantic arms folded in front of him—seemed to say, *Good morning! I'm a secret agent!*

I stopped in front of him and said, "Hello."

He said something in Hebrew that I didn't understand at all, and when I just looked at him in confusion, he said in heavily accented English, "Your ID."

"Oh," I said. "Sure."

I fumbled in my pockets for my passport and handed it to him. He opened it to the photograph and then glanced up at me, with a look that said, *Both you and I know, of course, that I could crush you.*

As he examined the passport for what seemed like an unnecessarily long time, I couldn't help but compare him to almost every other Jew I had ever known. First of all, he was the combined size of entire families with whom I was acquainted. He also readily exuded the threat of violence. I was quite sure that nobody who had attended Bialik Hebrew Day School with me had grown up to be anything like this.

"Why are you here?" he asked.

"For an interview for an internship."

"With who?"

"Ambassador Mekel."

At this point, still holding my passport tightly, he looked down at me with half-squinted eyes. I couldn't tell if he was suspicious or just trying to scare me, and I decided to just stare back at him. We squared off like that for a few seconds until he was confident that he had driven home his main point (which was that he could crush me).

Once it was clear that I had received the message, he handed me back my passport and told me what floor to take the elevator to. Then he folded his arms in front of him again, watching me as I got on and pressed the button. As the doors closed, he was still staring me down, and if my quickened heartbeat was any indication, his intimidation tactics were working just fine.

When the elevator doors opened and I stepped out, I found myself in a sort of antechamber. Two heavy metal doors looked firmly locked. Behind a thick glass window sat another, somewhat smaller security guard in a suit.

"I'm here for an interview," I told him.

"Give me your ID."

I slid it through a little slot at the base of the window, and he examined it studiously. He then picked up a phone and called someone else, speaking in rapid Hebrew.

"Go through that door," he instructed me, pointing at one of the two doors that flanked his window and pressing a button that released the door lock for me. I went through the door, expecting to be inside the halls or offices of the consulate. Instead I found myself in an even smaller room, this one dominated by a large walk-through metal detector of the type you find in airports. There was yet another locked door in front of me, and on my right another thick glass window looking onto the security guard's desk. There was another suit-wearing security guard in the room with me. He asked me to empty my pockets.

He took my wallet and, as he spoke to me, started going through every card and piece of paper in it.

"Gregory," he said. "It says on your CV that you speak a little Hebrew."

A bit taken aback by the continuous layers of questioning, I nodded. I noticed that he was actually holding a copy of my CV in one of his hands.

"Where did you learn this Hebrew?"

"I only know a little," I told him. "I learned it in school as a child, but I've forgotten most of it."

"What was the name of the school?" he asked.

I thought that this was getting sort of ridiculous, but answered. "Bialik Hebrew Day School."

He had now finished going through my wallet and, apparently finding nothing of note, handed it back to me.

"Pass through the metal detector," he told me, and I did. It did not buzz or make any other kind of sound, but he started frisking me carefully anyway. When he found nothing on me, he nodded at his colleague behind the glass, who buzzed me through the second door. I was finally in the consulate itself.

A woman about my age was waiting for me.

"Gregory, follow me," she said immediately, not bothering to introduce herself.

I followed her up a narrow staircase, down a long nondescript corridor, and into Ambassador Mekel's office. It was a large corner office with a big wooden desk, shelves full of books about the Middle East, a conference area with some couches and plush leather chairs, and a framed picture of Prime Minister Ariel Sharon hanging on the wall.

Ambassador Mekel was a stocky man in his late fifties with crinkly gray hair, large glasses, and a crooked smile. My first impression of him, though, had nothing to do with his personal appearance, and everything to do with the fact that it looked like he was precariously close to tipping over. Mekel's feet were both on the desk, but not in the usual relaxed, reclining manner. Rather, one foot was perched on the edge so that, because he was sitting very close to the desk, it was essentially resting on his chest; the other was splayed out far to his left. It was hard to say if his center of gravity was actually on his chair or on his desk, or somewhere else entirely, and so my immediate impression was that he was about to fall to the floor. When a second or two passed and he didn't fall, I realized that he had for some reason put himself in this position intentionally.

I'd done my research. Ambassador Arye Mekel, Israel's deputy permanent representative to the United Nations, was a man with a long and distinguished career of public service. At various times he'd served as a foreign policy adviser to a prime minister, as the head of Israel's state TV and Radio Authority, and in a variety of consulates and embassies around the world. *And apparently,* I thought as I reached out a hand to greet him, *he is also some kind of contortionist.*

Mekel adjusted his precarious position somewhat in order to shake my hand.

"It's an honor to meet you, sir," I said, but he brushed this off with a dismissive gesture, as if to tell me not to waste time with pleasantries.

The first thing he said to me was: "You look perfect on paper, so there must be something wrong with you."

I was not quite sure how to respond to this, and stared at him blankly, trying to think of a witty retort.

"Why are you here?" he asked me, after he had deduced that no witty retort was forthcoming.

"What do you mean?"

"You're applying for an internship?"

"Yes," I said, nodding.

He glanced down at my résumé on the desk in front of him, then looked up at me again.

"We don't offer internships," he told me.

Oh, wonderful, I thought. *Then what exactly am I doing here?* Why had I been put through their intense security procedures? And why did some disembodied voice named Yaron now know the names of most of my childhood friends, my opinions on the different law school classes I was taking, my sexual preferences, and the nationality of my roommate? I fought the urge to start yelling incoherently out of sheer frustration.

Ambassador Mekel asked, "Do you want a job instead?"

"Pardon me?" I replied, thinking I had misheard him.

"The chances of you getting a job here were exactly zero," he told me, which I thought was strange after he'd seemingly just offered me a job. "There is generally no chance for a résumé to reach me, and if it does, I usually just throw it away."

He paused to gauge my reaction. I must have looked like someone trying hallucinogenic drugs for the first time.

"I don't know how it got to me in the first place, or how you got in the door," he continued. "Normally I throw these things out without looking at them. It just so happens, though, that our speechwriter is leaving soon. Would you like to come on as a sort of deputy speechwriter on a part-time basis, and then if everything goes well, this summer you will become the actual speechwriter and take over?"

Slightly frazzled and more than a little bit shocked, I didn't know what to say.

Mekel smiled in obvious amusement, and repeated, "Because we don't offer internships."

I accepted Ambassador Mekel's offer, but told him that as a Canadian, I was not eligible to work in the United States. He shook his head before I even finished the sentence and said, "I can hire anyone I want. We'll just change your status from student to diplomat."

So that was it. From the U.S. State Department's point of view, I was going to be an Israeli diplomat, even though I wasn't an Israeli citizen. It was hard to take it all in. I had come in just hoping to get an internship.

There were still a few more details to deal with. First, a committee interview that Ambassador Mekel assured me was just a technicality, and then a much more intense security check, which could take up to a few months.

I was ushered into a small office, where one of his staff members was sitting, and told to wait there for the committee interview to start. I sat down and introduced myself. Almost immediately, the staffer volunteered that one of the people who would be at my committee interview was "a total bitch."

"I don't even know why she is part of the committee interview," he said. "She works for the consulate, not the Mission, and she's the biggest bitch you'll ever meet."

I wasn't sure how to respond to this. Was this some kind of intricate test of my social skills? I just smiled slightly, and nodded. I had no idea at this point that this was nothing more than typical Israeli directness, which can be a bit startling to North Americans accustomed to cordial pretense.

The woman in question would, in fact, turn out to be one of the most unpleasant people I had ever encountered. Without a doubt, "total bitch" was an accurate description. I was told that she was an administrative diplomat for the Israeli Foreign Ministry. When I heard her name I remembered that she had been one of the people I had called during my months of trying to find an internship. She had obviously just ignored my phone call.

In the committee interview, she sat directly to my right, leaning toward me in what seemed like a hostile manner. Also present were Ambassador Mekel and another diplomat. The difference between their behavior and hers during this meeting couldn't have been more stark. Whereas they would ask relevant job-interview-type questions like "What is your writing background?" and "Are you going to be able to handle the stress of this particular job?," she would ask things like "What is the big story in New Jersey politics these days?" and "Could you please give me a brief rundown of the United States' involvement in the Second World War?"

Her curt manner seemed to say: *Clearly this person does not know anything about the United States' involvement in the Second World War. Look at him. He doesn't even know how to put on a tie properly.*

I remember this question about the Second World War in particular because it made me think of high school history class discussions in which I'd wondered along with my classmates what the point of those classes were when they clearly would never help us get jobs. Outside, I did my best to keep a straight face.

I suppose that my answers satisfied her or, as actually seems more likely after having gotten to know her since then, that she herself had no idea what the correct answers were. Possibly, as Ambassador Mekel had said, this interview was more of a technicality anyway. In any case, after the other diplomat—for no apparent reason and with no explanation—briefly tested my very mediocre ability in French, they told me that the job was mine and that all I had to do now was get my security clearance.

In a state of mild shock, I went home to digest it all. I had no idea what lay in store for me.

2

The Only One Who Turns Me On

A few days after I was offered the job, the security people responsible for the Mission called me to arrange a "security interview." They told me that during this meeting I would be asked some questions to "get to know me better." Ominously, they refused to say how long the meeting would last.

Once more I had to face the giant bald man in the foyer, who again asked for my passport before allowing me in. If he remembered me, he certainly didn't let on. I then had to pass through the metal detector and the frisking again, and, as before, the whole procedure seemed unnecessarily long. This time, once all the obstacles had been overcome and I was inside, I was ushered into a little conference room and told to wait for the security agent responsible for my file. He eventually arrived, and after introducing himself and shaking my hand, he proceeded to close a latch on the door, effectively locking us in and anyone else out.

DID YOU JUST LOCK ME IN? I felt like shouting, but resisted, since it wouldn't have helped my chances of getting my security clearance.

Although much smaller than the behemoth in the lobby, my interviewer had the same shaven head and dangerous air about him. But, at first anyway, he seemed pleasant enough, welcoming me and asking if I wanted anything to drink.

Then the questions began, and suddenly Yaron's daily telephone inquisition seemed like polite chitchat. I was asked about all of my friends and family ("Tell me about your father"), about ex-girlfriends ("Explain to me why you didn't break up with her earlier"), alcohol use, drug use, gambling, petitions I had signed, and demonstrations I had attended. I couldn't help but laugh a little at some of his questions and about his reactions to some of my answers.

When he asked me about alcohol, for example, I told him that I drank occasionally, and he asked me what my favorite liquor was.

"Whiskey," I said.

"But whiskey is very harsh," he replied.

"I guess so."

"I don't like whiskey," he informed me. I wasn't sure exactly how I was supposed to respond to this, but he paused for a long while, seemingly waiting for me to change my answer to strawberry daiquiris. I said nothing.

He then asked whether I had any connections to mysticism, terrorist groups, extremist organizations, or cults. This last item—cults—was another question that made me laugh a little, particularly as my questioner came back to it several times, as if he had some information that I was in fact involved in a cult of some sort.

"Gregory, are you sure you understand what a cult is?" he asked me, after I had already told him that I was not a cult member. He clearly had not ruled out the possibility that he was dealing with an idiot, and not just any idiot, but one who might, in fact, be a member of a cult.

"Yes," I told him, smiling a bit. "I know what a cult is."

"And you are sure you have never been a member of one?"

I waited for a second or two before answering so as to suggest that I was considering my past carefully, and that my answer would be based on all the evidence available to my clearly limited intelligence.

"Yes, I am sure I have never been a member of one," I told him.

He didn't seem fully convinced, but moved on anyway. He asked whether I had any medical problems, whether I had taken any psychiatric medication, whether I had seen a psychologist, and several vague questions about how I dealt with stress and pressure.

After about two hours of this, he told me that for the next six weeks or so, "agents in the field" would investigate my story, my answers, and my life. My expression must have betrayed how foreign all this was to me. He smiled at the look on my face, and volunteered that even he did not know exactly what these agents did or how they did it.

So I went home, and for the next two months, I imagined that every Middle Eastern–looking person on the street was spying on me, every click on my phone was a wiretap, and every action of mine was being watched. I expected men in dark suits to visit my parents' home or the workplaces of my close friends. Instead there was nothing, or at least nothing noticeable—either they were very good at what they did, or as I increasingly suspected, they weren't doing anything at all.

Later, when I was finally working at the Mission, I spoke to an eighteen-year-old college student who was doing an internship with the Israeli consul general, and he told me that his security interview had left him spooked for weeks. While the person who interviewed me was relatively friendly and not particularly intimidating—except in the absurd amount of detail he wanted to know about my life— this intern had had a very different experience.

The security agent who interviewed him was a six-and-a-half-foot Russian Israeli, with a thick Russian accent. At first, though, despite his imposing appearance and manner, this interviewer had seemed very pleasant and spoke in a soft and reassuring tone.

"We are very open-minded," he said. "We just want to know the truth about your life and your past. It doesn't matter what you have done—we just want you to be open with us. Be honest and everything will be all right."

Suddenly, the intern told me, the Russian's voice got louder and sterner, and as he smashed his hand violently down on the table, he near-yelled, "THE ONLY THING WE WILL NOT TOLERATE IS LIES!"

He continued speaking loudly and angrily for the next two hours. The easy, relaxed attitude of the first minute of the interview had apparently been some sort of ruse.

Still another colleague had been subjected to an even stranger security interview. Whereas my interviewer had asked a little bit about past romantic relationships and why or how they had begun or ended, he had not asked for too many particulars. My friend's interviewer had demanded far more intimate details. My favorite of his questions was "Tell me—have you ever engaged in any abnormal sexual conduct?"

I suggested that my friend should have paused thoughtfully for a moment, asked, "Could you define abnormal?," and then touched the interviewer's leg.

After about six weeks of waiting, I received a phone call to say that my security clearance had come through. I was delighted, and very eager to start my new job. The secretary on the phone told me that Ambassador Mekel wanted to talk to me first thing in the morning on the day that I started. This sent my imagination spiraling. Would he reveal some hidden truth to me? Something top secret about the Israeli government?

"It's true," I pictured him saying. "Jews do control the media."

Or maybe even: "The Holocaust? We made that up."

I arrived at the Mission on my first morning in a brand-new suit, very excited to be there, and went into his office. Once again he was twisted into an impossible position in his chair, his left leg this time resting on the floor but pushed out far to one side and his right leg on the desk and bent so that his knee was almost touching his shoulder. I was pretty impressed with his flexibility.

At this first official meeting, I expected some serious briefing about what was happening in the Middle East or at the United Nations, an explanation of the responsibilities of my job, or even just some sort of introductory discussion. Instead, Ambassador Mekel told me an incredibly dirty joke—one totally inappropriate for inclusion here, but involving a beach, a genie, and a man whose wife didn't satisfy him.

After the joke, Ambassador Mekel gave me a very brief talk about how I should go about learning my job by shadowing the current head speechwriter and reading past speeches written at the Israeli Mission. He then passed me over to the Mission coordinator, Avi, an Israeli a few years older than me, whose job it was to handle the logistics of the Mission's daily activities. Avi gave me a tour of the Mission before showing me to my office. The Mission occupied one floor of the consulate building, with two halls lined with the offices of the diplomats and support staff. At the end of one hallway was the office of the ambassador. At the end of the other was the office of the deputy ambassador. My own office was tucked away in a corner between the bathrooms and the computer department. It was a very tiny room that not only had no windows, but was also lacking a doorknob, which I noticed as I was shown inside and had to open it by wedging my fingers through a little hole in the wood.

"Yeah," Avi said. "That."

When I took over the head speechwriter's position, he told me, I would move to a better office.

"In the meantime," he said, "hopefully you will also get a doorknob."

"That would be very nice," I told him.

"I'll put in a request," he said, "but let me warn you—things here take a long time to get done."

He smiled broadly at this revelation for several seconds, but didn't expand on it.

Avi left me alone, and I sat down in my chair with a folder of past speeches, trying to get my mind around the fact that this was real. I had brought two books with me, and I took them out of my bag and put them on the shelves in the corner. The first was a collection of some of history's most famous speeches, given to me as a congratulatory gift by my roommate Meny, an old friend of mine from Toronto. It had the inscription, "I know that you have always wanted to be the *smell* of our people, but for now, you will have to be satisfied with being the voice of our people. Hopefully this book will help you."

The second book was a Hebrew–English dictionary purchased for a Hebrew class I had been taking. Since the vast majority of people who worked at the Mission were Israeli and the working language was Hebrew, I'd started taking Hebrew classes three times a week.

Because I'd scheduled my law classes at night so that I could start work when my clearance came through, my Hebrew classes had to be at lunchtime. It turned out that the other people taking Hebrew classes in the middle of the day in New York were very old women.

Not everyone in the class was ancient, but the next youngest person to me was probably in her early sixties. The average age was somewhere in the seventies, and there were one or two women well over eighty. And yes, they were all women.

The whole thing was a bit awkward, but there were some particularly bizarre moments. Once, one of the women returned from a vacation to Israel with a box of Israeli chocolate. She distributed some to everyone, saying, "For your grandchildren." When she got to me, she said, "For *you*, Greg!" and, in addition to the chocolate, gave me a lollipop.

"Thank you," I said, looking down at the lollipop in front of me—I was the only one who had been given one—and at the old women arrayed around the table, smiling broadly at me. *I'm twenty-five!* I wanted to yell.

Another time, I was in the elevator after a class with one of my classmates on the older side of the spectrum.

"Greg," she said. "I have a question for you."

I had dealt with Israeli security's questions, so I figured I could deal with anyone's.

"Yeah?"

"Well," she said. "I have a granddaughter who just graduated college and came back to New York."

"Oh," I said, already queasy about the direction this conversation was taking. Although I was most definitely single, and always on the lookout for potential girlfriends, I still wasn't keen on being set up by grandmothers.

"She went to Cornell," she said. "That's Ivy League!"

"Yes." I nodded. "I know."

"Now, hold on," she corrected herself. "Actually, only part of the school is Ivy League. Part of it is not."

I nodded again, anxiously waiting for the elevator to reach the lobby.

"But she was in the Ivy League part."

"Uh-huh."

"But she hasn't been in the city for four years now, so she needs to make some new friends. I thought maybe you'd like to take her out."

"I'd love to," I told her. "I'm just very busy at the moment—with law school and everything."

She paused for a moment, clearly disappointed.

"Education *is* the most important thing"—she nodded—"but if you have time in the future, you must let me know."

We often performed little skits in class to practice our Hebrew, and whenever one called for a male part, the teacher assigned it to me. Many of the skits involved romantic dialogue or love scenes. In one interminably long scene where both parties pledged their undying love and devotion, I was reading opposite Ellen, who was well into her eighties.

In front of the rest of the class, we read the syrupy dialogue to each other. Then we did it again, translating to English as we went.

"You are the only one I long for," I told her as earnestly as I could.

"You are the only one I desire," she responded.

"You don't understand," I said. "You're the only one I could ever be with."

"I understand," she responded in her raspy Queens accent, "for you are truly the one that is made for me."

I looked at her, hunched over in front of me, the pages pressed up close to her wrinkled face so that she could read them. If any of my friends—investment bankers and medical students—knew how I passed my days, I would never live it down.

Things became worse when Ellen, who was straining her eyes even to read the words, came across a phrase that she translated as "You are the only one who lights up my world."

"No," the teacher said. "That's not quite the right translation. Can anyone figure out what the real meaning is?"

The rest of my geriatric class leaned forward, carefully examining the Hebrew script in front of them. It suddenly dawned on me, with a bit of horror, what the phrase meant, and I found myself forced to look toward this very old woman, bent over the page, still straining her eyes to read it, and say, "It means that I am the only one who turns you on."

"Exactly," the teacher said. "It means that Greg is the only one who can turn Ellen on."

These were awkward times.

But when my security clearance finally came through, it felt a bit like I was saying good-bye to my grandmother—only in plural. These women, though so much older than me, were the kind of

Jews I had always known. Had I actually met their granddaughters, they would probably have been exactly like the girls I had gone to school with back at Bialik Hebrew Day School in Toronto. Their world was one that I shared.

I knew, though, that I was now going to be surrounded by Jews of a wholly different kind, Jews whose world was entirely foreign to me.

So there they were on my shelf: the book of collected speeches and the Hebrew dictionary. And in that weird little office, with no windows and no doorknob, I sat down to sort through the file of previous speeches, statements, and official letters.

After a few days, they all began to blend together. Hezbollah or Hamas or Islamic Jihad or Fatah had shot at, bombed, tried to shoot, or tried to bomb Israeli targets, and Israel's ambassador to the United Nations, Dan Gillerman, was urging the international community to insist on the dismantling of terrorist organizations and a renewal of the peace process. Alternatively, Israel had taken some sort of military action against Palestinian or Hezbollah targets, the U.N. Security Council had been called to address the situation, and Ambassador Gillerman was explaining Israel's actions.

It became somewhat monotonous, and as I read the documents, there was a frequent distraction: *the constant screaming from down the hall.*

I had no idea who was screaming, or what they were screaming about, but every hour or so, I would hear the muffled sound of somebody screaming loudly and angrily. The first few times I ignored it, figuring that it was none of my business, but by the morning of the second day, I began venturing gingerly out into the hallway whenever I heard it. I stood out there, and was able to determine the direction from which the screaming was coming, but still not which office. The hallway itself was always completely empty.

It took me about a week of sneaking out of my office and down the hallway to locate the source. Eventually, I discovered that it was coming from behind the closed office door of the Mission's librarian, a man Avi had introduced me to during my tour of the Mission. Avi had told me then that the librarian served as our researcher and archivist. If I needed any documents, I was to call on him.

I had realized within a few days, however, that this was only marginally more useful than asking the watercooler to retrieve documents for me. Within my first two weeks there, in fact, I actually helped *him* find something, and when I told one of my new colleagues about this, he nodded knowingly. Nobody could quite figure out the librarian's purpose, I was told, or what he had been doing for twenty years.

The librarian had been at the U.N. Mission longer than anyone else in the history of the State of Israel—roughly two decades. He had seen ambassadors come and go, including one who would go on to become the prime minister of Israel, and had served through several wars and two Palestinian Intifadas. He had outlasted everyone else, and though he was well into his sixties, it seemed that he would outlast all of us as well. All this was impressive. The only problem was that nobody seemed to know what he actually *did*.

Much later on, in fact, a little birthday party was held for the librarian, and Ambassador Dan Gillerman, ever the diplomat, made a speech in which he said, "To be perfectly honest, I don't really know what you do all day, but I'm told you must be doing a good job. If you weren't, I'm sure something would go wrong here at the Mission."

Whatever he was doing in there, he seemed to consider it very important, even top secret. Unlike most of the offices in the Mission, which had regular doorknobs (or mine, which had no doorknob whatsoever), the librarian's door had a large bolting mechanism with a code, so that only he could open it.

"But there is no reason for that," Avi told me. "There is no reason why his door has to be closed all the time either. And nobody knows why he needs a code and all this security—it's just that he was here before anybody else and set it all up at some point. What the hell is going on in there?"

Now and then I would walk by the librarian's office just as he was coming or going to his strange little room, and I'd try to sneak a look inside to figure out why he needed so much privacy. The place was a ridiculous mess. There were books and papers piled everywhere, no empty tabletops, no order or organization of any kind whatsoever. Besides anything else—such as the fact that if his job was to keep ordered records, he was failing miserably—it was an enormous fire hazard. In fact, several times over the years, inspectors had come from Israel to survey the administration of the consulate building and had threatened to fire him if the room was not ordered in some way. After they left, though, nothing ever changed.

But the strangest thing about him was definitely the screaming. The librarian always seemed to be ridiculing the person he addressed; either he was yelling at himself and was filled with self-loathing, or he thought that whoever was on the phone was a complete imbecile.

Once I'd figured out who was doing the yelling, I asked Avi about it—perhaps there was some kind of under-the-table librarian diplomacy that occurred among the librarians of all the different U.N. Missions? He just shrugged his shoulders and said, "I have no idea who he's yelling at every day. To tell you the truth, I'm not even sure that he has a phone in there."

After about a week of familiarizing myself with both the documents and the screaming down the hall, the pattern of my days suddenly changed. One morning, Avi showed up at my office to take me on a tour of the U.N. itself.

Avi was about thirty, fit, and with a small build. He had been living in New York for many years already, and seemed to have adapted to it. Unlike, for example, the security personnel or Ambassador Mekel, he fit fairly neatly into the city's mosaic. Each morning before work he went to the gym, and arrived at the office listening to his iPod. He lived in Chelsea and often went to Broadway musicals. I had trouble picturing him in Israel or, actually, anywhere outside of Manhattan.

We walked out of the consulate building and toward the towering U.N. headquarters. It was only about a block's distance in physical terms, but I knew that politically it was light-years away.

"So," Avi said as we made our way there, "I still don't really understand how you ended up at the Mission."

"Yeah." I nodded. "Neither do I."

He laughed, then said, "Well, don't worry about it too much. Sometimes bad things just happen to good people."

Before I had a chance to explore this further, we had entered the U.N. grounds, and Avi announced, "You are no longer in the United States. You're now in international territory."

I considered this, watching a taxi speed by on First Avenue.

On the front grounds of the U.N. there was a large sculpture of a gun whose barrel had been twisted so that it would no longer work. Groups of tourists were taking pictures of one another in front of the sculpture.

There was also a very long line of them waiting to get into the building, each one having to pass through metal detectors first, but I followed Avi as he walked past the whole line, flashing the U.N. tag he wore around his neck.

"There's also a diplomat-only entrance," Avi told me as we walked into the palatial lobby of the United Nations. I had never been there before, even as a tourist, and I was duly impressed. The room was enormous and seemed calculated to make any individual feel like a small part of a larger whole.

"This is pretty cool," I said to Avi, sincerely.

"Don't let it fool you," he answered immediately, almost reflexively. "This place is falling apart."

Soon I began to see what he meant, at least in terms of the physical facilities. As we left the throngs of tourists in the lobby and entered the hallways and meeting rooms where the actual business of the U.N. took place, it seemed as if we were walking back into the past—or, rather, into a picture of what the past thought the *future* would look like. There was something of an imagined space-age quality to it all. The paint was peeling off the walls, the carpets were old and dirty, and the furniture looked like it had been purchased at yard sales.

I pointed at a pair of incredibly ugly bright orange vinyl chairs and said, "This stuff looks like something you'd find in my parents' basement."

Avi laughed. "To an Israeli, I think it looks like the kind of thing you store in your bomb shelter."

There were people in suits everywhere, some walking very quickly and urgently, others ambling along together, talking amiably. They all wore U.N. passes on chains around their necks, and on the passes it said what countries they represented. Within a few minutes, I saw people from dozens of countries, speaking numerous languages. At one point we passed a group of African delegates dressed in traditional dress, and Avi said, "The protocol is sort of that you can wear either a suit or your country's traditional dress."

He showed me the diplomat-only lounge, where all these diplomats congregated between official meetings and held less formal talks.

"Some of the most important things happen here, though," he said, and indeed, arrayed around the room were little clusters of diplomats, engaged in what looked like serious discussions.

For a few seconds I watched a diplomat who looked European holding a glass of wine as he talked to a small group of Asian diplomats in a hushed tone. Then my eye was drawn to an enormous tapestry that covered an entire wall. It showed the Great Wall of China in intricate color and detail.

"That tapestry's one of China's gifts to the U.N.," Avi said, and then explained, "All the countries give at least one gift. Like that twisted gun outside—that's Luxembourg's."

"That's a pretty nice gift," I said.

"Well, Luxembourg is very generous."

I laughed, and Avi added, "Wait until you see ours."

A moment later he stopped suddenly, and I looked at what appeared to be a big hunk of gray rock.

"Not quite as beautiful as China's gift, huh?" I said.

"Some people think that Israel could have done better than a rock," he answered.

The rock was obviously ancient, and had some Jewish symbols on it. A plaque next to it said that Prime Minister Ariel Sharon had personally sent it to the U.N. when he was Israel's foreign minister.

"I guess it has a message, though," I said.

"Everything here is political." Avi nodded. "Everything."

We got to a small, old-fashioned elevator operated by a man in a similarly old-fashioned uniform. He asked us which floor we were going to and pressed the button. I noticed that there were only four floors in this wing of the building.

"That's quite a job he has," I said to Avi, when we got off.

"It's pretty ridiculous," he agreed. "I think he's been there for like thirty years and isn't going anywhere anytime soon. Great benefits and salary, and a pretty easy and pointless job—at the expense of people all over the world."

We walked past a room that Avi said was the Security Council, the U.N.'s Holy of Holies. We couldn't go in because a meeting was in progress.

"Don't worry, though," he told me. "You'll spend a lot of time there, and eventually you'll be sick of it, like the rest of us."

Outside the room about a dozen journalists with cameras waited quietly behind a rope.

"They camp out here during meetings," Avi explained, "and then jump at the diplomats when they come out of the SC."

Next we went to the General Assembly hall. I was again a bit overwhelmed by the majesty of the U.N. It was exactly as I had seen it on television and in movies, with the desks for the various countries arrayed in neat rows in a sort of stadium-seating down toward where the secretary general sat. We went and sat down at Israel's table. On it there was a little microphone and a row of three buttons, and Avi explained that the microphone was for responding to speeches of other delegations and the buttons were for voting on resolutions: the green for yes, the red for no, and the yellow for abstain. There was even a big scoreboard that listed the votes.

"Up there"—Avi pointed at some glass booths near the ceiling of the huge chamber—"is where the interpreters sit."

He pointed at the earpieces at the table, and I put one in my ear. "You can listen to any speech in any of the U.N.'s six official languages," he explained. "You just turn the dial to whichever one you want."

I played with the earpiece dial for a few minutes, looking around the room and imagining the chaos that would be present when it was full.

"Oh, and see the jugs of water?" Avi asked, pointing at glass pitchers that sat neatly on every second desk throughout the room. "It used to be that there were two old women who went around delivering water to each delegate's spot. Then there was some kind of big commission established to cut costs at the United Nations, and they wasted a lot of money on that commission, and eventually one of the only decisions they made was to fire the old women, and that from now on, two delegates would have to share one jug of water instead of everyone getting their own. The commission itself wasted tons of money, and was essentially pointless."

"Like the elevator operator?"

"Exactly." Avi laughed. "You've come to a very strange place. I hope you're aware of that."

"I'm realizing that," I said. "A little more each day."

I sat for a few minutes looking out at the General Assembly hall, trying to take it all in. After a while I got up and walked down the aisle that ran between the different countries' seats, and made my way to the podium at the front of the hall where people made speeches. Avi followed me.

"That's where the ambassador will be delivering your speeches," he said, "right in front of where the secretary-general sits."

I looked back at all the seats behind us, where the various states' representatives would be when the speeches were delivered.

"Not intimidating at all," I joked.

"Why don't you go up there?" he suggested.

"Really?"

"Sure. Why not?"

So I climbed up to the podium—where so many historic words had been spoken, where presidents, prime ministers, and kings had stood—and stared out at the world, which was not, of course, actually there at the moment.

"Why don't the countries start at *A*," I said, suddenly noticing that they started somewhere halfway through the alphabet and moved backward from there.

"There's a lottery every year, I think," Avi said, "and the winner gets to be closest to the secretary-general. Then it's alphabetical from there."

I shook my head at how juvenile it all sounded, and he added, "I told you, *everything* here is political."

When we got back to the Israeli Mission, Ambassador Mekel happened to be in the hallway outside his office, and he beckoned us both in. He took a seat behind his desk and swung one of his legs on top of it awkwardly. Avi had no visible reaction.

"So did he give you a tour?" Mekel asked.

I nodded.

"I bet Avi doesn't seem like other Israelis you know," he said. "You see, I only hire Israelis here who understand America and the rest of the world, not those who just once visited a cousin in Long Island and so think they understand everything about this country."

I nodded again, unsure how I was expected to react to this.

"Look at him," Mekel continued, pointing at Avi. "He's more Chelsea than Chelsea."

I still wasn't sure what to make of this, and just continued sitting there.

"So what did you think of your tour?" Mekel asked.

"It was great. Very interesting. It's so amazing to be here. So thank you again."

"What did you see?"

"The Security Council was occupied," I told him, "but we pretty much saw everything else—the conference rooms, the General Assembly, the Delegates' Lounge."

"And?"

"And? It was great. Some of the art is great, even. I liked China's tapestry in the Delegates' Lounge especially—the one of the Great Wall."

"The Great Wall was designed to keep foreign invaders out," he said, "and to separate people from each other."

He swung his other leg onto the desk so that he was in full contortionist mode, then leaned back in his chair. "Think about it."

3

Damn! There's a Fish in My Pants!

I was sitting in my office one morning, listening to the librarian down the hall scream, when my phone rang.

"Greg, can you come?" a voice said when I answered, and immediately hung up. I would happily have gone to whoever it was who was summoning me, but unfortunately I had no idea who it was. Unsure what to do, I just stayed at my desk, and went back to listening to the screaming librarian.

A few minutes later, the phone rang again.

"Hello?" I answered.

"Greg, can you come?" the same voice said.

"Sure, but who is this?" I asked quickly, before he could hang up again.

"It's Antoni," he told me, and now I recognized the voice of one of the Mission's senior diplomats.

I walked past the librarian's office, where the screaming continued, and went into Antoni's office. It was a relatively big office, but seemed small because it was incredibly cluttered with papers and files. In one corner was a muted television showing an Israeli newscast, and on the wall was a framed and autographed photograph of Antoni shaking President George W. Bush's hand.

Antoni was an Israeli who had been born in Italy and raised by Italian parents. He spoke about four European languages, in addition to Hebrew and English, and had a sharp intellect. But organized he was not.

When he gestured for me to sit down, I hesitated because both the chairs he had for guests were covered with stacks of papers.

"Just move some of that stuff," he told me, and I lifted a stack of papers from one of the chairs and handed it to him. He put it squarely on his desk, teetering precariously atop the stacks of paper already there.

"Greg," he said, "I have an unusual request for you."

I nodded, waiting for him to go on.

"I have to be at two meetings at once this morning."

"That could present some problems," I said.

"Yes. So I need you to cover one for me."

"What does that mean exactly?" I asked, and he told me that I would have to go to a meeting of one of the U.N.'s main bodies—the Economic and Social Council—and serve as Israel's representative at the meeting.

"Nothing much is going to happen," Antoni said. "You just have to take notes about anything that comes up that might interest us."

To me, this seemed like quite an assignment this early on. I would be representing a sovereign state—of which I was not even a citizen—at the United Nations, and the responsibility seemed daunting, even if it sounded like I didn't actually have to do very much. And how was I going to know what might interest them? Wouldn't it make sense for someone to go with me my first time?

But I just nodded, trying to pretend that I wasn't unnerved.

Taking a notebook and the U.N. pass that I had recently been issued, I left the consulate building a few minutes later and headed toward the U.N. Once there, I realized that I didn't actually remember how to get to the room where the meeting was being held. At the thought of disrupting a U.N. meeting by coming in late, I became somewhat frantic to find it, dashing around the corridors in a decidedly undiplomatic manner.

I finally found the room and was relieved to see that the meeting hadn't started yet. It was sort of a miniversion of the General Assembly, with a seat for each country, but on a much smaller scale. There were people milling about everywhere, and nobody took much notice of me, as if in their minds I actually somehow belonged there.

I scanned the room to find Israel's seat. Antoni had explained to me before I left that at ECOSOC—the U.N.'s Economic and Social Council—Israel, like most countries, was just an observer, not a member. The members sat down below, and the observer states sat in alphabetical order in stadium-like seating around them. It only took me a couple minutes to locate our seat, but when I did I noticed something that worried me.

Whereas at most U.N. meetings, Israel was flanked by Ireland and Italy, at this meeting, Ireland was sitting down below with the other members. The placard directly to the left of my seat said THE ISLAMIC REPUBLIC OF IRAN. What's more, unlike at the General Assembly, where there was plenty of room between countries, here they were packed much closer together, so that Israel and Iran had to sit right next to each other. *This should be interesting,* I thought, making my way toward Israel's seat.

The Iranian delegate wasn't there yet, and I sat down in Israel's seat and carefully put the earpiece in. Other delegates were starting to sit down and do the same, and I was trying to convince myself that this was actually real—that I was sitting at the United Nations and representing Israel. Alone.

I happened to glance behind me, and noticed the woman sitting at the Netherlands' seat. She was the only other person in the room around my age, and she was very pretty. She saw me looking at her and gave me a wide, friendly smile.

Well, this is an interesting twist, I thought, trying to decide if maybe the United Nations was a good place to meet girls, and temporarily forgetting the whole awkward situation with Iran. That was the life with which I was more familiar, that of a normal single male in his midtwenties in New York, not of a diplomat for a foreign country.

I looked back at Iran's seat and saw that there was still nobody there, despite the fact that almost everyone else had taken their places. While I was looking at the Netherlands someone had passed out copies of the U.N.'s daily agenda, and I flipped through to the meeting I was attending. The list of speakers included Iran, which meant that its delegate would definitely be present.

The seat beside me remained empty as the chairman called the meeting to order. Other countries began giving speeches on the topic at hand, which was the economic aspects of peacekeeping operations. I took notes on everything I thought Israel might be interested in.

I looked back at the Dutch girl, who was busy scribbling notes on a legal pad. She noticed me watching her and looked up. She smiled again, and nodded. I nodded back, smiling as well.

Would an international romance be possible? I wondered, mentally playing with the term *diplomatic relations*.

The next speaker was called, and still the Iranian delegate was not beside me. According to the agenda, there was only one more speaker before Iran. When Thailand began speaking, and there was still nobody to my left, I really started to wonder what would happen.

Then the chair of the meeting said, "And now, the distinguished delegate from the Islamic Republic of Iran."

There was nothing for a second. Silence. Then the two rows in front of me all looked back to see who was sitting at Iran's seat, and because there was nobody there and I was sitting right next to the empty seat, they turned their gazes to me, as if expecting an explanation. I shrugged my shoulders. If they were looking for Iran, they were definitely asking the wrong country.

Another second of silence, and then I heard the Iranian delegate begin to speak over the speaker system. I looked down at where his plaque had been and suddenly noticed that it was gone; someone had walked by and taken it. Now that he was speaking I saw that he was sitting about ten seats away from me, completely out of alphabetical order—and completely breaking U.N. protocol. He had simply refused to sit next to Israel.

I glanced back at the Dutch girl and saw that she was watching. She had seen what had happened, and when I looked at her, she rolled her eyes at the Iranian's behavior.

I decided that when the meeting ended I would try to talk to her, and knew that this little incident would serve as the perfect fodder. When the speeches were over, though, she was approached by some other diplomats and engaged in discussion. Was she an actual diplomat, I wondered, or just a fraud like me?

When I returned to the Mission and sought out Antoni to give him my notes, I found him sitting with Ambassador Mekel. I told them both what had happened, and they laughed. They said that this was not typical, because usually Israel's enemies just didn't put themselves in positions where they could be seen to be openly breaking U.N. protocol.

"Have you ever thought," Mekel asked me, "that maybe Iran has no problem sitting beside Israel, and actually just doesn't want to sit next to *you*?"

"Greg," Antoni added, "did you take a shower today?"

They both laughed, and I left my meeting notes with them and went back to my office to think about the Dutch girl.

Right around this time, as I was being snubbed by foreign governments at work, I was also being snubbed by personal acquaintances at home: my roommate, Meny, decided to go back to Toronto, and moved out on me with very little notice. I needed to find a replacement for him before the next month's rent was due, but since I lived in a tiny basement apartment in Manhattan's East Village, there was little room for error when choosing a new roommate, and little room for anything else, for that matter.

My bedroom door couldn't fully open into the room because my bed was in the way; my bedroom window looked out at a brick wall; and you could easily reach into the kitchen fridge while still sitting on the living-room couch. We had a tiny patio out back—a luxury in Manhattan—but to get to it you actually had to crawl through the other bedroom's window.

Because of the close quarters, it was essential that I get along with my new roommate. I'd always had a list of traits I looked for in potential roommates: they had to be relatively intelligent, have a decent sense of humor, and be willing to keep the place tidy. But now that I worked for the Israeli government, I had a whole bunch of new factors to consider when screening applicants. After the intense security scans I'd been put through, I was certain that they'd want me to make sure the person I lived with wasn't going to present security issues, and given the nature of my everyday work, I also knew that it wouldn't be particularly pleasant to live with someone who had radically anti-Israel feelings. So I decided to look for the most apolitical roommate I could possibly find.

The roommate I wound up choosing was named Naoko. She was a Japanese girl the same age as me who had been living in the United States for ten years. A set designer for films, Naoko seemed as apolitical as New Yorkers get. To be on the safe side, though, I told her only that I "worked at the U.N.," without providing any more specifics. This seemed to satisfy any curiosity Naoko had, and she didn't ask any follow-up questions.

I thought nothing more about these security issues until a complication arose a little while later. I was at home doing some work for law school, and Naoko was making dinner for herself. She had assembled a collection of ingredients, all Middle Eastern, and was busily preparing some kind of salad. When I asked her where she had purchased the groceries, she told me the name of a Middle Eastern deli that she liked, and proceeded to assemble her dinner expertly. Offhandedly, I asked her where she'd learned so much about Middle Eastern cooking, and was a bit taken aback by her answer.

"Well, my dad lives in Syria," Naoko said matter-of-factly.

"Uh-huh," I said, trying to digest this answer.

I had no personal animosity toward the Syrian people or any of Israel's other enemies, of course, but I was aware that this little piece of information would not sit very well with the security officials at the Mission.

"Yeah," she said. "I just got back from visiting him in Damascus a few weeks ago. It's a beautiful city."

I nodded slowly. "That's what I've heard."

I watched Naoko slicing the vegetables and pouring on some kind of sauce, then asked, "What does he do there?"

"Oh, he works for a Japanese high tech company."

Okay, I thought, *that's no big deal. At least he's not involved in some sort of government work.* I was about to drop the subject, but just out of curiosity, I decided to ask one or two more questions.

"And how long has he been there?"

"Only a couple years," she told me.

Not terrible, I thought.

"And before that he was in Japan?"

Naoko shook her head. "No. Two years in Lebanon, and before that, five years in Saudi Arabia."

I dropped the conversation there. I wasn't a security screener for Israel, and since I hadn't yet fully picked up the paranoia of the security agents at work, I thought of this more as amusingly ironic than anything else. But when I casually joked about it to one of my officemates, she told me sternly that I should be very careful and that maybe I should talk to security about the situation.

Suddenly I couldn't help but look at Naoko with different eyes. I tried not to mention Israel around her, and didn't speak about work on the phone at home. Soon after these almost certainly ridiculous concerns began to dawn on me, I had a routine meeting with the deputy head of security for the Israeli consulate and U.N. Mission, and took the opportunity to ask him about the situation.

He questioned me a little about Naoko—how I had met her, what I knew of her, and so on—and then told me simply not to reveal that I worked for Israel. He instructed me to continue my story of "working for the U.N." around her. As I got to know Naoko better, my vague descriptions of my work began to seem a bit ridiculous, even to me, but what was funny was that Naoko never pushed me for any more information about what I did during the day. Wouldn't most people, I thought, be at least a little curious about the inner workings of the U.N.? It seemed that I'd really done a good job of picking an apolitical roommate.

"Don't worry about it too much," a different security official told me. "Just don't sleep with her."

I laughed at this, but he wasn't joking.

"Seriously," he said. "You could wake up in Damascus."

"I hear it's a beautiful city," I told him.

Again, he didn't laugh. I was starting to realize that, while many of my Israeli officemates used humor (even what struck me as inappropriate humor) to dispel the pressures of the job, the security experts took their jobs very, very seriously. When you cracked a joke, they seemed to immediately see you as a security threat. I learned to bite my tongue when I thought of something funny around them.

In any case, on the first security man's orders, my home life with Naoko became more and more like a sitcom about someone with a secret identity. I hid what I did during the day, speaking only in vague terms about my job, and squirreling away books about Israel in my bedroom so that Naoko would not see them. One day, not long after my discussion with the deputy security chief, Naoko brought home a little paper shredder, put it in the living room, and plugged it in.

"Feel free to use it anytime you want," she said. "Really. You know, for shredding personal documents."

I tried my best not to be as paranoid as my coworkers. Granted, it was a little weird that while all of Naoko's other possessions were in her room, this new shredder was left in a prominent position in our living room. And it was kind of strange that she seemed to be almost pressing me to use it, but I wasn't going to jump to any conclusions.

My friend Jacob, who was from New York but happened to have recently moved to Israel, had different thoughts on the matter. "Don't use that shredder!" he told me, when he called to check up on me. "It's faxing things to Damascus."

"It's not like I bring classified material home," I told him. "Why would Syria want my old credit-card receipts and bank statements?"

"Identity theft," Jacob quipped, and well past the point where it was still funny, we jokingly discussed the possibility of the Syrian regime deciding to steal my identity in order to make use of the free Canadian health care system.

In the end, I never needed to shred anything. But I never saw her use that shredder either.

I was beginning to understand the paranoia that surrounds everyone involved with the Israeli government. In fact, right around the time Naoko moved in, I saw firsthand how sensitive Israelis are to threats against their security—or even to anti-Israel statements. In fact, I may have actually played a role in escalating this paranoia. But I didn't mean to: my employers should have known that I don't really speak French.

Well, to be more exact, I speak a *little* French. Growing up in Canada, I was made to study it, but managed to retain very little, except, for some inexplicable reason, how to say, *"Zut! Il y a un poisson dans mon pantalon!"* (Damn! There is a fish in my pants!) I studied a bit more French later on in college and managed to achieve a moderate level of ability, which I listed on my résumé when I got hired by the Mission. And there had been that moment, during my committee interview, when one of the diplomats there had tested my French in a very cursory manner, and I suppose I convinced him that I spoke the language to some degree.

I had started the job fairly confident that, working for the Israeli government in New York City, I would not actually have to make use of my French. Unfortunately, I'd miscalculated.

One day early on, while I was sitting in the office of the head speechwriter, Julie, whom I was to replace, her phone rang. It was Ambassador Mekel, and he asked her to send me to his office. This was strange, because she was still training me, and the logical thing if something had come up would have been for her to go to his office for instructions. I was still very new to the Mission, and had not yet done very much there.

But I went to Ambassador Mekel's office, curious as to what this was all about, and without even saying hello, he asked me, "You speak French, right?"

This can only end badly, I thought. What I wanted to say was: *As long as you are not about to ask me any more questions or ask me to do anything at all using French—yes.*

Instead I just nodded.

"Quick," Mekel told me, handing me a document. "This just came in from France. It's a very anti-Israel statement from a U.N. official, but it's in French. I need you to translate it, and then we'll start writing Israel's response."

"Okay," I said, a little numb.

I took the paper from the ambassador and started back to my office, silently praying that the gist of the U.N. official's statement was that he had a fish in his pants.

Strangely, it turned out the statement was not totally unrelated to fish.

I went into my little office and closed the door. I quickly scanned the document, and saw that although I understood the basic nature of what was being said, a lot of it was in political and legal French, and there was no way that I could hope to translate it accurately. I didn't even have a dictionary.

I leaned back in my chair and looked around the room, not sure what I was searching for exactly, but hoping my eyes would land on something that could help me. Of course, there was nothing, not even a window. At that moment I wanted a window more than anything else in the world, even more than a doorknob. I wasn't sure if this was to stage some kind of elaborate escape, or just to ease the suffocation I was feeling, but I urgently needed a window.

Or someone who spoke French.

Unsure how to proceed, I called a girl I had recently gone on a few dates with, as I knew that her French was superior to mine, but she didn't answer her phone. I then called several other friends who spoke French, but couldn't reach any of them either. This left me with the internet, where I found a website that did online translation. I was very wary of using this software. I'd heard a story about translation software that translated the biblical verse "The spirit is willing but the flesh is weak" as "The vodka is good but the meat is rotten." I couldn't afford that kind of mistranslation in this context.

The website was my only hope, though, and using it along with my shaky knowledge of French, I set about trying to translate the document.

After a long, painful while I deduced that this U.N. official had ranted to a reporter about how all the problems in the Middle East should be blamed on Israel, and that the country was the root of the chaos in war-torn Iraq and elsewhere in the region.

Or at least that's what I thought he had said.

This was the usual sort of opinion that is constantly voiced by Arab governments and their proxies. What made this particular statement interesting and worthy of response was that it wasn't made by an Arab government spokesperson, a journalist, or an academic. It was the statement of a U.N. official, and seemed to show, a little more nakedly than usual, the politicization often at play in the U.N.'s nominally neutral corridors. The individual responsible for the inflammatory words was from an Arab country and had previously served in a high-ranking position in its government, but the fact was that he now worked for the U.N., and had the responsibility to maintain objectivity, or at least the appearance of it.

But I really wasn't sure I had the specifics of his statement correct. I checked a few phrases from it with the diplomat in our office who spoke French, and he confirmed my impressions, but this was done in a quick and somewhat superficial manner. So when I went into Ambassador Mekel's office and handed him the page of my translation, I was not at all confident, and quickly retreated back to my office, very much hoping that it was the last I would hear about it. But it was not.

Immediately after returning to my desk, I began having doubts about the veracity of my translation. I knew that if the official's statement had actually been less heated than my interpretation, and Israel responded too stridently, it could cause some serious embarrassment to the State of Israel and, perhaps less importantly, to me. With this in mind, I became less and less sure that my translation was faithful, and more and more worried that the *free internet page* that I had used for a serious matter of international relations was not reliable.

At one point in his statement, probably the most caustic part of it, the U.N. official had said—at least according to my translation—that Israel was the "great poison" in the Middle East. This was obviously a very hostile remark, and I knew that Israel's response would turn on that hostility. The only problem, I now realized, was that the French word for "fish" was very close to the French word for "poison," and I grew concerned that all the man had said was that Israel was the "big fish" in the region—probably inaccurate, but not really insulting at all.

I knew that if the Israeli government responded to something the diplomat had not even said, Israel would seem reactionary and paranoid—and I would probably lose my job—but there was nothing I could do about it, and so I sat there in my office, hoping against all odds that my translation was accurate and that absolutely nothing would come of this. I felt like I was in a cell, awaiting some kind of punishment. I sat there in this state of resigned terror for about half an hour before I saw, through the little hole where there should have been a doorknob, that there was someone outside my office. Suddenly one of the senior diplomats burst in, looking almost giddy with excitement. It was the first time that any of them had ever visited me in my office, and he seemed to have too much energy for the little room.

"Go to the Associated Press website!" he told me. "Quickly!"

When I did, he showed me that not only was there a copy there of Israel's condemnation of the U.N. official's statement, but it referred very directly to my translation. In fact, the AP itself seemed to be using my translation for their story about the incident.

"See!" the senior diplomat told me happily. "You're really making a difference already!"

I nodded uneasily, forced a smile, and said, "Great."

Within a few hours, Reuters picked up the story as well, and I started to realize that things were going to get worse before they got better. The only question: How bad would they get?

The next morning I got some idea. Just after I got to work, Kofi Annan's spokesperson held a press conference in which he said that his office had never used the word *poison.*

Great, I thought, my heart sinking. *He was talking about fish after all.*

Luckily, though, the spokesperson was referring to the secretary-general's *own* office having never used the word *poison,* and it seemed like the official who had made the statement had in fact done so. Still, it caused me no small measure of distress that the official spokesperson of the secretary-general of the United Nations was making use of my paltry translation.

Over the next few days, my translation was quoted by the *New York Times* and the *Washington Post,* as well as by papers in other countries—from Kurdistan to Japan. Columnists Charles Krauthammer and William Safire both quoted it in their articles, and that Sunday, Kofi Annan appeared on TV's *Meet the Press,* and his interviewer read my flawed translation for him to respond to.

Thankfully, by this time I had determined that the substance, if not the phrasing, of my translation was pretty much correct. Even so, I waited anxiously for it to disappear from the media, especially since by now a better, actually coherent translation was floating around. This translation was being essentially ignored, however, because having appeared first, mine seemed to be considered the official one.

At one point in the middle of the storm, I happened to walk into the office of one of the senior diplomats at the Mission. He was heatedly, and with some obvious satisfaction, talking in English to someone on the phone about how the U.N. official was getting lambasted in the press for his offensive comments. Barely noticing me in the room, he was staring out his window at the U.N. Secretariat building just down the street. I stood there for a while as he gleefully told whoever was on the other end of the line about how the U.N. official had started a fight with Israel, and was now getting what he deserved.

I watched him, and swore to myself that once this had blown over I would be far more careful. This was not the sleepy Toronto suburb I had grown up in—nor was it in any way similar to my regular life down in the East Village or at law school.

"You do not fuck with the Jews!" the senior diplomat began yelling into the phone, still looking out at the towering U.N. headquarters building. "YOU DO *NOT* FUCK WITH THE JEWS!"

4

Hamas, the PLO, and My Love Life

At around the same time as the translation incident, Israel began putting this "You do not fuck with the Jews" philosophy into practice by assassinating the leaders of Hamas. This had been something it had attempted to do in the past, but now pursued with increased vigor because of the continuing suicide bombings. The first to go was Sheikh Ahmed Yassin, a frail, wheelchair-bound cleric in his late sixties. He was the founder and spiritual leader of Hamas, and Israel held him responsible for the deaths of hundreds of Israeli civilians. So, as he was leaving a Gaza City mosque one morning, he was hit by a precisely targeted Israeli rocket, which instantly killed him along with a good deal of his retinue.

I heard this news while lying on the sofa in my living room. This was still early in my time at the Mission, and I was not yet working there every day. The day that Israel decided to deal death from on high was one of the days when I was theoretically supposed to be studying corporate tax law or some equally titillating subject. What this meant in practice was that I had the books open in front of me and was lying on the sofa in the "living room," periodically reaching into the refrigerator in the "kitchen" without really moving my position at all, and without ever looking at the books. The television was on.

The news suddenly reported what had happened in Gaza, briefly showing the scene of the Israeli attack: some rubble, something that could have been part of a wheelchair, a bloody shoe, and a lot of angry Palestinians. I snapped upright very quickly. The report then flashed to a scene of plenty more angry Palestinians—what could have been thousands of them—marching through a Gaza street in fury, shaking their fists and yelling something in Arabic that I didn't understand, but that didn't seem exactly conciliatory.

No good will come of this, I thought.

Then: *Wait, shouldn't I be doing something? Wasn't I just hired to do something?*

But what should I do?

I looked around, taking in the scene in my little New York apartment—some empty Chinese take-out boxes sitting on the kitchen counter, a stack of menus for other restaurants, a few copies of *Time Out New York* lying on the coffee table next to my law school books, and the constant hum of traffic on Second Avenue just barely audible in the distance—and contrasted it with what seemed like a very different scene in faraway Gaza.

Gunmen amid the angry marchers were now firing shots into the air in the background, and the reporter was saying that at the scene of Yassin's death, many of his followers had come to rub their hands into the mix of blood and gravel where he had been—a symbol, the reporter explained, of the preparations for revenge.

Should I be doing something? I thought. *What the hell should I do?*

More than happy to dispense with the pretense of studying law, I called Avi at the Mission to ask if they needed me to come in to the office. As we spoke, it sounded like there was a lot of yelling going on around him at the Mission.

"Need *you?*" he said. "Why would we need *you?*"

"Because of what happened in Gaza."

"Oh, no, I think we're okay without you," he replied, sounding amused by my call.

"Thanks," I said.

Hanging up, I continued watching the report from Gaza. After a little while longer, the front door opened and Naoko arrived home from work, even though it was just midafternoon. Because she was in film, she often worked strange hours, and had been gone since very early that morning.

"How's the movie going?" I asked.

"Great," she said cheerfully. "But it's pretty exhausting. I'm just here for a short break."

She slumped down next to me on the couch and looked at the television for the first time since she had come in. They were replaying the footage of the angry crowd and the gunmen shooting into the sky as various analysts gave their opinion of what would now befall the Middle East. Nobody seemed particularly optimistic, at least in the short term.

"Everyone in film uses these energy drinks, which are basically just concentrated vitamin C, in order to work the long hours and not get sick," she told me, not having seemed to have taken note of what was on television. "But I'm all out. I have to get more later."

I considered changing the channel, as my policy around her was essentially to avoid all mentions of the Middle East, but decided it might seem a bit forced.

She watched the screen seemingly absently, presumably still thinking about the energy drink she didn't have.

But then, suddenly, she said wistfully, "I worry about my dad a lot. Living over there."

"Of course," I said, but didn't push this line of conversation any further.

Soon she retreated to her bedroom, closing the door behind her, and I was left alone again to watch the increasingly heated riots in Gaza.

The next morning, the Mission seemed like a very different place than it normally did. Ever since I had received my security clearance, and the security agents at the consulate had started to recognize me and let me in wordlessly, I barely registered their presence as I entered the consulate building. Not so that day.

Almost immediately after I got off the subway and came out of Grand Central station, I saw one of the security agents I knew, even though we were a few blocks away from the consulate. At first I thought he was simply on his way to work, but then noticed that he was just standing there, lingering outside the station on Forty-second Street.

"Good morning," I said, smiling.

For just a fraction of a second he looked at me and made eye contact, giving me a very stern look, and pointedly refusing to respond. He looked away quickly and I walked off, suddenly understanding that he was "undercover"—or at least as "undercover" as was possible for an athletic-looking man with a thick Middle Eastern accent, dressed in a dark black suit, and loitering outside Grand Central station while constantly surveying the area with obviously acute alertness.

When I was almost at the consulate, and was waiting for the light to change so that I could cross the street and go inside, I saw two more of the security agents standing on the corner together, watching the foot and vehicle traffic go by. This time I did not try to make conversation. There was also one standing outside the doors to the consulate, in addition to the usual one inside the lobby. A group of NYPD officers was stationed outside as well, holding very heavy-duty firearms in what seemed like a threatening show of force—an interesting little addition, I thought, to my new work environment.

Once inside, I discovered that although I had arrived at the Mission earlier than most of us normally did, I was still one of the last there, and the atmosphere was more frenzied and chaotic than I had seen it before. The various diplomats were running around hurriedly, yelling to one another in jackhammer Hebrew, and Ambassador Mekel's door—usually open in the morning—was closed and behind it I could hear voices talking in serious tones. The secretaries and support staff were also scurrying around urgently, though it wasn't clear to me what anyone was actually doing. Or—and this was what concerned me most—what exactly *I* should be doing.

Adding to the general sense of disorder was the fact that lying in the middle of the main corridor in the Mission there was what appeared to be some kind of large mainframe computer being taken apart by one of the consulate's computer technicians and two people I didn't recognize. I couldn't fathom why this had to happen in the middle of the Mission's main thoroughfare on what was sure to be a very busy, important day for Israel's U.N. diplomats. Nevertheless, there were parts arrayed all over the floor in a wide circle, and the technicians seemed to be tossing them about carelessly. I noticed that as the diplomats and support staff ran about frantically, they would casually leap over the half-assembled machine and its parts, as if this obstacle was entirely natural. None of them seemed to notice me, and nobody gave me any direction about what I should be doing.

The only really recognizable aspect of this strange scene was that I could hear the familiar sound of the librarian screaming behind his closed door. In the midst of the frantic, surreal environment in which I found myself, it was somehow reassuring.

Eventually Avi appeared and, hopping gracefully over the half-disassembled machine, said, "Hi, Greg. How are you?"

He seemed chipper and less harried than those around him.

"You don't seem as stressed as everyone else," I said.

He laughed. "The gym is the trick. Even on a busy day like this, I go to the gym and work out before work. It relieves stress."

He then outlined how the day would unfold. There was going to be an emergency session of the Security Council to debate a resolution condemning Israel's assassination of Yassin, and although Israel was not a member of the Council, it would be invited to address the meeting and give a statement. A speech—and a very important one.

"You should ask Julie if they need your help on the speech," he told me, and as he walked me over to Julie's office, I gestured back at the technicians and the mess they were making and asked, "What's going on there?"

Avi rolled his eyes, and said in a slow, irritated tone, "I have no idea what they're doing, and I don't know why they need to do it in the middle of the hallway. Or why they have to do it on a day like this."

I went into Julie's office to ask what my role might be, and she told me that she and Martin, the Mission's legal adviser, were finalizing a draft of the speech.

Julie was a young, bubbly blonde who, on the surface at least, seemed even more ill-suited for this job than I did. But she had been there for some time already, and had apparently somehow gotten used to the surreal work environment.

She and Martin had worked on the speech the previous day and, it sounded like, until late into the night. Martin was now taking new facts that had come in on the situation in the Middle East and assimilating them into the speech. He would then give it to us to go over for language, stylistic, and rhetorical issues.

"On big things like this, he usually takes the lead," she said, "but then you're going to have to go over it and give your take on it before we give it to Danny for his approval."

"Danny" was Ambassador Dan Gillerman. While Ambassador Mekel, technically the deputy ambassador, ran most of the Mission's operations and strategy, it was Gillerman who was the real face of Israel at the U.N., delivering the most important speeches and meeting with the most senior diplomats from other countries and the U.N Secretariat. At this point in my tenure at the Mission, I had

had very little contact with him, and since nobody had bothered to introduce me to him, despite the fact that soon I would be the one writing most of his speeches, I still wasn't entirely sure that he actually knew who I was.

I saw Gillerman almost daily, walking down the corridor or going into Ambassador Mekel's office for meetings, but had not yet summoned the nerve to introduce myself. He was a distant, imposing figure. I was impressed with how polished he always seemed, especially in contrast to most of the other Israeli officials I had encountered so far. His suits were perfectly tailored, he was always flawlessly groomed, and his English was absolutely fluent. He seemed like the ideal diplomat.

And on this morning I was actually about to contribute in a small way to a speech that he would give before the Security Council. I tried to wrap my mind around this fact as I left Julie's office, jumped over the ever-more-disorderly broken computer in the hall, and went into my office to check my computer for the latest news from the Middle East.

The scene in the Mission was hectic, but the scene in the Middle East was pure chaos. All across the Arab and Muslim world, angry protests had erupted, condemning Israel's action and demanding revenge. Even moderate Arab governments were furious, and the Palestinians—especially in Gaza—seemed to have descended to a new level of murderous rage.

I tried to decide if the assassination had been a good idea on Israel's part. Without a doubt, Yassin had been an unhelpful element in the Middle East mix, and was undeniably responsible for the deaths of many civilians. On the other hand, murdering Palestinian leaders seemed destined only to fan the flames of animosity and drive the two peoples further apart. I tended to give Israel the benefit of the doubt on most issues, including this one, but I wondered if there was the potential for a more nuanced approach that neither the Israeli military men nor the angry Palestinian mobs saw.

After a little while I became aware of a new sound. It was yelling which, of course, was not at all unfamiliar in our office—but it seemed different from the constant yelling of the librarian or the urgent yelling of the diplomats. It was farther away, more rhythmic, and more chantlike. It took me a moment to realize that it was a protest outside the consulate, the Arabic chanting sounding very hostile and threatening. Trapped inside the building, a multitude of armed guards protecting us, while the Middle East threatened to explode anew and we represented the most visible symbol of Israel in New York City, I thought yet again, *What have I gotten myself into?*

Eventually my phone rang and I was told that the speech draft was ready for me to go over. I sprang from my chair, anxious to do anything other than just sit in my windowless office, watching the riots in the Middle East on my screen and listening to the near riot outside. I raced down the hallway faster than I needed to, and almost tripped over the mass of computer parts now strewn all down its length. Leaping over the main piece itself, as well as over one of the crouching technicians working on it, I noticed, as I flew by, that he was actually pounding one of the parts with a hammer.

I had time to think, for just a second, *What could that possibly accomplish?*

And then I was down the hall, the sound of the hammer smashing computer parts joining with the general cacophony of angry protesters, screaming librarians, and frantic diplomats yelling back and forth in machine-gun Hebrew.

It was to this symphony that I sat down to read over the draft of the speech that Ambassador Gillerman would be giving. The speech was short and to the point, and seemed designed to convey a reasonable tone. It articulated some requests to the Council, beseeching it not to have a double standard of condemning Israel's actions without condemning Yassin's behavior that had led to them, and pointing explicitly to a recent suicide bombing in Israel for which Hamas had claimed responsibility. Interestingly, it also seemed to cast Israel's fight against Hamas and other Palestinian terrorist groups as part of the larger "war on terror" rhetoric that had become paradigmatic over the preceding few years. It even alluded to the recent terrorist attacks in various countries, seeking to present the Israeli experience as part of the larger whole.

Not yet confident enough to give serious critiques, I made a few halfhearted marks on the page and then went to hand back the speech to Martin, a pudgy Australian-Israeli in his midthirties. I had been briefly introduced to him a few weeks before, but we had not really spoken yet.

I got to Martin's office, which was just across the hallway from Ambassador Mekel's, and found him staring intently at a folder full of papers, reading through them with an almost violent quickness.

"Martin," I said, from the doorway. "Excuse me, but—"

Without looking up at all, he raised one finger to indicate that I should wait a moment. I stood there as he rifled urgently through the papers, his eyes darting back and forth frantically, devouring whatever their contents were. He eventually looked up at me with a piercing expression that suggested that I should not waste his time.

"I have the speech here," I said.

He got up, took it out of my hand, mumbled something I couldn't hear, and marched quickly out of his office and toward Mekel's. I followed him, trying to get his attention for just long enough to offer some words of praise on his work on the speech, but he went directly into Mekel's office and immediately slammed the door behind him. I stood there for a moment, the door a few inches from my nose.

The speech was to be delivered at the Security Council in a few hours. In the meantime, I walked back out into the hallway to watch the technician smash computer parts with his hammer.

My first time at a Security Council meeting had occurred on a much less heated day. Out of nowhere one morning, Ambassador

Mekel invited me to join him at a session of the Council at which a U.N. official was giving a briefing to the Council's members on recent events in the Middle East.

"Sure," I agreed, genuinely excited by this idea.

Besides the fact that, unlike those of the U.N.'s other bodies, the Council's decisions are binding, it is also the forum where the most high-profile and sensitive issues play out: issues of war and peace, and of security. In essence, the Council's operations are the reason that the U.N. was founded at all. I was eager to see it in action.

When it was time to go to the meeting, I walked down the long hallway from my office to Mekel's, but found that his office door was closed. His secretary, a woman in her midtwenties named Tammy, told me that he was on the phone and to wait for him.

"How are you doing so far?" she asked me while I waited, "in this very crazy place."

"It's not that crazy," I lied.

"If you don't think it's crazy," she said flatly, "then there is something wrong with you."

Soon the door opened and Ambassador Mekel came out. He saw Tammy and me talking, and gave me a mischievous grin that I didn't really understand. Then he and I left the building together, turning the corner at Forty-second Street and walking toward the East River.

"So?" he said out of nowhere, and I looked at him, unsure of how I might be expected to respond to this.

"What exactly is happening at this meeting?" I asked, somewhat lamely. "What can Israel expect to hear in this report?"

"So?" he repeated, ignoring my question entirely. "I saw you talking to Tammy."

"Yes," I answered. "She's very nice."

"Absolutely," he agreed. "Very smart, too, and I know that I can always rely on her."

I just nodded.

"I couldn't help but notice that you two seem to get along well," he continued.

"Sure," I agreed.

"And she *is* pretty," he said, looking at me sharply and raising his eyebrows encouragingly.

When I walked into the Security Council chamber for the first time, the importance of the room hit me immediately. Or, at least, I immediately got the feeling that the importance was supposed to be hitting me.

Like the rest of the U.N., the room itself was decorated and designed in what seemed to be its creators' conception of what that grand place the future would be like. If they were correct, I thought, the future would be full of incredibly ugly and uncomfortable chairs and have a strange kitschy color scheme. Also like the rest of the facilities at the U.N., the Council's chamber was basically falling apart, and it showed.

Trying to take in the whole scene, I walked with Ambassador Mekel to our seats in the gallery section of the chamber. We were relegated to these bleacher-type seats because Israel was not—in fact, never had been—a member of the Security Council. There are only fifteen members of the Council at one time: five permanent members, and ten rotating spots, and states that are not members of the Council may only sit in the upper seats and observe the proceedings. The Council members themselves sat in an imposing semicircle on the floor, like some kind of sci-fi intergalactic council.

Depending on what is being deliberated on the floor, the gallery is filled to varying degrees. On high-profile issues like Israel's "targeted assassinations," it is usually full of people—delegations from other countries, U.N. officials, and other interested parties.

This time the room was only about half full because it was a routine, not particularly controversial meeting. Still, since it was my first visit to the Council, I was amazed to be there, and Ambassador Mekel clearly enjoyed impressing me with the magnitude of the experience.

"The whole world is represented here," he whispered to me, raising his eyebrows. "Bet you've never been at something like this before."

I smiled. He was right. I couldn't imagine what something "like this" other than *this* itself could possibly be, but his point was well taken. I knew that he was enjoying watching my first experience at the Council, proud of himself for his own capacity to take someone into this vaunted environment. Settling in, and listening to my earpiece to try to understand what was occurring on the floor, I took the opportunity to look around the room at the other people present.

And that's when I was shocked to see that I actually recognized someone there. Sitting a few rows over was a German woman I had known in graduate school but hadn't seen in a few years.

Ambassador Mekel rightfully expected me to be awed by the Security Council, but I was immediately more interested in finding out what my old friend was doing there. When the meeting was adjourned and all the delegates poured onto the floor of the Council, she and I went straight to each other. We tried to maintain our professional demeanors, but it was difficult given the novelty of running into each other at that particular place. She told me that she was now a diplomat, too, working temporarily at the EU's Mission. We hugged each other and laughed loudly about the weirdness of it all.

Ambassador Mekel was quite surprised by this turn of events. From his perspective, I had suddenly, for no apparent reason, left his side to go somewhat giddily hug one of the delegates from the European Union. I glanced over at him as I hugged her, and he looked very confused.

"So you ran into an old friend at the Security Council?" he observed drily as we left the room. "Now you think you're special?"

Needless to say, lighthearted moments at the Security Council were a rarity, and there were none of them on that very different day when the Council addressed the matter of the assassination of the quadriplegic sheikh, Ahmed Yassin. When our speech was finally ready—written and rewritten, then vetted by Ambassador Gillerman—much of our delegation marched out toward the U.N. Ambassador Gillerman would be the one delivering the speech, and he would perhaps need one or two of the senior diplomats to help with the debate strategy. The rest of the Mission was going for moral support.

Outside the Security Council chamber there was a tremendous hubbub, with journalists, diplomats, and U.N. officials milling about, and a combative energy in the air. Inside, Ambassador Gillerman gave an impassioned, emotional delivery of the speech that we had prepared. This was, of course, responded to in kind by the Palestinian delegation and its allies. It was, as I came to learn, a typical U.N. shouting match.

After the speeches and debating were over, another typical result was reached. A resolution that condemned Israel, without fully putting its actions in a proper context, was supported by most members of the Council but vetoed by the United States. The Palestinians could claim what they believed to be a moral victory, the Israelis a legal one. It was a result I would see again and again at the U.N., like a recurring diplomatic chorus.

In the days following the meeting, there was a sense of foreboding, both in our office and, according to the reports I was reading, among the Israeli public. Everyone believed that Hamas would live up to its word to take revenge. The average Israeli waited with trepidation for the next bus bombing or attack on a café to shatter the ominous, pregnant quiet that had descended on the country's streets. In our office, we could only wait for news from the Middle East, anxious to know what would be our next challenge.

It would be only a couple months until I took over as the head speechwriter, and as things heated up more and more in Israel, that prospect became increasingly daunting. Israel, and the Middle East conflict, had always been part of the background noise in my life. When I was at Bialik Hebrew Day School as a kid in Toronto, it had been the focus of my day-to-day education. Even later, though, when it had faded to a soft hum, it had still been tangible in how deeply so many people around me cared about it, and in the heated discussions it engendered among my family and friends. But in Toronto, or in wholly academic discussions during graduate school and law school, it had seemed more like an abstract idea. Now that I'd started to engage with it directly, it was becoming more real for me, and the people involved in it were becoming three-dimensional in their passions and beliefs. And although my knee-jerk reaction, because of my childhood and background, was to take Israel's side on most issues—which was probably a good thing, given my job—I was realizing that the mature thing would be to try to use my position to examine the situation without the encumbrances of the ideological clichés constantly thrown about in Middle East discourse.

But there was never much time to think. Almost immediately following Sheikh Yassin's death, a fifty-five-year-old man named Abdel Aziz Rantisi became the new leader of Hamas. Although a pediatrician by training, and an occasional poet, he was said to be more militant and violent than his predecessor. At a memorial service for Yassin, he made a speech in which he declared, in no uncertain terms, an acceleration of violence. In a fiery diatribe, he said that it came as no surprise that the United States had vetoed the Security Council resolution condemning the killing of Yassin.

"America declared war against God," he said. "Sharon declared war against God and God declared war against America, Bush, and Sharon. The war of God continues against them and I can see the victory coming up from the land of Palestine by the hand of Hamas."

Fighting words, indeed. Rantisi spent most of his tenure as the leader of Hamas hiding, and when he did emerge into the open, just a few weeks after the memorial service, he was almost immediately killed by missiles fired from planes.

I was shocked by how quickly he was assassinated. Whether these were the right or wrong decisions to make, the sheer efficiency and reach of the Israeli military was a bit staggering.

Shortly afterward my elderly grandfather, who knew very little about the Middle East, asked me to explain the current situation to him in terms that he could understand. He had been a businessman for most of his life, and that was the world with which he was familiar.

"It's going to be a very busy week in my office," I told him, "because the boys in the front office are having a record quarter."

And in fact it was a busy week. Immediately following Rantisi's death, the Mission was again involved in diplomatic warfare. Like before, the Security Council was hastily convened to discuss Israel's actions, and from an Israeli perspective, the Council was once again focusing its energies in the wrong direction—trying to condemn the response to terrorism, rather than the perpetrators of terrorism.

Other delegations voiced the opinion that the United States' veto in the vote after the Yassin killing had effectively given a green light to Israel to continue its policy of targeted assassinations. After the deaths of Yassin and Rantisi, the United States had voiced "concern" about Israel's actions, and a sort of measured skepticism about whether they would help the cause of peace. It had been very careful, though, to balance this with a reminder that it believed Israel had the right to defend itself against the terrorist elements that sought to disrupt peace and kill its citizens.

With Martin again taking the most active role in the drafting of the speech for the Security Council, and me playing a slightly more robust part this time around, we put forward Israel's case. The Palestinian Authority had the obligation under international law to arrest, disarm, and dismantle these terrorist organizations, we argued. It would be different if their "hosts" were taking actions against the terrorists who were targeting Israelis, but since they were not, Israel had no recourse but to go after them itself.

The scene at the Council and in the Mission, as well as in the streets of faraway Gaza, were pretty much the same as it had been following the Yassin assassination: dark and frenzied. Amid the chaos, I did my best to help Ambassador Gillerman and the other senior members of the Mission. Because I still didn't fully understand this new world I had found myself in, though, I remained somewhat removed.

At one point just after the Rantisi assassination, I was standing outside the Security Council chamber. There was the usual mob of journalists, delegates, and U.N. officials, accompanied by the frantic flashing of cameras and chatter in dozens of different languages. For a brief moment I saw on the far side of this great confusion the pretty girl from the Dutch Mission, whom I had not seen since the day Iran had refused to sit next to me. We made eye contact and she smiled at me—perhaps remembering which delegation I was a part of, and recognizing that it was our Mission that stood at the center of this madness. But then the surging crowd shifted, and I lost sight of her.

Suddenly I was jostled from one side, and turned to see that I had been bumped into by Nasser al-Kidwa, the Palestinian representative at the U.N.—and Yasser Arafat's cousin. It was the first time I had ever seen him so close. He was flanked by a collection of handlers, and he smiled briefly at the flashing cameras as he walked into the little antechamber right outside the Security Council, which was off-limits to the press crowding outside.

When I looked for the Dutch girl again—wondering if this was even a vaguely appropriate time to try to talk to her—I couldn't find her. The PLO and Hamas were ruining my love life, and I resented it.

5

No Such Thing as a Free Lunch

With my school term ending and two weeks until I became head speechwriter, I took the opportunity to visit Israel. If I was now going to be in charge of the country's voice, I thought I should take a look at it from a closer angle. In the weeks leading up to my trip, during the Yassin and Rantisi episodes, I became aware of an option that would make my trip a little more interesting, and might also help me deal with an issue that had emerged in my weird new life.

Because of the killings of Yassin and Rantisi and the deteriorating overall situation in the Middle East, there was a lot of concern that the lives of Israeli diplomatic personnel in the United States and elsewhere were in even more danger than usual. In the past, a few Israeli diplomats had been shot while abroad, and security at the New York consulate was now at a heightened level. I was warned not to take the same route to work and home every day, and not to come in at the same time, and also reminded not to tell anyone where I worked. There were often angry demonstrations outside the building, and I found myself getting used to them.

"We can protect you in or right near the consulate," one of the security officials told me sternly, "but when you're not in the area, you're on your own."

I was sitting in his office at the time, and as he spoke he was holding, for no apparent reason, what looked to be a handgun cartridge, casually gesturing with it as he told me that my life was in danger. He seemed pretty serious about the whole thing.

At around the same time I also happened to hear that a private organization in Israel affiliated with the Israeli Ministry of Defense offered courses in various kinds of self-protection to those who could justify their potential need for them—people who worked for the government, in private security companies, or for reputable organizations in dangerous areas of the world. The courses ranged from standard training in martial arts, to a course called "combat firearms," to "bodyguarding," to "defensive driving." This last course offered training in shooting at someone who was chasing you while you were driving, not in avoiding skidding out on ice, which is how I remembered defensive driving classes in Canada.

There was also a course on something called "offensive driving," which seemed, as best as I could tell, to be about shooting at someone while *you* were chasing *them* in a car. I tried to imagine myself in this situation in New York, where, on top of any other unlikely circumstances, I didn't actually have access to a car.

But probably the least practical of these course offerings for my daily life was the one that would teach me the proper way to shoot firearms on a plane while maneuvering around my fellow passengers. It didn't seem particularly likely that I would end up on a plane armed with a gun.

And the information about all the courses seemed to suggest that they would not be exactly pleasant, that a student signing up would have to suffer a little for the wisdom gained. One of the promotional pictures showed a student being punched in the face by a man in a black balaclava while bystanders looked on approvingly.

Despite these warning signs, I decided to do it. I would take the course in "combat firearms" now, and maybe a different one later, so that I would be able to better deal with, or at least understand, the potential dangers of my new career. *This is the life you have chosen*, I told myself.

In order to sign up for the class, I asked my friend Jacob—a New Yorker who had moved to Israel, and spoke Hebrew well—to call the organization for me. He called me back later that day sounding a bit unnerved by what he'd learned.

"First of all," he said, "his name is 'Name.'"

"What?" I asked, thinking I must have misheard him.

"His name is the Hebrew word for the word *name*, Shem. His name is Shem, which means 'name.' Don't you find that a little strange?"

I agreed it was, and asked, "Well, what did Name tell you?"

"He kept stressing that you would be served a free lunch with the course."

"Really?"

"Yeah. He seemed very proud of that."

"Okay, besides that?"

"Well, that was really all he was willing to tell me. He's very suspicious about the whole thing, about you, about me, how I know you, how long I've known you, why you want to do this training, how you heard about them, and a million other things."

The paranoia sounded familiar, and I sent Shem the information he said that he needed in order to do another background check on me.

When I told Avi that I was going to be away from the office for a week because I was going to Israel, he reacted with some surprise.

"Why would you go to Israel on vacation?" he asked. "Why don't you go somewhere more interesting?"

"Maybe you don't think it's interesting because you're from there," I said.

He nodded. "Okay, but why don't you go somewhere fun?"

"Like where?" I asked.

"Sweden," he said, getting suddenly excited. "You should go to Sweden!"

"Why Sweden?"

"Greg! Sweden is amazing!"

"I'm going to Israel," I told him. "If I work for the Israeli government, I should go visit Israel."

"Greg, I'm just saying that if I were you, I would go to Sweden."

When I told Ambassador Mekel that I was going to be visiting Israel, his response was even less encouraging.

"Okay," he said, "but you better be careful. We don't want to hear that your body washed up on the Tel Aviv beach."

These words ringing in my ears, I landed at the Tel Aviv airport a few days later, and found myself in the general chaos of the main terminal, which felt a bit like the U.N. Mission, but even less ordered and reasonable. People were shoving and yelling, children were screaming in Hebrew. Amid the chaos, I eventually made my way to the front of the line and told the immigration agent that I was visiting the country for ten days. I half expected her to ask what I did back in New York, but she didn't. More or less wordlessly, she stamped my passport and ushered me in. To her I was just another tourist visiting from America. Which, I supposed, was right, except that I was going to spend a lot of my time in Israel armed with a Magnum 45.

The next morning, I took a cab from Jacob's apartment in Tel Aviv to the nearby Israeli city of Herzliyya to meet Shem.

"Make sure they give you your free lunch," Jacob said as I was leaving. "He promised it on the phone."

Herzliyya is one of Israel's wealthiest cities, and I was supposed to meet Shem at a ritzy beachfront hotel. It occurred to me on the way there that I had no idea what Shem looked like. When I got there I looked around the busy lobby. There were dozens of people, standing around or sitting at tables in the bar area. A man in casual, nondescript clothes waved me over confidently.

He was no behemoth like some of the security guards at the consulate were, but he shared their hardened, dangerous look.

"Gregory," he said, standing up and putting his hand out. "Nice to meet you."

He gestured for me to sit down with him at the table, and only then did I notice that there was someone else there. She was a petite woman in her late thirties who introduced herself as Lydia, in an accent that sounded like a cross between British and French, but was certainly not Israeli. She did not say what her role in all this was, and neither did Shem.

Shem seemed coiled and tense, and had the air of someone who was *perpetually* coiled and tense. Even as he called over a waitress to order more beverages, he appeared poised to explode into violence at any moment, which I had no reason to doubt was actually the case. As the waitress came over to us, he scanned the room, alertly, almost nervously, and continued to do so for the three hours we were there.

Our drinks ordered, Shem turned back to Lydia and me, still glancing around the room from the corners of his eyes. He told us that we would be classmates in the course, and then immediately turned to me and said, "Tell her what you do."

I hesitated for a minute, a little embarrassed by the sudden attention.

"I'm a speechwriter for the Israeli government at the United Nations," I said.

"Wow!" she said. "That's a pretty big deal, isn't it?"

"Of course it is," Shem said proudly, as if he had something to do with it. "It's very important."

"What do you do?" I asked Lydia, trying to dodge the focus. I had no idea what she might say, what possible reason a very small woman apparently visiting from Europe would have for taking a class in combat firearms. In any case, whatever I might have expected her to say she did for a living, it wasn't what she did say.

"I'm the tour manager for Radiohead," she said.

I was entirely taken aback, but Shem seemed to brush it off as unimportant. Only because my mouth was somewhat agape did he reluctantly respond to it.

"That's a band?" he asked, vaguely and without much interest. And now I looked at *him* with a gaping mouth.

Radiohead, of course, was one of the most popular bands on the planet. With worldwide popularity, they were not just very well known in Israel, but had actually played in the country several times. It floored me that Shem had not heard of them; in his late thirties, he was well within their demographic. Within a few minutes, though, it became apparent he was not the kind of person who paid much attention to music. Shem saw the world as if through the sight of a gun.

He was a former security officer of some kind, that much was immediately clear. But he left any more details vague, and on a sort of need-to-know basis, and he didn't think we needed to know much. Over the next few days, as he alluded to his past and I compared it to what I knew about the Israeli security services, it became obvious to me that he was an ex-Mossad officer. They were even more secretive and paranoid than the rest of the Israeli security apparatus.

On that first day, still sitting in the hotel lobby, Shem provided us with the theoretical know-how necessary for working with firearms. This wasn't merely a lesson on how guns worked, or on the safety precautions needed to handle them. It went far beyond that to more esoteric topics like how to determine by someone's gait that they had a concealed weapon, and the psychology of what being armed did to a person's thought patterns. Shem drew diagrams on a paper in front of him, and questioned us Socratically about what our intuition told us about armed combat, which was entirely foreign to both Lydia and me. Meanwhile, he continued to look around the lobby suspiciously, and to glance alertly at the entrance when anyone new came in.

Whenever the waitress came near, Shem turned the paper over in front of him and stopped talking immediately. There would be an awkward silence as she was clearing something from our table or checking if we wanted anything else, and he would only resume the lecture again once she had departed. She took to giving him a strange look.

At one point, Shem's cell phone rang and he answered it, standing up from the table. He walked away from us toward the hotel doors, but as he went I was surprised to hear that he was speaking in what sounded to me like fluent Portuguese.

While Shem was on the phone, I found out a little bit more about Lydia. She was French, but had been living in England for many years, and she did indeed run Radiohead's multimillion-dollar world tours.

"But why," I asked, "are you studying combat firearms?"

She laughed. "It is a bit odd, isn't it?"

I nodded, and she explained that although when the band was on tour, she worked eighteen hours a day for months at a time, when they were on vacation or recording an album, she really had nothing to do. So, she explained, she often spent those months working for nonprofit organizations in foreign locales, sometimes in dangerous regions. She was about to go on one such job, and the organization she was going with had demanded that she take the course.

"I don't usually get all that nervous about this sort of thing, but everyone keeps telling me that it doesn't help my safety that I'm a woman—and a Jew."

She pointed at Shem, who was still talking seriously on the phone, and said, "His advice to me has been that I shouldn't go at all, but he says that if I am going to go, he'll teach me how to protect myself."

We watched him silently for a while, and then Lydia volunteered that the previous day he had actually driven her to tears.

"I wanted to quit, and they wouldn't let me," she said, and then explained that she had been going through intensely physical martial-arts training for the few days prior to my arrival. Besides being petite, she was very gentle and refined, and seemed even more out of place than me—which was saying quite a lot. "You're lucky you weren't there yesterday. I'm all bruised up today. I almost didn't come."

When Shem returned, we spent the next hour or so practicing our analysis of whether someone constituted a threat or not.

"Do you see that woman with the baby carriage?" he said. "Don't assume that there is a baby in it."

I looked at the woman and her carriage, trying to decide the likelihood of there being something other than a baby in it.

"And what about that man by the desk?" Shem continued. "Notice how he keeps touching his hip every few moments—that could mean that he has a gun there."

It all seemed a bit silly to me, or at very least foreign, and maybe my expression betrayed this thought, because Shem added sternly, "You have to take this seriously. It could save your life one day."

It continued like this for a while—me, the former Mossad officer, and Radiohead's tour manager, discussing which of the hotel guests were potential assailants.

Eventually we left the hotel and drove to a café, where Shem dutifully bought us lunch.

"It's included in the package," he reminded me, then spent the next twenty minutes eluding my questions on what exactly he had done for the Israeli security services.

Then we got back in the car and pulled up at a street corner, where we stopped, without any explanation, to pick up a large man in his twenties who looked incredibly disheveled and was carrying a large duffel bag. Wordlessly, he got in and sat in the back beside Lydia.

As we drove off, Shem said to me, "This is Sagi. Last year he was the jujitsu champion of Israel. Later on you'll fight him."

There was absolutely no sign that Shem was joking, nor that he ever joked. I looked back warily at the large man in the backseat, who nodded at me. Before I could ask any questions, Shem's cell phone rang again and he answered it, immediately speaking in quick, fluent French to whoever was on the other end of the line.

His French—like his Hebrew, English, and, apparently, Portuguese—seemed absolutely perfect, and I thought that it would have been good to have him around during the whole "Israel is the great poison" incident at the U.N. I tried to understand what he was saying, and could only make out every fifth word or so. It did not seem to have anything to with either fish or poison.

Herzliyya is a small city, but the traffic was terrible, even in the middle of the day, and all the drivers seemed determined to kill themselves and as many other people as possible at the soonest opportunity. I was homesick for the safe, sane drivers of Manhattan.

Eventually, when we had successfully made our way through the death trap of the roads, we parked at a mall where, Shem said, there was a firing range in the basement.

The range had a little waiting room with pictures of weapons and soldiers on the walls, and cases full of guns, ammo, holsters, and other accoutrements. The staff working there seemed to know Shem well. As he spoke to them in Hebrew about what firearms we would need, and Sagi admired some knives that were on display in a glass case, Lydia and I watched a training exercise that was going on in the main shooting gallery. It was one of the most intense displays I had ever witnessed.

In the gallery, there was a life-size cardboard cutout of a small house, with windows, a doorway, and some actual tables and chairs. The person training was standing next to one of the tables, peering out the window and then ducking back behind the wall, as if he were on some kind of police mission. After a minute or two he leaped in front of the window, fired five shots through it at targets against the back wall, and retreated again. Then he threw the table over with a loud crash and ducked behind it, before releasing another volley of bullets at the target. It left both Lydia and me stunned and apprehensive about what we were about to do.

Shem showed up holding two large guns, looked at the frightening training in front of us, and said, "See, that's sport training, not real stuff like what we're going to do."

At first I thought that I had misheard him, or that this was a joke, but I had heard right.

"Our training will be much more combative," he said.

And our training *was* more intense, and more combative, than what the person before us had been doing. It was the first time either Lydia or I had ever held a handgun in our lives, and we went through a couple hours of rudimentary handgun training ("This is where the bullets come out of") and safety basics ("Don't ever point this side at anyone you care about"). After a while, a recognizably *Israeli* edge emerged.

For one thing, Shem told us that Israeli security services, in whose style we were being trained, never used safeties—the little mechanism that prevents a gun from firing by accident—on their weapons. This had the result, it seemed to me, of making an already dangerous activity that much more dangerous.

"On some of our guns," he told us, "we even remove the safety."

The reason, he explained, was that Israelis believed that the fraction of a second it took to disable the safety on a gun could be fatally pivotal in real battle. That may be so, I thought, but he had already told us that we would be working with real ammo, and I felt like having the safety on might be a good idea, at least for the time being. (ISRAEL'S U.N. SPEECHWRITER ACCIDENTALLY SHOOTS RADIOHEAD'S TOUR MANAGER, I imagined the newspaper headline.)

"I have trained with American agents," he told us, "and they use safeties. It makes them slow."

I looked at Lydia, who was holding an enormous gun in her tiny hand, her shoulder looking tired from the effort, and saw by the look on her face that she was as skeptical and uneasy as me.

"The attitude we use in the Israeli security services," Shem continued, "is simply attack, attack, attack. Even if you're defending, you do it by attacking. So safeties serve no useful purpose."

But a few minutes later, when I had the gun tucked into my hip pocket without the safety on, and was practicing drawing it into a firing position, I could think of at least one useful purpose: not shooting myself in the genitals.

Before long we were drawing our guns when Shem shouted to do so, and firing at the targets. At the next stage, Shem and sometimes his large jujitsu champion assistant, Sagi, kicked us in the stomachs—not with full force, of course, but firmly—while we aimed the loaded guns at the targets and struggled to shoot.

What the hell am I doing? I thought, tensing my stomach muscles to make the kicks hurt a little less while firing round after round of live ammunition.

"The next thing we're going to do," Shem said, "is run toward the target while shooting it, and then, if necessary, beat it with the gun."

Lydia and I stared at him blankly. I was wondering what particular set of circumstances would make it necessary for me to beat a paper target with a gun.

"If you think about it," he continued, "killing someone is fairly simple. All you do is shoot as many bullets as you can into them. Aim for the chest area, though, and just put as many shots as you can into there. A head shot is great if you can get it, but the problem with aiming for the head is that you have a good chance of missing."

He paused and stared at me sternly, as if I had a reputation for trying to shoot people in the head and missing.

"So in this exercise," he continued, "your task is to run straight at the targets, firing as many bullets as possible into their chest area. Just empty out the cartridge altogether, and if it's not empty when you reach it, shoot the rest of the bullets from up close. Then you can beat it with your gun until you are satisfied."

Shem went to set up the targets—large human figures cut out of paper—at the other end of the range, leaving Lydia and me standing alone.

As we watched Shem methodically aligning the targets, Lydia leaned close to me and whispered, "I think he's daft."

Then Shem came back and said, "Remember not to run like you've seen on television, in a sideways manner. That's how American agents—FBI and so on—are trained to run as they go after a target, because they're trying to minimize the space on their body that they are presenting to their opponents."

Here Shem demonstrated, moving forward in a sort of stealthy sideward manner that I actually did recognize from television and movies.

"It might protect them a little bit," he told us, "but the Israeli philosophy is to run straight at the target, even if it opens us up a bit more to being shot. The idea is to attack, attack, attack very quickly, and we think that is the best defense."

Lydia and I took turns charging aggressively while firing at the targets. When we got within a few inches of our targets, Shem told us—screamed frighteningly at us, that is—to unload the rest of our bullets, savagely destroying the paper cutouts.

Over the next few days we shot round after round of bullets, from different angles, distances, and positions. We enacted one particularly unlikely scenario wherein I was told to sit at a table and pretend to be in a restaurant or bar, then was prompted to knock the table over, draw my gun, and shoot at a target from behind it. In the process of landing on the hard floor behind the clattering table while drawing my gun, I wondered what exactly would have to befall my East Village life in order for me to start eating at restaurants with a gun on my hip. I didn't think that the proprietors of the little French bistro on my corner would appreciate it.

For a few years now, I had found something appealing in the Israeli concept of Jewishness. It involved being tough and assertive, and rejecting the concept of the "weak Jew" or the "ghetto Jew." It seemed, much of the time, to have very little to do with religion, which was another draw. Outside of Israel, being a Jew seemed connected much more to religion and ritual than to the proud self-sufficiency and Jewish national identity on which Israel was originally founded. But now, throwing tables onto the floor, being smashed around by Shem, my arms aching from firing round after round of ammunition, I was beginning to realize that maybe this wasn't exactly my idea of Jewish identity either.

All of it was just as foreign to Lydia, if not more so, and I wondered if Shem picked up on our bewilderment. He certainly didn't seem to.

But he did occasionally try to make this training relevant to our daily lives. One day he brought in a women's handbag, a small pistol, and an even smaller electric stun gun. He showed Lydia that the handbag had a secret pocket where the pistol could be stored but drawn quickly.

"Nobody will even know you have it," he told her.

She nodded.

"Another option that would be good for you is this," he told her, indicating the stun gun. "It's very effective in putting an enemy out of commission, but is almost never fatal."

"So you can't kill someone with it?" Lydia asked, and I could tell by her tone of voice that she thought this was a good thing, that perhaps the stun gun *was* something she would be interested in—for her protection, but not for accidentally murdering someone.

Shem, however, didn't understand her question in the same way.

"No, you can't kill someone with it," he allowed, almost reluctantly, "but don't write it off just for that reason."

As my time in Israel wound to a close, Shem asked me if I would return in a few months for the next training module.

"Probably," I said unconvincingly, aching all over and eager to leave.

Shem told us that he had prepared one final exercise for Lydia and me, to synthesize all that we had learned. I didn't like the sound of this at all.

Soon I found myself alone atop a staircase, wearing boxing gloves, with a loaded, safety-less gun tucked uncomfortably in my hip pocket. The boxing gloves had come out of the duffel bag that Sagi had been carrying the first day, and I had been told to put them on but not why I would need them. I had no idea what was about to happen.

"Okay!" Shem shouted from down below. "Run! Run!"

I took a breath and raced down the staircase, bracing myself for the worst.

Weighed down awkwardly by the gun in my pocket, I thought of how my father, always very paranoid about safety, had drilled several habits into me as a child, among the strongest an absolute prohibition against running with scissors or even carrying them pointing upward. To that day, I could not help but hold scissors very gingerly, always with a mild sense of fear, their tips pointed downward and away from my body. I was glad my father wasn't here to see me with a loaded *gun*—without a safety—lodged beside my crotch.

But when I reached the bottom of the stairs and turned the corner into the training hall, I was immediately more concerned with fear than irony. Standing there waiting for me, geared up in boxing gloves, was Sagi. He was twice my size.

"Fight!" Shem yelled. I looked at him blankly, unsure exactly what he wanted me to do. Then Sagi punched me in the head.

I sent a punch right back at him, which he easily parried, and suddenly I was involved in a boxing match with Israel's jujitsu champion, my gun bobbing awkwardly as I moved.

Sagi threw two more punches at me, which I somehow avoided, and I responded in kind, catching him lightly in the chest with one of them. I was quickly becoming winded, and my head was ringing a little from the first punch he had landed, but I danced around, trying my best to make some headway against him, or at least survive the encounter.

Then Sagi launched a very aggressive series of punches, and I stumbled backward, narrowly missing smashing into Lydia, who was standing to the side and watching this absurd spectacle. She jumped away with a little yelp, and I dropped my hands in surprise. Sagi took the opportunity to hit me twice in the face, firmly but definitely using only a fraction of his strength. Then he stopped, as it had become clear who had won.

I stood there gasping for breath, my face stinging from these two last punches, but Shem gave me no opportunity for a respite.

"Push-ups!" he yelled. "Get down! Now!"

I more or less fell to the ground at this, stripping off the boxing gloves and getting into my best estimation of the push-up position.

"Go! Go! Go!"

Barely able to breathe as it was, I started doing push-ups.

"Faster!" Shem yelled, walking over so he was standing right beside me. "Faster!"

Up and down I went for what felt like forever, and the gun in my pocket not only made this harder to do but also made me very nervous. Then, just as my arms were reaching the breaking point, Shem did something to make things that much harder, and more dangerous. He kicked one of my hands out from under me, so that I collapsed, my already stinging face landing on the hard floor with a smack, my body landing on top of the gun.

I lay there for a moment, stunned, looking up at him.

"Get up and shoot at the target!" Shem yelled. "Don't lie there. Get up, draw your gun, and shoot, shoot, shoot!"

I began struggling to do so.

"Now!" he continued. "Don't be a weak American!"

"No," I tried to say, but found I couldn't catch my breath, let alone speak. "I'm a weak *Canadian*."

6

Note to Self:
Don't Knock Over U.S. Senators

I returned to New York bruised, tired, and with a new, improbable skill: I was now pretty good with a handgun.

"How was Belgium?" Naoko asked excitedly when I got home, carrying my suitcase with an arm still aching from Shem's training. On the advice of the security officer at the Mission, I had told her that I had been sent by "the U.N." on a business trip to Europe. She was sitting on the couch and drinking a beer as I came in.

"It was good," I answered, collapsing wearily beside her. "Have you ever been?"

We proceeded to discuss Brussels for a while, with me straining to recall a trip I had taken there some years before.

"I got you this," I said after a while, giving her a little plastic figurine I had purchased in Herzliyya, and that I thought looked somewhat European. Only on the flight over had I remembered to take off the little price sticker that had Hebrew writing on it.

"Thanks!" she said, looking at it. "It's so cute, and it looks so Belgian!" Then she said, "You look tanned. Was it very hot there?"

I had spent a day on the Tel Aviv beach before coming home. "Yeah." I nodded. "It really was."

Back at the Mission, I started to be given more speechwriting responsibility. Some of these speeches—on technology, medicine, arts, the U.N.'s own organizational structures, and a slew of other topics—were not the sort of thing that makes front-page headlines, and were often given by the senior diplomats instead of by the ambassador.

For one of the more important ones, on international efforts against terrorism, I only finished getting all the necessary information two hours before Ambassador Mekel was to present it to the Security Council. It felt like barely enough time to make the final changes, and I was in my office plugging them in when someone from the computer department came in and said, "We need to borrow your computer to test something."

"What?" I asked. "I'm writing a speech for the Security Council."

"It will just take five minutes," he said, and promptly turned my computer off, disconnected it, and took it out of the room while I watched with my mouth agape. Ten minutes passed. Then twenty. At the forty-five-minute mark, I started to get nervous that I wouldn't have enough time to finish, and went to Ambassador Mekel's office.

"Do you have it ready?" he asked, and I explained the situation. Shaking his head angrily, but not seeming particularly surprised that this had happened, he picked up his phone and called the computer department. After a few seconds of talking calmly to whoever had answered the phone, he yelled, "He's writing a speech that will be given to the Security Council in one hour!"

After slamming down the phone, he said evenly, "They're bringing it back to you now."

But even when I did have a computer, things were never exactly orderly. Nothing was ever really planned out ahead of time, even when it was clear that other countries were working on their speeches weeks in advance. Occasionally, if an upcoming speech was deemed particularly important, I would be given notice with some time to spare, but the general procedure was chaotic and last-minute.

One of the senior diplomats would summon me to their office, or even just happen to pass me in the hallway, and they'd say, "Greg, we need a speech on science by tomorrow afternoon."

"Tomorrow afternoon?" I'd ask, alarmed.

"Yes, or tomorrow morning if possible, because I might have to give the speech tomorrow afternoon."

"But what *about* science? What do you actually want to *say*?"

"Eh," they'd answer dismissively. "It doesn't matter that much. But we need to say *something*."

"Something about science," I would mumble to myself, staggering back to my office, pained by the fact that I knew very little about science but now had to prepare something coherent and preferably substantive to be presented *on the record* as the viewpoint of a sovereign state at the United Nations.

The same scenario played out again and again with many different topics. Sometimes officials in the Foreign Ministry in Jerusalem would actually email me talking points or incoherently written drafts of speeches they wanted revised, but far more often I was left to my own devices. I often showed finished speeches to Martin, who seemed to care about the content and wording more than everyone else, and whose competence seemed somewhat foreign to this whole enterprise. He would sometimes edit it, which I welcomed.

Then I'd go to the debate with the diplomat who was presenting the speech, and sit with them at Israel's place in the assembly hall. There, in my suit, the earpiece in my ear and the little placard that said ISRAEL in front of us, I would try to pretend that any of this made sense or felt normal.

The fact that Israel is not exactly just another country heightened my sense of being a stranger in a strange land. In addition to Iran, other members of the U.N. refused to even talk to the Israeli diplomats, and many of the debates, even on issues that really have nothing to do with the Middle East, turned into near shouting matches between the Israeli diplomats and their counterparts from the Arab and Muslim world. On these occasions, I was often tasked with writing quick replies to the opposing side's arguments, sometimes with only a few minutes at my disposal. And sometimes on absolutely ridiculous discussions.

"Look at this," one of the senior diplomats once said, coming into my office and throwing a pile of pages on my desk. "This is what the Syrians said at this morning's meeting. We need to rebut this in half an hour."

I looked at the Syrian speech, which had certain sections underlined. Some of them made serious claims, but others seemed frivolous. One, for example, spent a good deal of time complaining that the Israeli occupation of Palestinian territory was causing increased sibling rivalry among Palestinian children. A second made the claim, without any backup argument, that the occupation was causing acne in Palestinian teens. The occupation had never seemed like a positive thing to me, but acne?

I looked up at the diplomat and said, "Am I reading this right? Are they claiming that the occupation causes pimples?"

He nodded gravely. "You need to write something countering that."

"How?" I asked.

"It should be *easy* to counter it," he said. "It's ridiculous. The occupation does *not* cause pimples."

For the moment things were relatively quiet for Israel at the U.N., but something very big was brewing. Some time ago, Israel had begun constructing a barrier to separate itself from the West Bank. Those in favor of it argued that by stopping Palestinian terrorists from entering Israel, it was contributing to an atmosphere conducive to peace. Those opposed to it believed that the tremendous burdens the barrier imposed on the Palestinians were not justified by security concerns, and that it was above all else a tremendous landgrab.

Several months earlier, the General Assembly had voted to refer the issue to the International Court of Justice in The Hague, the U.N.'s judicial branch, and the Court had been considering it since then. Now, the ICJ was about to issue its legal opinion on the barrier, and all hell was set to break loose. Martin told me to think about what Israel's main messages should be in the wake of the Court's impending decision, and to start considering how those messages should be conveyed.

I read piles of documents and reports about the "barrier," which was the neutral term chosen by the U.N. The Israeli government was calling it the "security fence," and some of its most strident opponents were calling it the "segregation wall," or even the "apartheid wall." Much of it was indeed a fence, but the images that were most frequently seen in the press were of the section that was a stark, gray wall. It was ugly and depressing, and it had some undeniably tragic effects, like separating families and cutting Palestinian farmers off from their land, but I still believed that there was some sound basic logic to it. The Middle East crisis had gone on for too long, and too much blood had been spilled. Under the leadership of Prime Minister Sharon, the guiding principle of the Israeli government was not to seek some kind of peace or reconciliation, but simply to divide the two warring peoples from each other. After all, nothing else had been successful. The barrier and Sharon's tentative plan to withdraw from the Gaza Strip in the near future were tools to this end.

The problem was that while I mostly agreed with the basic premise behind the barrier's construction, I had some misgivings about its particulars. Rather than following the Green Line, which divided the West Bank and Israel proper, at many points it protruded well past the Green Line into the West Bank. In part, this was just a security measure, and a way to make sure that there was a reasonable partition. I worried, though, that there was more than a grain of truth to the accusation that it was, in effect at least, an attempt to take Palestinian land. If it had just stuck closer to the Green Line, I thought, it would have been much easier to justify.

In fact, my creeping concern was that the route chosen was a grab for land not as much for economic, political, or security reasons as for religious ones. On the other side of the Green Line, of course, was where the exceedingly controversial Israeli settlements were located, and with the planned route for the barrier, many of them would be included on the Israeli side of the divide. The official Israeli position was that the "security fence" was not meant to mark a permanent border anyway, but was just a security measure, and that it could be changed according to any future diplomatic agreements.

But I worried that, with a wink and a nod, Israel was actually constructing a de facto geopolitical border, and a problematic one at that. The religious settlers, bent on redeeming biblical Israel and not particularly interested in the idea of a modern state, did not fit in with my view of Israel as it was founded and as it should be: a democratic, secular home for the long-suffering Jewish people. Not only that, it seemed possible to me that their fanaticism could in the long run actually derail the whole state by fatally wounding its credibility. Those around me in the U.N. Mission, and our superiors in Jerusalem, were almost all secular, but because of the power and fervor of the religious right in Israel, national projects like the barrier had to accommodate those who didn't really even see the need for the secular national government. Studying the details of the barrier issue, I increasingly wished that this was not the case.

But I had to deal with the situation as it was, not as I wished it to

be. The senior diplomats began setting the foundation for the strug-
gle we knew was coming, and I did my best to help Martin plan for
it, too. Our diplomats met quietly with other delegations, seeking
to lay out the Israeli case for the barrier in as reassuring a manner
as possible. The hope was that when the General Assembly came to
consider the Court's opinion, these other countries' representatives
would remember the Israeli point of view.

I wasn't usually invited to these discussions, so I just heard about
them in the morning staff meetings we had begun having on a daily
basis. But I did accidentally end up at a couple of these sessions with
other delegations.

Since my arrival at the U.N., I had started to liken it to high
school. Among the various member states, there were the popular
kids, the bullies, the class clowns. But the aspect of U.N. life most
akin to high school was the many social and activity clubs. Founded
and joined by middle-aged U.N. diplomats, the clubs were advertised
by amateurish flyers and, I was told, showcased a few times a year at
a "clubs fair" in the main lobby. As a U.N. diplomat, you could join
the canoeing club, the knitting group, the outdoor adventure club,
or an intramural sports team. There were also informal "mixers."

"Secretary-General Kofi Annan," I told Avi, "must be our student-
body president."

"Yes," he said, "and maybe you could be the prom queen."

With that tantalizing possibility in mind, I went to one of these
"clubs fairs" during this period when we waited for the ICJ to give
its opinion about the barrier. The lobby was normally just a cross-
roads for diplomats moving from one chamber to another or coming
in and out of the building, but now it was set up as if for high school
orientation. Little booths lined the room, each devoted to a different activity or club (SALSA CLUB! BRIDGE LEAGUE!), and U.N. diplomats
milled about in front of the tables, taking brochures. They looked
like they were discussing which extracurricular activity would look
best on their college applications.

I walked by the Salsa Club's table, where half a dozen male, middle-aged diplomats were talking animatedly in what sounded like Serbian. The last thing I wanted to do was salsa dance with a bunch of middle-aged Serbian men, and so I quickly walked on. I made my way slowly through the hall, and then went to the cafeteria to grab something to eat.

The cafeteria was also reminiscent of high school. I took my tray and moved around to different stations, where cafeteria workers slopped mediocre food onto my plate. Then I went into the main seating area, where the diplomats sat at the cafeteria tables in cliques. Higher-ranking diplomats usually sat together, and everyone seemed to sit according to geographic or political alignment. The French were happy to sit with the Italians, but you'd never catch the Americans eating with, say, the Cubans or the Iranians. And, of course, many groups wouldn't sit anywhere near Israel. We were the outcast. If you were seen sitting with Israel in the cafeteria, you'd never get a date for homecoming.

I held my tray, feeling awkward as I looked around for a place to sit. It was crowded and there were no empty tables. Then I saw someone waving at me; it was Ambassador Mekel, eating by himself at a table near the windows. I walked over, and he gestured for me to sit down.

"Greg," he said. "What are you doing here?"

"I came to see the clubs fair."

"The what?"

"In the lobby there's a clubs fair for all kinds of activities that diplomats can do—salsa dancing, canoeing . . ."

He looked at me like I had gone crazy.

"Really," I said. "Avi told me about it."

"You're going to go salsa dancing with U.N. diplomats?" he asked, laughing.

I started to reply, but he cut me off, suddenly serious. "Greg, are you ready to take over and be responsible for all our speeches?"

I paused for a moment, then said, "I think so. At least I hope so."

"Because you know, if you screw up, all we do is point at you and say, 'Hey, it's not our fault. Some Canadian wrote that.'"

I laughed, mostly sure that he was joking.

"Seriously," he said. "You're taking over soon, and after this fence thing is done, the rest of the summer will be very quiet, but then in September when the General Assembly starts, you will be busier than you have ever been in your life. You'll be working late at night and on the weekends. But it will be interesting. You'll be working with the foreign minister, writing his speech, working with all kinds of other people who come in from Israel—"

"The foreign minister?" I asked, taken aback.

"Oh yeah," he said. "You'll be working on his speech for the opening of the General Assembly."

This was news to me, but I tried to act casual. Mekel was finished eating now and was leaning far back in his chair, although not quite engaged in the same level of acrobatics he did back in his own office.

"Okay," he said, looking down at my half-finished lunch. "I have some meetings with other delegations about the fence now. You should come."

"Really?" I asked. "But I left my tie and suit jacket back at the Mission."

He shook his head. "It doesn't matter. Let's go."

We went to the Delegates' Lounge, and sat around the corner from the giant tapestry of the Great Wall that China had given to the U.N. The first meeting, he said, was going to be with representatives of the African Union, and the second was going to be with none other than Canada. I had the fleeting thought that maybe my presence at this meeting was not so random after all, though I couldn't come up with a particularly solid justification for it either.

A middle-aged Arab diplomat walked by us, and I knew that I had seen him in at least some of the U.N. debates I had attended, but couldn't place him. There was a flicker of recognition on his face when he saw Mekel, but he made a clear effort to remain stone-faced and avoid eye contact as he passed by us on his way farther into the lounge. Mekel leaned in toward me and whispered, "That's the Syrian ambassador."

We were waiting for Antoni, the Italian-born Israeli diplomat from the Mission, who would be attending the meeting as well. When he arrived he gave me a confused and surprised look. Sitting down next to me, he said, "What are you doing here?"

I just shook my head vaguely, as if to say that I really had no idea, and pointed at Ambassador Mekel.

"I found Greg wandering around, looking for salsa lessons," Mekel told him, and Antoni looked at me quizzically.

When the delegates from the African Union arrived, I was introduced to them as an Israeli diplomat, and after greeting them, I spent the next few minutes observing the Israelis outlining their position. The African Union delegates nodded, gently asking a few questions, and seeming fairly sympathetic.

"What did you think of this?" Mekel asked Antoni in Hebrew after they had left, and Antoni just shrugged. I wasn't sure if I should really be a part of this discussion, but I jumped in anyway, first in my broken Hebrew, and then switching to English after a few seconds.

"But that seemed to go pretty well," I said. "They seemed fairly supportive."

Mekel and Antoni exchanged a knowing smile, and then Mekel turned to me.

"When a diplomat says yes," he told me, "it means maybe. When a diplomat says maybe, it means no. And if a diplomat says no?"

I shook my head, not knowing how to answer.

"It means he's not a diplomat," he finished.

A few minutes later the Canadians arrived—a middle-aged man who was apparently a senior diplomat, and a woman a bit younger.

I was introduced to them, as I was to the Africans, but then Ambassador Mekel said, "And guess what? He's Canadian!"

They both looked at me, confused and scrunching their brows.

"Really?" the woman asked, and I nodded.

"Yeah," I said, "I'm from Toronto. I grew up there, and went to high school there and everything."

"Wow," the man said. "But you must be an Israeli citizen, too."

"No." I shook my head, shrugging. "Just Canadian. You guys represent *me*."

They were both clearly perplexed, and their faces showed it. Out of the corner of my eye I could see Ambassador Mekel smiling wryly, and I wondered again if I was actually at this meeting for a reason. But even as the Canadian diplomats were still trying to figure out what I was doing in the Israeli Mission, the meeting got under way. Antoni and Ambassador Mekel set about delivering the same sort of argument as before, only now geared more to a Canadian audience. The need for the "security fence" was couched in terms of a democracy's responsibility to protect its citizenry, and Canada's importance in the community of democracies was emphasized. The Canadians seemed receptive to the messages they were receiving, nodding, seeming to agree, and, of course, being unfailingly polite.

There was a familiarity and friendliness between the two delegations, though not necessarily closeness, and they could not have seemed more different from one another. The Canadians acted properly and according to protocol, refrained from making any jokes at all, and, in general, seemed utterly bland. *But of course,* I reminded myself, *don't forget who you're comparing them to.*

After the meeting, the two Canadians gave me their business cards and wished me luck. I could tell that they still couldn't quite figure out what to make of me.

"Those are your people," Antoni said to me as they walked off.

"I guess so," I replied, nodding slowly.

———————

One weekend, during the calm before the storm of the Court's opinion, Naoko invited me to a party at a bar near our apartment where some of her friends from the film world were celebrating someone's birthday. It would be one of the first times I would spend time with her outside our tiny home. Naoko had been accepted to graduate school for the fall, and would soon be leaving New York, and despite my bizarre security concerns, I knew that I would be sad when she went. Besides the fact that she was clearly a nice, sensitive person, she also provided me with a little glimpse into a world that interested me but that seemed very far away. She spent her time with filmmakers, artists, and writers. I spent mine with diplomats, security agents, and former assassins. But I knew that I wasn't wholly suited for the world I inhabited, and that a part of me would have enjoyed hers instead.

When I got to the bar, Naoko, obviously drunk, rushed over to me and put a Hawaiian lei around my neck, giggled, and ran off. She did not seem like a Syrian spy. And as I spent the rest of the night talking to her artist friends, that became increasingly apparent. But it didn't really even matter anymore. She would be gone within a couple months, and this world would disappear from my sight.

When the International Court of Justice finally delivered its advisory opinion, the storm that had been threatening erupted with a force even beyond expectations. On the morning that the opinion was released, I got to work very early, and was walking tiredly down the hallway of the U.N. Mission toward the little kitchen. Suddenly Martin appeared from around a corner, blocking my path.

"Have you read it yet?" he asked urgently. I shook my head. It was first thing in the morning and the document was dozens of pages long. My main priority at this point was coffee.

"It's very bad," Martin said. "We knew it would be bad, but not this bad. Go read it and then come talk to me."

"Okay," I said, heading away from my office and toward the coffeemaker in the kitchen.

Once properly caffeinated, I went back to my office and closed the door on the chaos that was quickly developing in the Mission, though it only partly muted the growing cacophony. I sat down to read through the document; it was almost cartoonishly scathing. In its dozens of pages, it included very little about Israel's concerns about terrorism and promptly brushed them off. By a tally of fourteen to one, the one being the American judge on the Court, the Court deemed the construction of the barrier contrary to international law and recommended that it be torn down. It seemed that, along with the Israelis and Palestinians, the rest of the world was not seeing the nuances in the situation. Israel's most vocal supporters were cheering on the barrier wholeheartedly, while the Court and other critics were lambasting it in its entirety. I worried about the route, but thought that the barrier as a whole made sense. Was it not possible, I wondered, for anyone in positions of power to see the gray areas?

I went to Martin's office, and we discussed how Israel should act. I was still leery about giving my own opinion on matters that seemed well beyond the scope of my experience, but after Martin outlined his basic strategy to me, I gave my two cents as best as I could, and he agreed. We were going to try to keep Israel's response moderate and restrained. The words we wanted to use and messages we aimed to convey were going to be conciliatory, if not accepting— because, despite the Court's opinion, construction of the barrier would continue apace. The problem was that there were a lot of people involved in the decision-making process, both in New York and in Israel, who were eager to take a more typically Israeli—that is, offensive and argumentative—approach.

"Our strategy," Martin said, "has to be to show that the Court is the reactionary one, and that Israel is reasonable. But to do that, we have to keep all the loudmouths in check."

It was at this heated time, about three months into the job, that I rather unceremoniously became the head speechwriter for the Mission. If I had followed my original plan to enlist in the Israeli army, I would by now have already been in basic training somewhere in the desert. But immediately after being hired at the Mission, I had given up all thoughts of joining the army, and removed myself from the list of foreign volunteers scheduled to enlist. It was a decision I was happy about. This seemed like a much better deal.

After a little going-away party for Julie, my predecessor, I went to get my few belongings from my pathetic little windowless office. Clutching them under one arm, I wedged my fingers through the hole in the door where a doorknob should have been—in the end, it had never arrived—in order to close the door behind me. I had become quite adept at this.

My new office was much closer to the heart of the Mission, near both Ambassador Mekel and Ambassador Gillerman's offices. Directly beside it was Avi's office, and just outside was a little cubicle belonging to a middle-aged woman named Hanna who had some kind of administrative job I had not quite figured out yet. I had been briefly introduced to her at some point, but as I moved into my new office, she barely even made eye contact, and said nothing in response when I greeted her, despite the fact that we would now be sitting just a few feet away from each other every day. Focusing intently on her computer screen, her face stern and businesslike, she gave the impression that she was involved in something very important and could not spare a moment to look away.

I was excited enough about my move that this didn't faze me much as I went into my office and surveyed it. There were big windows through which actual natural light was coming in, and out of which I could see the neighboring buildings, including the U.N. Secretariat building. I had a big desk, lots of space, and best of all, a doorknob. After putting my things down, I sat proudly behind the desk. From there I could see Hanna's computer screen, on which there was a video game where a player had to shoot at pink and yellow bubbles in order to pop them and get points.

In the following days, as we prepared for the General Assembly debate on the barrier, things were very busy for me. I wrote various smaller speeches and statements for Ambassador Gillerman and the other diplomats and did what I could to help Martin prepare the big speech on the barrier. Our morning staff meetings, presided over by Ambassadors Gillerman and Mekel, had turned into frenzied strategy sessions where different views on the proper course of action were shot back and forth in rapid-fire Hebrew. I tended to keep quiet at these discussions, just trying to absorb as much as I could with my limited grasp of the language. It was especially difficult because much of the talk involved military, political, and legal Hebrew lingo that my senior-citizen Hebrew classmates and I had never covered. Then I would go back to my desk to work on whatever writing was needed, and to watch Hanna play her video game, which she started first thing in the morning every day and played for eight straight hours, stopping only for a lunch break.

One day during this time, a woman in her late thirties named Dalia arrived from Jerusalem, where she had worked in the Ministry of Communication, to be the Mission's new spokesperson. I introduced myself to her while she unpacked some photos and other little decorations for her workspace. One of the photos was of Ariel Sharon, and had a little handwritten Hebrew inscription, thanking Dalia for something, and signed "Arik," Sharon's nickname among Israelis.

"You know the prime minister?" I asked.

"I've been working for the government for a long time now."

I looked down at the picture, trying to decipher his Hebrew scrawl.

"Sharon is such a cute man," she said, "and so sweet!"

On the day that the General Assembly was to discuss the Court's opinion, I crafted press releases for Dalia to send out, and we worked together to provide the media with copies of our talking points and of Ambassador Gillerman's speech. He delivered the speech with passion and force, holding up photographs of the graves of Israelis murdered by Palestinian terrorists and playing to an atmosphere that was even more circuslike than usual.

Afterward, a long debate ensued about the resolution resulting from the Court's opinion and, of course, the vote went overwhelmingly against Israel. All the meetings and strategy sessions seemed to have largely been for nothing. But then again, I thought, maybe it was the machinations of our opposition that were pointless. After all, over in the Middle East, the barrier was being built as if nothing had happened at all.

Late one night in the aftermath of all this, I was sitting at home on the couch with Naoko, watching a movie, when my phone suddenly rang. It was close to midnight, but when I looked at the call display I saw that it was Martin calling. *What now?* I thought as I reluctantly answered it, conscious of the fact that a possible Syrian spy was sitting next to me in her pajamas, sharing my popcorn.

"Hi Martin," I said.

"Did you write this?" he yelled frantically into the phone, without even saying hello. "Were you there?"

I had no idea what he was talking about, and told him so.

"I'm getting all sorts of angry cables from the Foreign Ministry in Jerusalem about this. Who let this happen?"

"Martin," I said, trying to calm him down. "I really don't know what you're talking about."

"You weren't with Danny at the GA when he said that stuff?" he demanded. "You didn't write it?"

I assured him again that I had no idea what he was talking about, but that I had not been with Ambassador Gillerman at the General Assembly in the last few days.

"I'll call you back," he said, and hung up.

"What was that all about?" Naoko asked.

"Oh, just a work thing."

"So late at night?"

"I work with a bunch of crazy people," I said, and she just nodded.

Martin didn't actually call me back that night, but, saying good night to Naoko, I went into my room to log onto the internet to investigate what the call was about. It didn't take long to figure it out because it was all over the media. The post-vote General Assembly discussions about the "security fence" resolution—where countries commented on each other's votes and explained their own—were still going on, and continued to be heated and acrimonious. At one session, with nobody there to help him craft his words, Ambassador Gillerman had apparently just been winging it. Among other things, he told the Assembly that for the Palestinian Authority to "lecture anyone about the rule of law or accuse others of being outlaws, we have indeed reached a point where the inmates are running the asylum."

This comment was being interpreted as a comparison of the U.N. and an asylum, and was resulting in a lot of angry responses not only from Arab delegations, but also from European ones, U.N. officials, and the media. The ambassador was taking a firestorm of flak from around the world, and I went to sleep very glad that I had not written those words.

The next day, though, I was tasked with formulating Israel's official apology, which was to be distributed to all the U.N. member states, as well as to the secretary-general and the president of the

General Assembly. Ambassador Gillerman was making the argument that he had meant that the Palestinian Authority, and not the United Nations General Assembly itself, was being run by lunatics. This was also the gist of the formal explanation I was told to write. I was instructed, though, not to come off as *too* apologetic.

Entirely undeterred, Israel continued building the barrier. The general belief in the government was that the United Nations was a politicized organization that was biased against Israel, and that the country's foremost responsibility was to protect its citizens. And because the Court's opinion was not actually legally binding, ignoring it would not have any substantive repercussions. In any case, the United States was supporting Israel's right to construct the "security fence," and to the Israeli decision makers, that was all that really mattered.

For me, the most memorable part of this whole barrier episode, and the most potentially embarrassing, happened across the street from the U.N. While we fought diplomatic battles in the building, and dueling parties fired potshots at each other in the national and international press, there were continual protests and counterprotests outside the U.N. Adding to this circus, various American politicians took the opportunity to grandstand a little, seizing the moment to bolster their pro-Israel credentials. One of these was Senator Hillary Clinton.

Ambassador Gillerman had just participated in a question-and-answer session outside the Security Council for a throng of journalists from every media outlet imaginable, and was now scheduled to do a joint press conference with Senator Clinton. Several of us from the Mission were trying to stay by his side while he did these and many other events throughout the day, both for moral support, and to do our best to help avoid further firestorms sparked by any less-than-perfectly-crafted phrases.

The Secret Service had closed off First Avenue, and as we followed Ambassador Gillerman out of the U.N., we darted across the street toward the mob that was already standing on the other side. Because it was apparent that the press conference had already begun, we ran quickly, flanked by both our Israeli bodyguards and by armed members of the U.S. State Department's Diplomatic Security Division, who were sometimes lent to us on occasions that demanded heightened security.

I found myself near the front of this little group, hurtling toward the crowd on the sidewalk, where some members of the Secret Service stepped aside for us. Before they moved, I hadn't quite realized how close I already was to the crowd or that we were coming in behind where Gillerman and Clinton would be standing. I was going too fast to stop quickly, and I saw that in a split second I would crash into a woman who stood facing the crowd, her back to me.

My first thought was: *Oh my God! I'm going to smash into that woman.*

My next thought, as I struggled to avoid knocking her over, was: *Oh my God! That woman has a HUGE head!*

Then, as I careened to a stop inches away from her, I thought: *Oh my God! That woman with the huge head who I'm about to knock over is HILLARY CLINTON!*

I actually did brush into her—very lightly, thankfully—and she glanced at me for a second. She was already talking to the horde of journalists, photographers, and onlookers arrayed around her, and didn't let this interruption distract her or break her poise. For my part, embarrassed by this, but relieved that it didn't end as badly as it could have, I leaped away from the senator just as Ambassador Gillerman smoothly strode in, greeted her, and joined the press conference amid a flurry of flashes from the photographers.

One of Clinton's Secret Service guards gave me a very stern look. He had clearly seen what had almost happened, but recognized that it was unintentional. I glanced around to see if anyone else had seen it and caught the eye of a woman around my age who was clearly one of Clinton's staffers. She was standing right behind her boss and holding an official-looking clipboard.

"Do you work for the ambassador?" she whispered to me, and I nodded.

"I work for Senator Clinton."

"It's nice to meet you," I whispered back, and we shook hands as our two bosses fielded questions from the audience, angrily and righteously affirming Israel's right to build the "security fence."

Clinton's aide leaned in to me, and said, "You almost smashed into her, didn't you?"

I smiled guiltily. She was probably imagining the same newspaper headline I was: IDIOT ISRAELI SPEECHWRITER KNOCKS OVER HILLARY CLINTON.

After this, at least at the U.N., the fuss over the barrier subsided for the time being, but it was poised to be a continually controversial issue well into the future.

7

My Name Is Joey Shmeltz

Everyone had warned me that September was going to be hell for me, because that was when the new session of the General Assembly would open, the U.N.'s most chaotic time of the year. Throughout August, though, things were exceedingly quiet. A lot of the diplomats and other officials at the U.N. went back to their home countries for the month, and so there were very few meetings or debates, almost none of them of much importance. The need for the smaller speeches or statements that I had been writing for months now, to say nothing of the high-profile speeches like the one on the barrier, dropped off. I suddenly had very little to do, and New York's sweltering summer days started to drag endlessly.

"What am I supposed to be doing?" I asked Avi one afternoon. He was in his office, leaning back in his chair and watching what appeared to be a Swedish music video on his computer screen. He shrugged, fanning himself with a piece of paper, and shook his head.

"I don't know," he said. "Enjoy the summer! Maybe you can start getting your speeches ready for the fall. Just look at the schedule and try to figure out what Israel will want to talk about."

"And decide myself what Israel will want to say?"

"Sure," he said, his eyes straying to the Swedish pop stars on his screen. "Why not?"

On another excruciatingly slow August day, Avi came into my office.

"Do you want to come to a meeting with me?" he asked.

"Yes," I said immediately. I had no idea what the meeting was about or why I should be there, but I was getting bored just sitting in my office and staring out at Hanna playing her bubble-popping game.

"Great," he said, and I followed him out into the hallway and past the office of the librarian, who was in the middle of one of his louder fits, shouting, "No, you listen to me! You don't understand!" As we went out into the street, Avi explained that we were headed for one of the routine logistics meetings he attended on behalf of Israel.

"I just thought that you might want to get out because there's nothing going on at the Mission."

Avi and I took our seats at Israel's place in one of the U.N.'s large conference rooms. I looked over at our neighbors, the Italians on one side and the Irish on the other, and exchanged smiles with them. Since the incident when I had been shunned by Iran, I always appreciated their presence as a buffer. Although their delegations were bigger than ours—most countries' were—I had started to recognize some of their diplomats, and it seemed like some of them had begun to recognize me.

Avi was involved in the actual substance of the meeting, but it had very little to do with me, so I let my eyes wander hopefully to the Netherlands' seat. There was only an older man sitting there alone. My Dutch girl was nowhere to be seen.

"How are you?" one of the Irish representatives, about ten years older than me, asked me at a short break in the meeting, when Avi had gone to the restroom.

"Good," I said, smiling. "It's sort of nice and peaceful now, before the new General Assembly session starts in a few weeks."

"Sure"—he nodded—"but today's a bit of a busy day, isn't it?"

I wasn't really sure what he meant, but I just nodded slowly. He must have picked up on my uncertainty because he asked, "You guys *are* going to be at the General Assembly this afternoon, aren't you? It seems like a debate that directly concerns your country."

My country.

I had no idea what he was talking about, but I nodded again. "Right, right. We'll be there."

There were very few people at the Israeli Mission that day, and I didn't know of anybody going to the General Assembly that afternoon. This was definitely not something I would always be aware of, so I wasn't too concerned, but when Avi got back, I quietly mentioned it to him. He was most definitely aware of everyone's schedule—it was part of his job—and he hadn't heard of this debate either.

"Are you sure?" he whispered to me, and I just pointed at the Irish delegate and shrugged. He must have realized we were talking about him, because even though the meeting had started again, he turned toward us and smiled questioningly. Avi leaned forward. I could see that he was trying to figure out how to phrase this properly without making the Israeli Mission look amateurish.

"There's a debate in the General Assembly this afternoon, right?" he asked, and I thought he'd done a pretty good job of saving face.

"Yes," the Irish representative said. "On resolution . . ."

And he said a specific resolution number. The number meant absolutely nothing to me, and I wasn't sure if it meant something to Avi, but he just nodded. When the Irish representative was again focused on the meeting at hand, Avi whispered to me, "I don't think anyone in the Mission knows about this, and it sounds like we should."

Right after this meeting we went quickly back to the Mission, where Avi told our superiors about the debate. There was almost nobody at the Mission at all, and those there already had their afternoons planned. "You should go," one of them said to me. "It won't be a big deal. Just take notes."

Nobody thought to explain to me what the resolution was about, and I didn't think to ask, but I was happy to agree, seeing as I had very little else to do. And although I had not yet done it at a meeting of the General Assembly, I had gone on a few of these little note-taking missions at the U.N.'s other organs. I went to the meeting hall and took my seat at Israel's place, the little placard ISRAEL in front of me. Thankfully, Italy and Ireland were there, so I didn't have to deal with Iran sitting—or refusing to sit—right beside me. But these were not the same one or two relatively young people who had been beside Avi and me that morning. They were older, much more senior people from the delegations, each with several assistants, and when I sat down between them, they both gave me a sort of bemused look, as if they were surprised that it was me representing Israel at this meeting. Also, there seemed to be a bit more tension in the room than usual, and a few more people than would normally be present at a regular discussion. Something was clearly up.

Although I didn't recognize him, the Italian representative greeted me and shook my hand. Then he leaned in a bit and said, "So you know, the vote is definitely going to happen today after all."

I smiled and nodded, as if I knew what he was talking about. But I was suddenly numb. *The vote? The vote? What vote? Nobody said anything about a vote!*

"So have you decided how you're voting?" I asked, more than a little awkwardly. I had absolutely no idea how this sort of discussion normally progressed.

Clearly that was not how, because he gave me a strange look and nodded. "Yes, we've worked it out."

I knew at very least that the "we" was not just the Italian delegation, but the whole European Union, who always voted together on issues of foreign policy. Still, that cleared up nothing for me.

"Would you excuse me?" I said to the Italian as suavely as possible—which is to say not suavely at all—before darting out of the room to the hallway, clutching my cell phone. There were still lots of people streaming in, and many had not yet taken their seats, so I knew there was still some time and was not yet totally overcome by the situation.

I called the Israeli Mission, trying the extensions of various senior diplomats, but none of them picked up. Finally I reached Ambassador Mekel's secretary, Tammy, and started to tell her about the situation, but the phone connection dropped. I had previously noticed that cell-phone reception at the U.N. was terrible, but it had never really affected me until now. I tried again, and was not able to get any signal whatsoever.

I went back into the conference hall to see how things stood. Although there were more people sitting down than before, some were still milling about, so I figured I had at least a couple more minutes. Running back out into the hallway, I raced to a set of windows, hoping that my reception would be better there. I managed to make the call, but lost the connection before anyone picked up.

I swore quietly to myself, unsure what to do. This bad cell-phone reception problem, I thought, probably didn't affect most diplomats here quite as much because *they probably actually knew what they were doing*. I was not so lucky. I raced back into the assembly hall, desperately trying my cell phone again. It rang a few times, and Tammy picked up again.

"Greg," she said. "What's wrong?"

"I need to talk to someone who can tell me how to vote," I said urgently.

"Greg, are you there?"

"Tammy, please give me Ambassador Mekel or one of the other diplomats."

"Greg? Can you hear me, Greg?"

And then she hung up.

I scanned the room, noting that most people were now seated, and those up front who ran the meeting were clearly getting ready to proceed. Starting to get a bit desperate—*Should I vote at all? Will there be repercussions if I don't vote? What are we even voting about?*—I looked around the room again, hoping that some solution to this problem would present itself. Then one did: the United States of America.

There, on the other side of the room, was the place where the United States' delegates were going to be sitting. Standing just beside it was a middle-aged male diplomat, and two other diplomats, a man and a woman in their late thirties. I decided that they were probably from the American delegation and walked in their direction. I knew that Israel usually voted along with the Americans, their closest ally and supporter. And since there were no Israelis around to tell me what to do, I figured that I might as well just ask the Americans.

I walked up to them, and after quickly confirming that their U.N. tags listed their country as the United States, I greeted the one who appeared to be the senior diplomat. He was in his mid to late fifties, and was quite clearly an important official from the U.S. State Department. Just as clearly to him, I was sure, I was a fool.

"Um, yeah . . ." I said, drawing it out awkwardly and almost stuttering. "I'm, uh . . . representing . . . Israel at this meeting . . ."

His brow furrowed a bit, and while still trying to remain diplomatic, he gave me a look that seemed to say, *What are you, fifteen?*

"Anyway," I went on, leaning in a bit so that nobody else would hear me, "I don't really . . . exactly . . . know how I'm supposed to vote, and—"

"You don't *know*?" he asked incredulously.

"Not as such," I said slowly, and paused for a second on this note. "There has been some miscommunication in the Israeli Mission today."

He'd clearly had experience dealing with the Israeli Mission, because this part didn't seem to surprise him at all; he just nodded.

"Anyway," I continued painfully, "I just wanted to know if you would mind telling me how *you guys* were going to vote."

He paused for a moment, looking around warily to make sure that nobody was around. Then he leaned in even closer to me. His two assistants did the same, until the four of us were essentially in a huddle on the floor of the assembly hall.

"This is just between you and us," he warned me, and when I nodded, he whispered, "We're voting no."

Our huddle broke then, and I fought the urge to give the American diplomats a high five.

"Thank you very much," I told them instead.

"Good luck," the senior diplomat said, and I walked away, aware that they were probably puzzling over the fact that Israel was now sending very young-looking North Americans to handle its diplomacy.

Heading to my seat, I thought, *No. They're going to vote no! But what does that mean? No to what?* I was not about to ask the Americans to explain to me exactly what the resolution they were voting against was actually *about*, since that would make Israel look even more ridiculous, so I just made my way across the hall, trying to decide whether or not to vote the same way as them. Shortly after getting back to my seat, I could see that the voting was about to begin, and I quickly tried my cell phone again. This time, miraculously, I managed to get through to someone with authority at the Israeli Mission. He didn't even know there was going to be a vote, or what the vote was about, but he said he'd find out and get back to me. He then hung up.

It continually astounded me that things were done in such a haphazard fashion in the Israeli government. I knew that Israel's supporters rallied around its policies and actions with the implicit belief that there was some kind of council of wise elders guiding them. I was realizing, in fact, that I myself had always intuitively subscribed to this feeling. On the flip side, I knew, Israel's opponents, especially its more anti-Semitic ones, saw a sinister, all powerful, and well-oiled machine of a state that pulled the strings behind so much of what went on in the Middle East and beyond. But now, while I prepared to vote at the U.N. General Assembly on behalf of the country, Israel seemed as adrift as could be imagined. There was no wise council of elders benevolently running the show, and there was no secret Zionist cabal. Instead, there were just humans—and, it was clear, wholly fallible ones at that.

After another few seconds the vote was called, and there was no longer any choice but to go for it. I put my earpiece in and looked down at the three buttons—green, red, and yellow. *Well*, I thought, *red it is.*

The Irish and Italian representatives on either side of me had already voted, and I reached forward and gingerly pressed the red button. I looked up at the big scoreboard at the front of the room to make sure that Israel's vote had been cast.

The chairman of the meeting then announced that if anyone needed it, we had a moment to change our votes before they were locked in. *No*, I thought, determinedly. *I'm sticking with no.*

The final tally was clear. There were several dozen abstentions, over ninety votes in favor of the resolution, and two votes against it. It would have been inaccurate, I thought, to say that the votes against it were cast by the United States and Israel, and more accurate to say that they were cast by the United States and Greg.

Literally moments after the vote I got a call on my cell phone. Now, of course, the reception was fine. On the other end of the line was one of the senior diplomats from the Mission, speaking urgently.

"Greg," he said, "are you still there?"

"Yes."

"We found out what the resolution is about. Vote against it, okay?"

"Sure," I said. "No problem."

Only later did I find out that the resolution was about weapons of mass destruction.

When I got home that night, still reeling from the day's events, I felt the need to tell somebody about the situation I had found myself in. *Too bad my roommate is possibly a Syrian spy,* I reminded myself as I unlocked the front door. But as I entered the apartment, a sound quickly wiped these thoughts from my mind. Someone was crying.

It was Naoko, who came out of her room as I entered, holding the phone and bawling. Instinctively, I moved toward her, and although we had never gotten close in our months living together—the fact that I had been instructed to hide what I did from her had created something of a wall between us—she came quickly to me and we hugged.

"What's wrong?" I asked, holding her.

Between sobs, she explained to me that she had been on the phone with her mother, who lived in Japan, not Syria, and had simply been trying to tell her that she missed her. When Naoko spoke with her mother it was in Japanese, but after ten years in the United States, she was finding that not everything translated.

"There is no way to say 'I miss you' in Japanese," she told me. "I want to tell her that I miss her, but I can't. It's impossible in Japanese."

She paused, and I considered this poignant situation. My strange afternoon at the General Assembly was temporarily forgotten.

"But I *do* miss her," she continued, and collapsed into me again.

I held her as she cried for another few seconds. Naoko was going to be leaving New York a few weeks later, and I had already found a new roommate who didn't raise any red flags, but as I held her, I knew that I would miss her, security risk or not.

"It's hard," she said, "to live between two different cultures."

"I know," I said, holding the possible Syrian spy as she wept. "I know."

At the end of August, I decided to take another quick trip to Israel to see Shem and his colleagues. This time I would mostly be learning about "intelligence" and "counterintelligence" so that I would have a better understanding of the threats inherent in this dimension of life in the Israeli government. After a quick one-day review of my earlier gun training, I was told to meet at the same hotel in Herzliyya again, but to look for a man named Gil instead of Shem.

"Gil?" I asked someone fitting his description.

He paused for a moment and then said yes in a manner that made me believe that this might not actually be his real name. He was much older than Shem, dressed nicely, and had the air of a retired spymaster—unlike Shem, who had the air of a retired killer. We sat there in the lobby and he outlined some of the very basic lessons of intelligence and counterintelligence work. He was articulate, intelligent, and urbane, and I wondered to what ends he had used these attributes in his career.

After a few hours of this, he told me that he was going to send me on a first trial assignment that afternoon. He told me, as well, that I shouldn't worry if I made mistakes, because I had only had a scant amount of training, and it was important at this stage just to recognize where I went wrong. This was going to be a test in "intelligence" rather than in "counterintelligence," he said, but it would give me a good sense of how spies worked so that later we could work on how to counter them.

He gave me the name of a different hotel and told me that my assignment was to locate the hotel, get as much information as possible about its layout, security systems, and anything else I could learn, get into one of the hotel rooms and map it out, and as a bonus task, find out the names of the last few guests who had checked in. I was to do all this without letting on what I was doing—which, of course, wasn't really too clear to me—and without arousing any suspicion. He also gave me a strict time limit.

Wondering how any of this would help me as a speechwriter, I went out into the bright Israeli sunlight to consider my plan of action in this strange little game. I was standing on a strip along the water, lined with big gaudy hotels of the kind that cater to wealthy foreign tourists and host conferences. I walked along looking for the name I had been given but came up empty-handed, so I asked a series of passersby if they knew where the hotel was. None of them had any idea.

I went into one of the large hotels to ask at the front desk. The concierge disappeared into a back room and then returned after a few minutes, shaking her head.

"Sorry," she told me. "We don't have any information for a hotel by that name."

I went to the big hotel next door, and the same scene was repeated there. At a loss, I went to a pay phone and called Jacob, whose apartment I was staying at again. He was at his job at an internet company in Tel Aviv.

"I need you to find a hotel for me," I told him.

"What?"

"Please go online and look up this hotel," I said, and gave him its name. "And let me know the address."

"Why?"

"Look, I don't have much time, but basically I have to go spy on the hotel."

There was a long pause.

"When will all this end?" Jacob laughed.

"I know this is a bit ridiculous, but can you please help?"

He agreed, and when I called him back ten minutes later, he had the directions for me.

"It was *very* hard to find, even online," he told me, "like they're trying to hide or something."

I got a taxi and, following Gil's advice, was careful not to give the driver the name of the hotel, but instead asked to be taken to a location a few blocks away. *What the hell am I doing?* I asked myself as I got out of the cab.

I was in a secluded residential neighborhood very far from the beach and all the big tourist hotels. It was no wonder that nobody seemed to have heard of this hotel, and I couldn't imagine what kind of place it was. I walked along the street until I saw the hotel. Compared to the big, luxurious hotels where I had come from, it looked pretty pathetic. It was a motel, really, and probably only had a couple dozen rooms.

I lingered out front for a while, taking down the license-plate numbers of all the nearby cars in the little notebook I had brought with me. Crouching behind one of them, and hoping that no neighbor would spot me and call the police, I also drew a little schematic of the property. Afterward, I emerged from my hiding spot behind the car just as a man walking a dog appeared out of the park. I smiled at him as he went past.

I was still scanning the property when the door to the reception area opened, and a woman looked out at me curiously. I waved and smiled at her, as if I had just been waiting for an invitation to come into the hotel, and started up the walkway. Inside the reception area, I pretended not to speak Hebrew at all, as part of the "cover story" I had been instructed to develop, and asked, "Do you speak English?"

Perhaps because it was weird for foreigners to show up at all at this strange little hotel nestled in an obscure residential neighborhood, she gave me a surprised look before answering that she spoke a little English.

"My name is Joey Shmeltz," I said, extending a hand. "I work for a film production company in Hollywood."

She immediately seemed impressed, and shook my hand enthusiastically. "How can I help you, Mr. Shmeltz?"

"Please," I said, "call me Joey."

I told her that I was visiting Israel on instructions from my bosses back in Hollywood, who were planning to come to Tel Aviv to film a major Hollywood movie. The problem, I told her, was that the movie had very big stars in it. On this I paused to gauge her reaction, noting that she was clearly riveted.

"Can you say which ones?" she asked, her eyes wide.

"I can't," I told her, "but they're *very* famous ones, and that is why we're looking for an out-of-the-way place for them to stay. Somewhere where they won't be bothered. Somewhere like this hotel."

I could see her mentally trying to figure out which Hollywood stars might be coming.

"They'd want to stay here?" she asked, gesturing to the shabby little reception area. I told her that yes, they wanted to make sure that they were out of the public eye.

My story sounded ridiculous even to me, but she seemed to be buying it, and she told me to wait for her to get the manager. She went into a back room, where, in Hebrew, she told him almost breathlessly that there was someone in the lobby from Hollywood who wanted to rent out the whole hotel so that big movie stars could stay there.

While she was there, I set about trying to find out who the last few guests who had checked in were. Very quickly, I reached across the counter and grabbed what seemed to be a logbook. I flipped through it to that day's date, but found no names or other information listed. Then I heard her coming back and quickly threw the book back on the counter, imagining what absurd and problematic situation I might find myself in if she were to catch me doing this and call the police or, even worse, the Israeli security services.

The receptionist came back with the manager, who seemed more than a little surprised that Hollywood stars would want to stay at his run-down hotel. But with a bit more convincing on my part, he quickly took to the idea, and brought out his calendar so that we could look at the dates in October in which I told him these big celebrities would be visiting.

After we had arranged the tentative dates, I told the manager and the receptionist—who was still standing there transfixed by the whole thing—that the movie stars in question were very concerned about their security in Israel. They then proceeded to spend the next ten minutes or so showing me where the alarms and emergency exits were located, and telling me that the police were not automatically summoned if the alarm sounded.

"But there is always someone at the desk," the manager told me, "and he does rounds every hour on the hour, so if something goes wrong, he is always here to call the police. And he is armed."

I nodded solemnly, taking this all down in my notebook, including a schematic of the alarm system and which doors triggered it and which did not. Then I told them that, of course, I would need to see the rooms, and they promptly took me on a tour of several. All of them were quite obviously worse than anywhere Hollywood stars would store their luggage, let alone stay themselves. Nevertheless, I nodded approvingly as I took more notes. After that, they stressed that I should call as soon as I knew any more details, and I told them I would.

"Thank you, Mr. Shmeltz," the manager said to me.

"Please," I said again, "call me Joey."

Getting back to the big hotel with just a few minutes left in the allotted time, I went into the lobby.

"How did it go?" Gil asked.

I went through what I had learned about the hotel and its security apparatus, and how I had gone about learning it. Gil congratulated me on a "job" fairly well done, but then proceeded to chastise me for all the mistakes I had made. There were a lot of them. For starters, he told me, I made the faulty assumption that just because it was a hotel I was seeking, it would be like one of the big beachside ones we were sitting in. This mistake cost me a lot of valuable time.

Also, he said, I should never have called Jacob because I couldn't trust him. I should not have lingered outside for so long in view of the neighbors and let myself be seen by the man walking the dog. I had failed at getting the names of the last few check-ins, even if I had made a valiant effort at it. It was good that I had told them that I didn't understand Hebrew so that I could eavesdrop on their conversation, but it was important to realize that it is often very hard to feign a lack of understanding. I had left them with a very memorable experience and conversation, when it would have been much more strategic to leave them nothing much in their minds to think back on about the encounter. And the main problem was that, although my film cover story had been just the kind of thing that gets people talking and opening up, it was a little too unbelievable that celebrities would want to stay at that hotel.

"Do you know what that hotel is normally used for?" Gil asked me.

I had been trying to figure this out myself. It was definitely not a hotel geared for tourists or business travelers, and although dilapidated and exceedingly modest, it wasn't quite run-down or seedy enough, and was in too nice an area, to be a hotel that catered to prostitutes. Gil smiled, and said, "This is a hotel where people go who are having affairs."

At the end of cataloging this long list of errors in judgment and analysis, Gil looked at me with a smile clearly meant to be reassuring. The Jewish James Bond, it seemed, I was not.

But he said, "This was not bad for a first time, though. So, maybe one day you will decide to switch from diplomacy to the world of, eh, more *subtle* ways of doing things for Israel. If you ever want to look into this line of work, you should call me."

Then he gave me a little piece of paper with his name and phone number handwritten on it, which I was pretty sure I'd never use.

8

The Foreign Minister Has No Clothes

Back in New York, I returned to a very different Mission and a very different United Nations. Gone were the quiet August days—broken only by the occasional surprise vote at the General Assembly—and in their place was burgeoning chaos. The new session of the General Assembly was now beginning, and there were dozens of important meetings and debates being held, with kings, presidents, and foreign ministers arriving to be present at the loftiest of these discussions. The size of our Mission had temporarily doubled, as a slew of Israeli diplomats and policy experts had been flown in from Israel and added to our staff in order to deal with the demands of this busiest time of year. In just a few days, the foreign minister of Israel, Silvan Shalom, would be visiting to attend high-level meetings and to deliver his speech at the opening session, a speech I would be working on.

There was a frenetic level of energy and activity in the office. People, many of whom I didn't recognize, were running about frantically, and the sound of printers, ringing phones, and Hebrew chatter was overwhelming. Temporary workspace had been arranged for some of our new officemates in a large communal office, but some of them had still spilled out into other areas of the Mission. When I got to my own office on my first day back from Israel, in fact, there was a balding man in his forties whom I didn't recognize sitting at my desk, calmly typing on my keyboard.

I stood at the door, looking at him, and assuming that he would explain himself, which he didn't. I knew, though, that unlike a few weeks earlier, I would have a vast amount of work to do, and was in a hurry to get started on it. He had obviously registered my presence in the doorway, but he didn't look up at all from the computer screen.

"Hi," I said, and he glanced up at me briefly.

"Hi," he said, eyes going right back to the screen.

"I'm Greg."

"Uh-huh," he answered very slowly, not really listening.

I stepped a few feet into the room and put my briefcase down against the wall, and then politely said, as an explanation, "This is my office."

He flicked his eyes up again quickly, seeming surprised that I was speaking English, and then looked back down at the screen.

"I'm just finishing something," he said in English, continuing to tap at the keyboard with one finger. "I should be done pretty soon."

Breathing out a sigh of frustration, I left the room to wait until he was done.

"What's with you people?" I asked Avi, next door. "First Palestine, and then my office?"

He laughed, and said, "Don't worry. They're setting up a space for him now. He'll be out of there soon. Things are getting crazy here."

For Avi, who handled the daily logistics of the Mission's operations, things were particularly busy. He was coordinating who was handling which responsibilities, as well as administrative details like diplomatic visas for all these visiting representatives, the scheduling of Israel's speeches at the U.N., and small things like making sure that everyone had desk space. In any office this would be daunting at a busy time like this. In ours it seemed more or less impossible.

Another thing that made the office particularly disorderly at this time—and, I imagined, Avi's job particularly onerous—was that Ambassador Mekel had left the Mission. A couple of weeks earlier, he had very suddenly been given the position of Israel's consul general in New York, and to add to the confusion, his replacement would not be arriving for months to come. While Ambassador Gillerman was the official head of our delegation, he didn't sully his hands with operational matters. As we headed into the U.N.'s most hectic season, nobody seemed to be in charge.

When I eventually got my office back that morning, I found that there was a multitude of speeches for me to write: for Ambassador Gillerman, for our regular diplomats, and for the imports from Israel. They were on a variety of topics and for a variety of forums, but they were all coming up quickly, to say nothing of the foreign minister's imminent speech, on which I had yet to be given any information.

Every few minutes over the coming days, as I struggled to make headway on these speeches—taking my cues from talking points sent from Jerusalem, old speeches, the speeches of other delegations, and just plain guesswork—a new person would come into my office, sometimes someone I hadn't even been introduced to yet, and hastily give me some sketchy information on yet another speech that needed to be quickly assembled. The pages and requests began to pile up on my desk, and I was soon coming into work early each morning and leaving late every night. But with all this chaos, there was not anyone telling me, or anyone else, what should take priority, what should be our strategy, or what were our general goals. With Ambassador Mekel now based elsewhere in the building, I was unsure how things would proceed without his eccentric but reassuring leadership.

As the various diplomats gave me their speech requests, I was amused and increasingly frustrated that they would often argue with me, not so much about the policies and platforms I presented in their speeches, but about my use of English. Even the ones who had just been flown in from Israel and didn't regularly use the language tried to "correct" my wording.

"Eh," they would say, "how you are about saying 'fight on great opposition to terror' is not being right here."

"Pardon me?" I would ask.

"You are writing here, in our speech statement, 'combat terror.' Should you not be of writing here 'fight on great opposition to terror'?"

Unsure whether to laugh or cry, I would gently suggest that my phrase choice was better. They would then insist on some negotiation, and in the end I would reluctantly agree that the speech could include some compromise, and we'd end up with a phrase like "we should greatly combat terror" or some other piece of syntactical nonsense. Then I'd send the diplomat off to give the speech, cringing at the stupid wording.

Once, one of the new diplomats who had been temporarily brought in suddenly appeared in my office, looking a bit harried.

"What's wrong?" I asked her, assuming that there was a speech that needed to be written for that afternoon that nobody had bothered to tell me about before. That happened a lot.

"I think there might be a problem," she told me in a worried tone, and then proceeded to explain that down the hall, behind a locked door, there was somebody screaming frantically, and that this had been going on all morning. I told her not to worry, that was a normal state of affairs.

And speaking of lunatics, the foreign minister was arriving in a few days.

For the past few months, I had been repeatedly told that during the opening weeks of the new General Assembly session, one of my more interesting assignments would be working on the foreign minister's speech. It certainly did sound interesting to me—as well as extremely intimidating—but everyone who told me about it seemed to do it with a smirk, or a hint of something that sounded like pity.

In my time working for the government so far, in fact, I had noticed something strange about the role of Silvan Shalom, the foreign minister. Because I worked for the Foreign Ministry, he was technically, way up the ladder, my boss. Even so, most of the strategies and policies we took at the Mission were derived from those of Prime Minister Ariel Sharon, and not from the Bureau of the Foreign Minister. Several people had told me that this was because nobody really thought that Shalom had a good understanding of the world outside Israel. From the delivery of the speeches he gave in English, in fact, he seemed to have no mastery of the language.

"Or Hebrew either," one of my colleagues at the Mission once quipped to me.

"He's just a joke," another said, "who probably would never have gotten where he is if he weren't married to the heiress to one of Israel's biggest media empires. And she's a joke, too."

But still, he was the foreign minister, the country's chief diplomat—even if nobody seemed to care—and I would soon be working on his speech for the General Assembly. Despite all the negative things I kept hearing about him, I was excited. In the next few weeks, in a sort of diplomatic circus, a very high-level representative from each country—in Israel's case, the foreign minister—would speak about what they saw as the key objectives for the new session of the GA.

But when, just as the foreign minister arrived in New York, I was given my first instructions for working on his speech, they didn't make it seem so high level after all.

"In this speech, you should avoid sentences that are more than six words long," a superior told me, in all seriousness. "The foreign minister has trouble with sentences that are more than six words long."

All the visiting foreign dignitaries, including the foreign minister, were staying at a luxury hotel near the U.N. and attending various meetings with one another, the secretary-general, and some influential New Yorkers. Early on the first morning of Silvan Shalom's visit, a messenger arrived from the hotel with a copy of a very early draft of the speech put together by his main foreign policy adviser. It was immediately clear from the short, staccato sentences, and the very simple thoughts conveyed in the speech, that what I had been told about the foreign minister was true. I went through the draft and jotted down some ideas that I thought might help, and later that day received a call from someone in the foreign minister's entourage telling me to come to their improvised headquarters in the hotel to help prepare the speech.

The hotel was a madhouse. The whole area around the U.N., in fact, was swarming with NYPD cars and officers, patrolling for threats and shutting down roads, and the hotel was one of the central hubs of this chaos. Its lobby teemed with staffers from dozens of different delegations, as well as security people, who stood around alertly, eyeing everyone, including one another, suspiciously.

Waiting for the elevator, I heard a mass of different languages being spoken urgently all around me. It was the U.N. itself, only more condensed and energized. When I got out on the Israelis' floor, I found a few people I knew from the Mission and the consulate, along with an enormous number of people I'd never seen before— the minister's retinue. The scene was characteristically chaotic, with Israelis chattering away in quick Hebrew and sometimes yelling for no apparent reason. Everyone was busy doing their parts to make the minister's visit a success, and there was a sense of heated energy in the room. I eventually managed to locate the minister's main foreign policy adviser, a man in his forties who called himself D.J., to talk about the speech.

As we spoke I pulled out my laptop and set about adding new developments and ideas to the speech, and editing it to make it both more readable for the minister and more substantive for his audience. With the six-words-per-sentence guideline, as well as a mandate to avoid words with too many syllables, it was hard to write a coherent and useful speech. Obviously, I knew I shouldn't criticize someone just because they couldn't speak English well. My Hebrew, after all, was pretty pathetic. But I couldn't help thinking, *In a country full of English-speaking immigrants, should such a person really be the FOREIGN MINISTER?*

And I wasn't the only one having to deal with what seemed like infantile needs stemming from the foreign minister's visit. One of my colleagues had been tasked with coordinating when he would deliver his speech to the General Assembly, and even this brought some trying requests. The way it generally worked was for the foreign dignitaries to speak in descending order of rank, with heads of state speaking before foreign ministers. This sounded reasonable to me. Apparently, though, Israel's foreign minister wanted his place in the order to be shifted. The reason I heard for this: he wanted to be on Israeli television at a time when he thought the maximum number of viewers would see him.

Because Israeli ministers, unlike American cabinet members, were elected politicians in their own right, they had to deal with the demands of domestic politics even as they went about fulfilling their own official roles. Some of them were able to strike a balance, and not let one job completely overtake the other. Silvan Shalom, it seemed, was not one of these.

"The minister wants as many Israelis as possible to see him looking like a leader," my colleague told me. "And he doesn't care what it takes to get him that spot."

The foreign minister's handlers had requested ahead of time that the Israeli U.N. delegation call in whatever favors it could from other countries at the U.N. in order to trade spots with another delegation to satisfy the foreign minister's ego.

"You know," my colleague continued, "we could use these favors for other, well, more important things."

But whatever it ended up taking, the minister got his speech slotted into the time that he wanted.

At one point, the foreign minister and a group of advisers and security people came into the room where a bunch of us were working. He was a smallish, stocky man with a pudgy face, a receding hairline, and thin-rimmed glasses. He stopped in briefly, said something to one of his staffers who sat there working, and departed, followed by most of his entourage. It was the first time I had seen him in person.

Over the past few months I'd become reasonably confident in my ability to write speeches. This one, though, was something of a challenge, not just because it had to be simplified for the minister to be able to pull it off intelligibly, but also because it played into domestic Israeli politics in a way that most of my other speeches up until this point had not. At this time in Israel, the biggest political hot-button issue was "disengagement," Prime Minister Sharon's controversial plan to unilaterally withdraw from the Gaza Strip the following year.

For me, the plan seemed like a flash of hope on the Middle East's otherwise dark horizon. It was terrible that, after decades, no solution acceptable to both Israel and the Palestinians had been found, but at least this was something. Israel would pull out of the Gaza Strip, taking its soldiers and settlers with it, and give the Gaza Strip Palestinians some room to decide their own destinies. It seemed like a totally obvious and reasonable course of action to me, and I had come to hope that it would extend to withdrawals from the West Bank as well, which in turn might lead to a real Palestinian state and a peaceful existence for the citizens of Israel. I knew also that although the international community would have preferred a bilateral solution, it was largely in favor of the plan. Ignoring the opinion of the rest of the world and continuing to build settlements in the Occupied Territories would only lead to a further degradation of Israel's image. Disengagement seemed like a way to salvage that image, and maybe some optimism for the future as well. I was very eager for it to succeed, and wanted to do whatever I could, in my limited capacity, to help it.

But although Sharon's plan had tremendous support from the left and center in Israel, the right wing was stridently opposed to it. In fact, politicians in the prime minister's own Likud Party, such as Foreign Minister Shalom, were still trying to formulate their own positions on the issue, potentially putting them at odds with their boss. But this wasn't the Israeli parliament. It was the United Nations, and I knew that the plans to withdraw from Gaza were precisely the kind of thing that would score some badly needed points for Israel in the world body. And since the Foreign Ministry was already promoting the plan, including in some of our speeches at the U.N., I thought it was reasonable to include it in the foreign minister's speech. This earned me a rebuke.

"That's the prime minister's policy," one of the foreign minister's advisers told me sternly. "The foreign minister won't mention that."

The more I delved into the way things worked, the more dysfunctional it all seemed.

I was still attending law school at night, and the first term of my last year had just started up. Because I had spent the first week of the term lying to some poor hotel manager in Israel, and the second week working very late nights with the foreign minister's staff, I had missed a good chunk of the first few classes of the year. On the night before the minister's speech, though, I ducked away to that evening's class. Afterward I would have to return to the hotel for a final meeting, this time with the foreign minister himself.

I came in and took a seat at the back of the class, unsure if my absences had been noted by the professor, whom I didn't yet know at all. My plan was to approach him after class, explain the situation, and apologize. Waiting for him to come in, I took out my laptop computer and opened the foreign minister's speech to continue working on it during class. Most of my classmates used laptops, so I knew this wouldn't be a problem.

How do I rescue this speech? I wondered.

Then the professor came in, a little man with a big, bright red bow tie. He went straight up to the podium at the front of the room, and when the class stopped chattering and went quiet, without even greeting us, he immediately said into his microphone, "Gregory Levey? Gregory Levey?"

I thought, *This cannot be good.* Unsure what was going on, and pretty exhausted from working long hours, I decided not to respond, and just watched him as he surveyed the room, apparently trying to locate me.

"Gregory Levey?" he asked again. "Gregory Levey?"

I didn't know what he wanted, but the fact was that I was stressed enough about the foreign minister's speech, and I wasn't in the mood to be grilled about legal cases I hadn't read or questioned on my absences in front of the whole class. I stayed silent and figured that at the end of class, I would explain everything to the professor.

"Does anybody *know* Gregory Levey?" he asked. Everyone shook their heads. I had never really spoken to any of the students in this particular class, and I shook my head with them to indicate that I didn't know this distasteful "Gregory Levey" character either.

"Okay," the professor said, marking something down on the sheet he had in front of him, "let's start the class now."

I knew that this little episode didn't bode well for me, but for the moment I was more concerned about the speech, and went immediately back to work on it as the class proceeded. When the professor asked questions, I didn't volunteer any answers, and he didn't call my name again. I was immersed in my work on the speech, trying to get a final draft ready to give to the foreign minister just a few hours later, and I was confident that I would make it through the class unscathed.

But five minutes before the end of the class the professor asked a question, and then looked straight at me, calling out, "Mark."

Well, I thought, *that isn't my name, so I don't need to respond.* He called out "Mark" again, and again I didn't respond. He looked frustrated. In some law school classes, and apparently this was one of them, professors wielded seating charts with everyone's names so that they could call on whomever they wanted.

"Who is that sitting in the back row," he pressed on, "four seats in from the left?"

"Oh, I'm not actually in this class," I said immediately, realizing as I did that I was only digging myself a deeper hole. "I'm just observing."

"You can't just do that without permission," he said. "What is your name?"

What would Shem and Gil tell me to do? I wondered.

"Oh . . ." I scrambled. "It's Joey Shmeltz."

"Come see me after class, Mr. Shmeltz," he said. He wrote something else down on his little pad and proceeded with the class, but I knew that I now had some major explaining to do.

"Professor," I said to him after the lecture, now in a hurry to get back to the hotel. "I have to admit that I just lied to you. My name is not Joey Shmeltz."

"Oh," he said reprovingly. "So you *are* Mark."

"No," I said, and he furrowed his brow in confusion.

"Then who *are* you?"

"I'm Gregory Levey," I told him, and he looked even more perplexed.

"Where have you been?" he asked angrily.

I shrugged, defeated in my deception, and in a rush to go.

"In the Middle East," I told him.

When I got to the hotel suites, there were far fewer people than there had been over the previous few days. Most of the visiting Israeli delegates, as well as those based in New York, were at a cocktail party for the foreign minister at Ambassador Gillerman's swanky apartment on the Upper East Side.

I pulled out my laptop and finished editing my take on his speech, and when D.J. and a few others from the delegation filtered back to the hotel, I showed them what I had. We went over it a bit more and at last completed a final draft. Then D.J. went to see if the foreign minister was ready for the meeting scheduled to discuss his speech.

"I'll see if he's in the mood for you to be there," D.J. said to me.

I just nodded weakly at this, too exhausted after what had been a string of fifteen-hour days even to be offended. D.J. disappeared down the hall with a printed copy of the speech, and I waited in one of the common rooms, chatting wearily with a secretary from the foreign minister's staff. After a while, D.J. popped his head in the door and said, "Okay, he's willing to have you in the meeting."

I followed him out into the hall, and we passed through a little station where the foreign minister's own set of bodyguards had positioned themselves in the hallway, to separate him even from the rest of the delegation. Then D.J. told me to wait outside the suite's doors, and he went inside. I waited outside, and suddenly my exhaustion was gone: I was about to have a meeting with the foreign minister of Israel in his luxury hotel suite. I straightened my tie, brushed off my suit, and waited, nervous but full of excitement.

After a minute or so, D.J. reappeared and called me in. As I entered, he stood to the side of the doorway in a vaguely ceremonial manner. Then he said, "Gregory Levey, meet His Excellency, the Foreign Minister of the State of Israel, Silvan Shalom."

Incredibly proud to be there and smiling broadly, I strode in and put my hand out in greeting. Then I realized that the foreign minister was wearing just his underwear.

I left my hand out, dangling for a moment, and thought, *Oh my*

God! Why is this man only wearing underwear? He was wearing a pair of light blue boxer shorts and a thin white undershirt, and was sitting sort of slumped over at a large conference table on one side of his luxuriously appointed private suite. Apparently not embarrassed at all by this situation, he raised himself briefly from the chair and shook my hand limply before settling back down again.

"Thank you for your help on the speech," he said, immediately ingratiating himself with me, but not really distracting me from the fact that I was in a suit and he was in his underwear.

"It was an honor," I answered. "Thank you for including me."

"Have a seat, Greg," D.J. said, "I'll be right back."

As he slipped out the door I sat down in one of the chairs across from the foreign minister, not sure exactly what to say. We were alone in the room. He gave me a half smile, but didn't say anything. *Well, this is awkward,* I thought, wondering why he wasn't bothering to get dressed.

Thankfully, it was only a moment before D.J. came back in, accompanied by the other people who were to be at the meeting. Following D.J. in was a large middle-aged man named Ron who had been introduced to me at some point over the previous few days as the director general of the Foreign Ministry, the top professional in the entire ministry and second only to the foreign minister in importance. Then came Ambassador Gillerman, who looked very surprised to find me sitting in the minister's hotel room, but not all that surprised to see that the foreign minister was only wearing underwear. Everyone but the foreign minister, of course, was wearing a suit.

The purpose of the meeting was for everyone present to read over the final draft of the speech and make any last-minute changes, and then for the foreign minister to try it out in front of us, in case he needed any coaching. Which he desperately did. The early part of the meeting, where we discussed the features of the speech, and additions and deletions that were needed, was conducted in

Hebrew. Then, when the minister started practicing it, reading it in his excruciatingly clumsy accent and struggling to make out the words, I fully understood why I'd been given such strict parameters.

We sat there for what seemed like an eternity as the foreign minister struggled to pronounce the words that D.J. and I had written. It was painful. Each word, even the simplest monosyllabic ones, was a challenge for him, and I couldn't imagine that any audience would be able to decipher these cracked, guttural utterances. The speech was to be delivered the next morning in front of hundreds of dignitaries, including Secretary-General Kofi Annan, and suddenly the immense number of hours we had put in over the previous few days seemed almost wasted. It was funny, I thought, to imagine that he had actually *wanted* his constituents to see him on TV giving the speech like this.

It was very close to Yom Kippur, the Jewish day of atonement, and, on D.J.'s initiative, we had mentioned this in the speech. While we had been writing it, I had questioned the use of the potentially difficult-to-pronounce word *atonement*, but D.J. said the minister himself had requested that it be in the speech. Now it was very unclear why, because he kept fatally tripping up on it on each run-through. When he did manage to articulate it completely, it was always totally unintelligible. Eventually we decided to set the rest of the speech aside and just concentrate on his performance of this one word.

"At-won-ment," he said, and someone stopped him.

"Ate-ony-ment," he tried, and was corrected again.

"A-tun-meent."

"Look," someone said in Hebrew to the foreign minister, "why don't we just not use that word?"

But the minister quickly brushed off this idea. He was, for some reason, wedded to using the word.

"A-toon-mant," he continued.

My exhaustion started to return. It was now past midnight, and it was taking a very long time to get through a not-very-long speech as the minister vainly tried to master this one word.

I wondered if American secretaries of state often sat around in their underwear with their advisers. And as the minister continued, and I struggled to push images of Henry Kissinger in his underwear out of my head, a camera crew burst into the room.

They didn't knock or anything, just swung the door open and marched right in. With some grunted hellos and a couple questioning glances at the minister's attire, they began setting up cameras and microphones. It turned out that they were part of the Foreign Ministry's own internal television crew, which recorded segments for the Ministry's own purposes and, I gathered, for distribution to the Israeli press. Tonight their task was to film the foreign minister as he prepared and practiced for his big speech to the General Assembly the next morning.

They were about to start shooting when, at the very last second, someone suggested that maybe the foreign minister should not be wearing just his underwear in the footage. Everyone agreed, and with apparent reluctance, he went into the other room in the suite and came back with a dress shirt, but still no pants.

He put it on and buttoned it, and then sat back down, so that from above the line of the table, it looked like he was properly dressed for a high-level meeting.

The camera crew started filming, panning around the table and taking us all in, one by one: the foreign minister, his top foreign policy adviser, the director general of the Foreign Ministry, the U.N. ambassador, and an errant law student who had just gotten chewed out by one of his professors.

"At-om-enent," the foreign minister said, slowly and seriously. "A-twone-ement."

9

Weekend at Arafat's

On a beautiful Saturday afternoon that September, shortly after the foreign minister and his entourage had left New York, I was in an ice-cream parlor in Little Italy with some friends. With the new session of the General Assembly in full swing and endless speeches to write, I was often working on weekends, and free afternoons like this one were a rarity. And so, looking out at the sunshine blanketing Little Italy, happy to be with the friends I now saw all too infrequently, I started to eat my ice cream, savoring the peacefulness of this idyllic moment.

Then my cell phone rang. Taking it out of my pocket, I saw that the call was from a number I didn't recognize, and was immediately wary.

"Hello," I answered, with some trepidation.

"Greg," said a heavily accented voice that I didn't at first recognize. "We have some information received for you from surveillance drones in Gaza."

I signaled to my friends that I would return in a moment, and slipped outside.

"What is it?" I asked quietly.

The caller turned out to be the diplomat at the U.N. Mission who dealt with the most sensitive issues. Still eating my ice cream, I listened as he explained that Israeli spy drones flying above the Gaza Strip had picked up images of Palestinian terrorists using U.N. ambulances to transport missiles. It was precisely the kind of abuse of U.N. resources that Israel often felt targeted by, and we were going to respond angrily. He told me that he would email me some information from sources in Israel, and to use it, along with some guidance from Martin, to start putting together an official statement of complaint. I went back into the little ice-cream parlor with what must have been a sour expression on my face. This job was starting to take over my life.

"I think I have to go."

"Why?" my friend Dave asked, alarmed. We had met in graduate school, when our lives were pretty similar. Now he was working in finance, and I was being hassled by phone calls about surveillance drones in Gaza. "What's wrong?"

"I just got information received from surveillance drones in Gaza," I told him flatly, and he looked at me questioningly, unsure whether I was joking. "Apparently, Palestinian terrorists are using U.N. ambulances to transport rockets."

Suddenly I noticed that the guy selling the ice cream was listening intently, his eyes narrowed slightly, and his hand holding the ice-cream scoop hovering in front of him. I gave him a dirty look and said to my friends, "Let's go outside."

I bid them a reluctant good-bye, thinking that my life had changed radically, and weirdly, in the last year.

After a call to Martin to get some guidance on what Israel's official line should be, I made my way to my law school library, since I would have needed special permission from security to go into the consulate on a weekend. It was the latest of several recent times when I had mixed my studies with my job at the Mission, because the combination of the two left me with almost no free time and I needed to use what I had as efficiently as possible. Not only did I now routinely work on speeches while sitting in my law school classes, but when I was sent to various U.N. debates, I often brought my law school books with me and used the time in the endless, sometimes tedious sessions to read for class.

I chose a computer beside a wall so that nobody could see what I was working on. When I was well into formulating a first draft of the official Israeli position to be sent to the secretary-general and all the other U.N. Missions, a woman from my corporate law class appeared beside me.

"Sucks to be studying on a day like this, huh?" she said.

I nodded, making sure the screen was angled away from her. This wasn't the kind of thing I was supposed to let people see.

"Are you working on an essay?" she asked.

"Yeah," I said slowly. "An essay."

When she left I checked the online Israeli and international press and was startled to read that Israel had sent an official complaint to the U.N. about what its intelligence had sighted in Gaza.

No, we haven't, I thought. *Not yet. I have it right here.*

In addition, I saw that a shouting match had already begun, with Ambassador Gillerman speaking to the press and angrily condemning what the U.N. seemed to be allowing to occur. U.N. officials were responding defensively, and a new battle had erupted before I even got to work on Monday morning to deliver Israel's official complaint. Over the next couple weeks, barbs were thrown back and forth, with some people demanding more proof than the very grainy video that Israeli intelligence had provided. Others in the U.N. hierarchy, meanwhile, were saying that Gillerman should have complained through the proper channels—the letter I'd drafted and eventually sent in—instead of through the press.

But Israeli officials, both in Israel and New York, characteristically refused to back down at all. One of them arrived from Jerusalem to brief the staff of both the U.N. Mission and the consulate on the situation, showing us an electronic presentation of the Israeli case and a copy of the wholly unclear video footage that the surveillance drones had taken. On this video it was possible to see some people loading *something* into what could have been a U.N. ambulance, but since I had a totally untrained eye, I simply had to take their word for it that it was a rocket.

And soon it became clear that it was actually not a rocket. What the surveillance drones had seen being loaded into an ambulance was, of all things, a *stretcher*. Israeli intelligence sheepishly admitted this determination well after the situation had already escalated into a big international incident, to which I'd contributed an assortment of statements and letters claiming that it had been a rocket.

It was clearly an embarrassment, but we didn't backtrack all that much. We should not have gone to the press before filing an official complaint, Israel admitted, but the fact that this particular incident did not seem to involve an actual rocket did little to counter the Israeli certainty that U.N. resources were sometimes used to further terror against the Jewish state.

"Besides," one high-ranking Israeli official quipped in a meeting I attended, "a stretcher can be a very dangerous thing, too. If you throw a stretcher at someone, it can really hurt them."

From that point on, the fall months progressed at a wild pace. Between speeches that needed to be dashed off and numerous U.N. meetings, other crises, like the ambulance incident, kept springing up, making life that much more chaotic. Every moment of quiet in the Middle East and at the U.N. was a pleasure, but they seemed rare.

My colleagues felt it, too. Martin came into my office one Friday afternoon on his way home.

"Okay," he said, "I'm going home, and hopefully you won't hear from me until Monday."

He paused, looking exhausted, then added, "If you hear from me, something has gone wrong."

Meanwhile, as these trying weeks continued, wearing everyone down, outside my office Hanna continued playing her bubble-popping video game, seemingly having no other duties. I watched it as I worked on my speeches, and it started to drive me a little crazy. I couldn't understand how she was still so obsessed with it, and why she was getting paid a salary. And then one morning I came into the Mission to find a new middle-aged woman sitting with Hanna, staring at the computer. Hanna introduced me to her and told me that she had just arrived from Israel. Then she said, "Today is my last day. She's going to be replacing me, so I'm training her."

This was the first time that Hanna had spoken to me at all in several months, despite sitting a few feet from me all day every day, but that wasn't what caught my attention. *Replacing her? Training her? In what?*

I took a quick glance at the computer screen and saw some kind of word-processing software that I had never before seen there, despite the fact that I had a constant view of Hanna's screen as I worked. Shrugging to myself as I went into my office, I closed the door behind me. Two hours later, when I opened my office door again, Hanna was gone, her few belongings removed from her workplace. Sitting in her chair was this new middle-aged woman, staring intently at the screen. And playing the bubble-popping video game.

But most of the time I was preoccupied by larger absurdities. One of these began innocuously enough when early one morning, one of my colleagues stuck her head into my office and said, "Greg, I have a favor to ask of you from Jerusalem. Could you meet me in my office in five minutes?"

This seemed strange, especially since as far as I knew, most of our superiors in Jerusalem didn't know of my existence. But when I arrived at her office a few minutes later, I found out that they did have some vague idea that I was there.

"Yes," she told me, "they said, 'Isn't there some guy there who isn't really Israeli? Ask him if he can do this.'"

Some of the officials in Jerusalem had heard that a little planning conference was being held in New York, organized by some pretty radical anti-Israel activist groups. They wanted to find out what was being said at the conference, but didn't want to send someone who was obviously Israeli, or someone who was known to work for the Israeli government. So they were asking me to go to the conference, which was open to the public, and to take notes.

"It won't be a big deal," my colleague said. "It will probably be a big room with lots of people there. Just sit in the back and take some notes."

So I went. But it was not a big room and there were not a lot of people there. Instead I found a small room with about twelve people sitting around a table. There were some empty seats against the wall, and I sat in one of those until one of the organizers waved me over.

"There won't be that many people here, so we're all going to sit around the conference table," she said.

I was unhappy about it, but I took a seat. A few more people came in, and then the meeting was called to order. This was certainly not, as it had been described to me, a conference where I could just take notes. Instead I was apparently participating in some kind of round-table discussion. One of the organizers announced that we had to go around the table, giving our names and the organizations we were representing. I thought of bolting, but made myself stay there, and as the others introduced themselves, I tried to come up with my cover story, just as Gil had taught me back in Israel.

"Hi," I said to them warmly, when it was my turn. "My name is Joey Shmeltz. I'm from Canadian Law Students for Human Rights in the Middle East."

I had, of course, entirely made up this group, but everyone around the table nodded in greeting, as if they had heard of CLSHRME and thought very highly of it.

"Welcome, Joey," the organizer said.

Letting out a deep sigh of relief as the focus shifted to the next person, I took out my notebook. The last few people started introducing themselves, and then one of them, a tall guy with a neatly cropped beard and square glasses with thick frames, said something that caught my attention. He gave his name, and told the group he was a lawyer in Toronto, where he was involved in Middle East advocacy. Then he smiled at me and waved, thinking, I was sure, that we would certainly have a lot to talk about after the meeting, and perhaps wondering why he had never heard of Canadian Law Students for Human Rights in the Middle East. I smiled back and gave him a short, contrived wave, then quickly looked away, making a mental note to dash out of there as quickly as I could at the meeting's end so as to avoid talking to him.

The meeting started, with the group brainstorming various plans to injure Israel's reputation in the PR arena and planning different ways to work together. Some of those present were entirely reasonable, and seemed justifiably concerned with the plight of the Palestinian people under the Israeli occupation. Others just spewed naked anti-Semitism with a virulence I had never witnessed firsthand. It was so different from anything I had ever heard in the comfortable Jewish neighborhood where I had grown up, or in my New York City law school, and it helped me put the ubiquitous Israeli paranoia and insecurity into context. I wrote it all down, knowing that I would never find out what use this intelligence was put to.

Now that I had grown somewhat more familiar with life at the Mission, I'd become aware that some of my colleagues would occasionally provide themselves comic relief from the pressures of our bizarre work environment. One of them, for example, once found a small ladder and brought it into our office suites. He hung it on a wall in the Mission—in a place where visiting diplomats from other countries would sometimes pass—with a note that read, "This is not a ladder." The ladder and the note remained there for months.

A couple of the more high-ranking Israeli diplomats would amuse themselves in a more provocative way, by going up to the diplomats of enemy states after U.N. debates and casually trying to shake their hands, knowing full well that they would just be greeted by an awkward, squirming refusal. All this, it seemed to me, was a way to take the edge off the stressful environment the Israeli delegation inhabited.

So I felt license to seek some comic relief of my own. I still couldn't get over the fact that the diplomats from the Iranian Mission and many of the more hard-line Arab states would not even make eye contact with us Israeli diplomats. I could almost accept that they wouldn't *speak* to us—their countries had no diplomatic relations with Israel and they were diplomats after all. But adamantly refusing to make eye contact in meetings or in the halls seemed to me to be the sort of dehumanizing cruelty common only among twelve-year-olds.

And so for some time now I had been testing them. During tedious U.N. sessions, I would look straight at the Syrian, Libyan, or Iranian diplomat until they felt that they were being watched and turned to face me. When they saw who was looking at them, they would quickly turn away, desperate not to make contact with the Israeli delegation. The game was even more fun when the seating arrangement had them behind me. Then I would turn and stare at them, following their eyes when they tried to avert them, as they squirmed around so as not to make eye contact with the accursed "Zionist entity."

What's the worst that could happen? I thought. *They lodge a formal complaint with the U.N. saying "the Zionist entity was looking at me"?*

But I was getting more ambitious. I figured that if the Israeli government was going to constantly have me do strange things, I would see if I could respond in kind. And so I hatched a plan.

At this point there were literally dozens of speeches for various Israeli diplomats to deliver at the U.N. They ranged from the less important ones, like those on the U.N.'s funding structures, which were delivered to the small committees of the U.N. by midlevel diplomats shipped in for the occasion, to the very high-profile ones, like those about terrorism, given by the ambassador.

Although I was frequently not given guidance on what to say in these speeches, I was still at least told on what subject to write and for which U.N. meeting. But now I decided to push beyond this, just as a little experiment. I scanned through the long list of debates scheduled over the next few weeks, looking for one that Israel had not decided to speak at, but that wouldn't be too controversial. A debate about nuclear weapons or terrorism would not do. I would need something more benign, and soon I found it—a meeting about how sports could be used to foster peace.

I went over to the office of the diplomat whose portfolio dealt with issues like this and, holding the schedule of meetings in my hand and pointing at the debate about sports, asked, "If we're going to talk about this, what ideas would you have for the speech?"

"The ambassador wants to speak at that debate, huh?" he asked, seeming surprised. I didn't reply.

"Well," he began after a moment, and then gave me a few offhand ideas for meaningful things for Israel to say at what promised to be a somewhat insipid debate. Later I went to Ambassador Gillerman's office. I told him about points I planned to make in the speech, as well as the ideas that the other diplomat had for it, and asked him if they sounded okay with him.

"I didn't know the Foreign Ministry wanted us to speak at that meeting," he said, "but those ideas sound fine with me."

"Great," I said, and went off to write the speech.

When I had finished a draft of it a day or so later, I showed it to the diplomat, who glanced at it briefly and shrugged, "If it's okay with the ambassador, it's okay with me."

So when the day of the meeting came, and Ambassador Giller-man asked me if the speech had been vetted, I was able to honestly tell him that it had. Then he and I, along with his security detail, went off to the U.N. so that he could present the speech as Israel's official statement, translated into all official U.N. languages, and transcribed for the official record.

The General Assembly hall was far more sparsely filled than it usually was for the meetings Ambassador Gillerman attended—the ones on high-profile issues—and as we came in, he said to me, "Where is everyone? I thought you said there would be a lot of media here."

I didn't remember ever saying that, and didn't know where he got that idea, so I just shrugged as we took our seats and waited for our turn to speak. And when it came, and Ambassador Giller-man went up to the podium at the General Assembly to deliver a speech on behalf of Israel that I had simply concocted out of nothing and for no reason, I couldn't help smiling and congratulating myself.

But then something happened to wipe the smile off my face. At the most recent Olympics, as it happened, the Iranian government had forced one of its judo athletes to resign from competition rather than face off against his Israeli opponent. I had thought that this manufactured speech of mine was a good opportunity to mention this in a relatively gentle manner, and so I had written in a subtle line about how it was unfortunate that "some countries" decided to use international sporting events as a forum for political attacks. Written like this, I didn't think it would cause any real problems, while still lending a bit of substance to what was, after all, a pretty silly speech.

But when Ambassador Gillerman reached that part of the speech, he decided to improvise and amp up the rhetoric a bit. After saying "some countries," he paused, looked straight across the room at the Iranian delegate, and added sternly, "like Iran," before continuing on with the speech as written.

Alarmed by this turn of events, I looked over at the Iranian, who had been suddenly jolted to attention. He looked a bit stunned, and stared up at Ambassador Gillerman, listening closely. Iran and Israel's Arab enemies were masters at politicizing U.N. discussions on nonpolitical topics in order to use them as forums for attacking Israel. It must have been something of a shock that Israel had just done it in return at one of the most apolitical meetings imaginable.

For my part, I hoped that I had not, with Ambassador Gillerman's help, just started another international incident. The Iranian representative at this meeting was probably a low-level functionary, but I was anxious that after the lunch break, when the meeting continued, Iran would see fit to respond. Then, of course, Israel would have to reply. All because of my little experiment. Luckily, though, Iran didn't retaliate, and nothing came of it in the end.

Iran again, I thought. *Now they'll never sit beside me.*

But not everything was fun and games. The Middle East was suddenly on the verge of yet another earth-shattering event: Yasser Arafat was gravely ill, and had been taken in a French jet to a hospital in Paris. As the whole Middle East held its breath, we tried to foresee the diplomatic repercussions of his death.

The initial reports about his condition had been so dire that it seemed like his demise was imminent, but he remained in critical condition in Paris, and outside of the public eye, for several weeks. Eventually it all started to seem a bit suspicious, and some in the Israeli government started to suspect that Arafat was already dead and those close to him were not admitting it so as to keep a temporary grip on his power.

"What's that American movie where they pretend the dead rich guy is still alive and move him around like a puppet?" Avi asked me one day.

"*Weekend at Bernie's.*"

"So this whole situation is like that," he said. "It's Weekend at Arafat's."

I tried to determine how various speeches we had lined up would have to be altered if Arafat died. Political speechwriters often write various versions of speeches, or even totally different speeches, to be used according to what situation presents itself. I'd frequently altered speeches at the last minute to assimilate the latest events in the always fast-moving Middle East. In this case, I did not want Israel to come off as insensitive to the sadness of so many of the Palestinian people in a speech that came right after Arafat's death.

On the day his death was announced, I happened to get to the Mission before anyone else, and saw the bulletin on my computer screen. I knew that we had a speech about Israeli-Palestinian relations scheduled in about an hour, and that it was not particularly kind to the Palestinian leadership. In light of that morning's announcement, it would certainly appear callous, so I set about softening its wording, working frantically to have it ready in time for the meeting.

Finally, with just a few minutes to spare and my head spinning from this harried drafting effort, I rushed into the office of the diplomat who was to be delivering the speech. He looked it over, approved my changes, and was about to leave for the meeting when his phone rang and a superior—either in the Foreign Ministry or at the Mission, I wasn't sure—told him that the decision had been made several hours before that, because of Arafat's death, we weren't going to do the speech at all. Instead, we were going to just remain silent, and see what happened in the Middle East and at the U.N. in the coming hours and days.

"I'm glad they let me know," I said, still reeling from the last frantic half hour.

I also had a personal concern in the wake of Arafat's death: I had a new love interest. Her name was Abby, and she was an American girl I had met on one of my visits to Israel. She had been living there for a few months, but eventually decided it wasn't for her. We had kept in touch, and now that she had moved back home to Washington, D.C., we had reconnected.

My plan had been to go to Washington that weekend to visit her, but now that Arafat had died, I wasn't sure if I would be able to go because it was uncertain how events would unfold. My weekends had been ruined by my job at the Mission because of far less serious events, and so I dashed off an email to Abby to tell her that I might not be able to make it to visit her because Yasser Arafat had died.

"You have a weird job," she replied.

The following week, things continued to be chaotic. In the Middle East, Arafat was controversial even in death. He had requested to be buried near the Muslim holy sites in East Jerusalem, and the Israeli government was refusing to accept this request, stirring up a political storm. In addition, conspiracy theories were swirling around, causing further uproar. One held that Arafat had died of AIDS. Another claimed that he had been the victim of poisoning.

At the U.N. we had our own problems. Typically, when a world leader of Arafat's stature dies, the General Assembly meets to honor them. Other countries offer their condolences and give eulogies. One such session was now being planned for Arafat, which put Israel in an awkward position. On the one hand, Israel would never participate in honoring someone it had more or less seen as the devil, and even just the presence of Israeli diplomats at the session could be interpreted as doing just that. On the other, it couldn't snub the U.N.

itself by not being there. Over the next few days there were a series of meetings at the Mission and in Israel, trying to determine how to deal with this conundrum. Someone eventually floated a tentative solution that I thought was a terrible idea.

They couldn't send anyone high ranking to the session, so one of my colleagues said, "Why not send just Greg?" Others nodded approvingly, and everyone in the room looked at me. Someone suggested another junior person at the Mission as a possibility, and then they all looked at both of us.

I glared back. I had been asked to do a lot of strange things since my arrival at the Mission, but this was going a bit far. For the last few years Israel had kept Yasser Arafat isolated in his compound in a state of siege. It had threatened to assassinate him on multiple occasions, and even destroyed parts of his headquarters, forcing him to live in ruins. He may very well have deserved all this, but the fact was that now that he had died, much of the world, in the form of the General Assembly, would be paying at least respectful condolences. Diplomacy aside, I did not really want to be there, alone, representing Israel.

I was very relieved when it was decided that Israel would not send anyone at all to the session.

10

Ariel Sharon Was a Hard Man to Turn Down

In the wake of Yasser Arafat's death, while we waited to see what the approaching months in the Middle East would bring, the fall session of the General Assembly came to an end. Although there were still speeches and statements to write, the volume lessened considerably. By January, all of the diplomats sent over from Israel were gone, as was the woman who had replaced Hanna at the bubble-popping game. In fact, I was not sure how much longer I would last either. My relationship with Abby, who lived in Washington, had progressed quickly, and since I only had one more semester of law school left, I was now seriously considering moving to Washington after that and leaving all this madness behind.

In the meantime, something pretty big was on the horizon. For the first time in its nearly sixty years of existence, the United Nations General Assembly was considering holding a session to commemorate the Holocaust, which had been a major impetus to found the organization in the first place. Israel joined with a handful of other countries to sponsor the resolution calling for the special session, and was working with them to garner support for it among the U.N.

membership. It was hard to believe, but some countries were actually opposing it, even as the collection of countries pushing for it—the Americans, Canadians, Israelis, Europeans, Australians, New Zealanders, and some others—tried to amass the necessary votes.

"Japan's on board," one of the Israeli diplomats would announce gleefully after returning from a meeting, or "It sounds like Ecuador is going to go along with this."

We kept a constant, running tally until, with only a few days to go, we were sure that the resolution would pass a vote in the General Assembly. At that time, when it became clear that this would be the result, dozens more countries suddenly sided with us, including some of those who had been quietly opposing it, apparently unwilling to appear defeated. And so preparations for the event began. Luminaries like Elie Wiesel were invited to speak, and the U.N. itself planned to host a big reception after the special assembly, at which Secretary-General Kofi Annan would be present for the inauguration of an exhibit about the Holocaust.

Israel, along with many other countries, would of course give a big speech to the General Assembly. Our spokesperson, Dalia, and I put out various statements and releases to trumpet the event, but the big speech was so high profile that there were a slew of people in the Israeli government vying to work on it, and I knew I wouldn't have much chance to contribute. That suited me fine, though, because it would be Foreign Minister Silvan Shalom who would be delivering the speech. A collection of people in Israel and New York wrote it, and on the day of the session I just did some tinkering to a few word choices, and gave it to the foreign minister's people.

After his speech, the foreign minister was standing on one side of the hall, surrounded by his aides and some of the people from the Mission and consulate. I was watching whoever was addressing the Assembly at the time, when an administrative worker from the consulate came over and told me that one of the minister's aides needed me. I made my way across the chamber to the little mob around the foreign minister, and after I had dutifully congratulated him on his speech, the aide who had requested that I come over took me aside.

"We need your help with something," she said, and I wondered if it was another speech or a statement. "We need you to walk an old man to the other side of the building for us."

"Excuse me?"

She pointed to a very old man sitting slumped in a chair, watching the person now addressing the General Assembly with obvious boredom. He was short and plump, and wearing a rumpled gray suit. It looked like he was about to fall asleep. I assumed he was one of the half-dozen Holocaust survivors Israel had flown over for the commemoration. The foreign minister's aide explained that one of the American Jewish organizations in New York had organized a meeting for the Holocaust survivors who were visiting to speak to one another. It was in a small room on the other side of the U.N., and I led the man out of the assembly hall toward it.

"Was that interesting to you?" I asked, trying to make conversation as we made our way slowly down the hall.

"No," he said quickly, and then went silent.

I pointed out various features of the U.N. as we walked, trying to play tour guide, but he didn't seem to care at all, so I switched tacks.

"Where do you live in Israel?" I asked, and he answered simply and without much elaboration.

"Do you like it there?" I asked.

"No," he said, and then added, "This walk is too long."

"I'm really sorry," I told him, "but your meeting is all the way on the other side of the building."

"Isn't there a shorter way?"

"I'm sorry," I told him. "Do you want to stop somewhere and rest for a few minutes? There are some chairs over there."

"No," he said, walking on resolutely. I was feeling pretty bad for him because I could see that this was all a major effort and that his legs were straining. The walk would normally have taken about two or three minutes for me, but with the speed he moved at, we had already passed the ten-minute mark.

"Are you sure you don't want to rest?" I asked again.

"Isn't there an escalator?" he said.

"Yes, but it doesn't go where we need to be."

"You chose a bad route," he told me. "This is too long."

We walked on slowly and silently for a long time, an air of bitter anger surrounding him. It had been established by now, I thought, that we didn't like each other. He was old, and he was a Holocaust survivor, but his attitude was starting to irritate me. *Look,* I wanted to say, *didn't you survive the HOLOCAUST? This is nothing! Stop complaining!*

After a very long time, we finally reached the meeting room. There were some people already inside and a few more standing outside talking in English, Hebrew, and Yiddish. I brought him to the doorway, where one of the organizers introduced him to another elderly man, who looked positively frail. They immediately began talking in Yiddish.

"I'll be back afterward to pick him up," I told the organizer.

But before I could leave, the two men, both well into their eighties, began talking in heated tones, and seemed to forget all about going into the meeting. I watched with alarm as their exchange grew more intense, until they were actually yelling at each other, but because I did not speak Yiddish, I had no idea what had precipitated this or what they were shouting about. The one I had escorted moved closer to the other one, and pointed an angry finger in his face. The other man was yelling back. I got worried that they would come to blows. Several Asian diplomats walked by, and looked more than a little stunned to see these two old men yelling violently at each other, in Yiddish, in the halls of the U.N.

"Okay, okay," I said, putting my hand on the shoulder of the man I had escorted and trying to gently pull him away. "It's all right."

They ignored me and continued on. By now, everyone else had gone into the room. The organizer noticed the fracas outside, and came out to find me looking embarrassed.

"What's going on here?" she asked me.

I shook my head in bewilderment, and tried again to calm the situation down. The organizer tried to do the same, physically turning the other man toward the room and telling him it was time to go in. He yelled one more thing, which sounded obscene, and went in.

"Okay," I said to the man I had brought over, who was still visibly agitated, "why don't you go into the meeting now, and I'll be waiting here afterward."

"He's wrong," he said to me in English. "He's wrong. He has no idea what he's talking about!"

I waited a moment, and then told him again that it was time to go into the room.

"I don't want to go in," he said, seething. "I'm not interested."

Now the organizer came to the doorway, gave me a questioning look, and then closed the door.

"Why don't you go to the meeting," I said, "since you walked all the way for it?"

"No, I want to go back to my hotel."

And so we began the long walk back to the other side of the U.N. building, with him lumbering slowly through the corridors in an angry silence. I offered him several opportunities to sit down and rest, but he declined them all, apparently determined to leave as quickly as possible. After what seemed like an eternity, when we were finally approaching the exit, he suddenly broke his silence.

"They stole my coat," he snapped. "Where's my coat?"

I tried to remember if he had had a coat with him when I had first met him in the General Assembly or at any time since, and decided that he had not.

"Where did you put your coat?" I asked him.

"They stole it. They took it when I came in."

The coat check, I realized.

"Nobody stole your coat," I said. "They're just keeping it for you. We can go get it now."

We were actually almost there already, and when he saw the coat-check booth, he darted toward it, moving far quicker than I had seen him do so far. There was a long line of people waiting for their coats, dignitaries and invited guests for the special session, but he didn't seem to notice the line, and just barreled toward the counter. Surprised at his sudden speed, I followed, smiling in embarrassment at all those waiting patiently in line.

As he reached the counter, he produced a little ticket and jammed it into the hand of a surprised coat-check attendant, who went to get his coat. In the meantime, still entirely oblivious that there was a line at all, he smashed into the person who was standing in front of him, almost knocking the man over and causing him to drop his own coat. This other man reached down and picked it up, and then turned to look at us.

Oh my God, I thought, *it's the Syrian ambassador.*

I was anxious to get away from this ridiculous encounter, and when he had his coat, we walked the few steps to the exit from the building, and went outside into the cold. I had been told what hotel he was staying at, and I hailed a taxi and told the driver.

"It was very nice to meet you," I said, opening the door and helping him in. "Enjoy the rest of your time in New York."

I wasn't sure if he heard me or not, but he didn't answer. I closed the door and watched the taxi drive off.

Shortly after the special session on the Holocaust, I started receiving reports from military intelligence about Hezbollah forces in Lebanon compromising the integrity of the Israel-Lebanon border, and requests to write letters of official complaint to the U.N. and the secretary-general. Most of the time, such as when the Hezbollah would shoot toward Israeli troops or place mines in the border region, this appeared reasonable. It started to feel less reasonable, however, when the army seemed to become overzealous about what they wanted to protest and sent me lists of complaints about youths on the Lebanese side who had gotten lost and accidentally crossed the border or, quite frequently, complaints about Lebanese shepherds who had taken their flock across the border to graze.

To be clear, the Israeli army was not alleging anything besides that these were actually shepherds, but was nevertheless asking me to write official letters to the secretary-general. I complied, though I had the increasing feeling that this was a bit ridiculous. Then I got another sheet of information from the military that showed me what ridiculous really was. On this one there were several entries where they wanted me to complain about the fact that sheep had crossed the border—not shepherds *with* their sheep, but simply *sheep*.

This sort of thing was starting to bother me, not just because it was silly, but also because I worried that it was actually harmful to Israel. The country had many legitimate reasons to be concerned about its security. There were constant threats from many directions, and they were wholly serious, but I was beginning to dislike the knee-jerk and hostile military and diplomatic reactions to imagined threats. Like the earlier allegation that U.N. ambulances were being used to transport rockets, this made the country as a whole look a bit unhinged, and it diluted the international response to real threats. *Is this jumpiness something I will never understand?* I wondered. *Is my lack of understanding just a product of the fact that I am from a very different place?* I didn't know, but I went to one of the senior diplomats to show him this latest request.

"Have you seen this?" I asked him. "I think it just makes us look silly. This month the Lebanese are complaining that we are flying air-force jets over Lebanese airspace, and we are complaining that their sheep are wandering across the border."

The diplomat told me to go ahead and use my judgment about which of the army's complaints to actually provide to the secretary-general.

"But remember," he joked, "they could be jihadi sheep."

In Israel, meanwhile, Prime Minister Sharon was struggling with a host of legal and political obstacles that stood in the way of implementing the main item on his agenda: a withdrawal from the Gaza Strip after a decades-long occupation. This was a huge reversal for Sharon, who had always supported the settlements, and it had earned him the animosity of much of his own constituency and even of many within his own party. His opponents were trying to block him from realizing his ambition, but true to his reputation, it seemed like he would be able to bulldoze through all of them. In the midst of this he would make a quick trip to the United States, where he would visit the White House and come to New York to give a speech to influential members of the American Jewish community and some American politicians in order to garner support for his plan.

It was strange to me that they needed any convincing. But although there was some tentative support for the plan from mainstream American Jews, some conservative religious Jews in the United States, like their counterparts in Israel, were putting up a good deal of opposition, as were certain groups of American Evangelical Christians. To my mind, so much of the future of the Middle East increasingly depended on the success of the disengagement and its aftermath. That it might be derailed by people who seemed almost fanatical was terribly discouraging.

A few weeks before Sharon's arrival, I got a call from Dalia, the spokesperson, asking me to come to her office. When I got there, she closed the door behind me and said in a hushed voice, "Greg, I got a call from a friend of mine who works for the prime minister, and he wanted to know if you could help the prime minister with something, if you're not too busy."

"Help the prime minister?"

"Yes," she said, talking very softly, "if you're not too busy?"

"I think I can make time to help the prime minister."

"Great," she said. "Let's call my friend, who works with him."

She dialed the phone number, and I looked up at the autographed photo she had on her wall of Sharon. Dalia's friend answered, and they spoke briefly, and then she handed the phone to me.

"Greg," a male voice said. "Dalia tells me that you can write pretty good speeches. The prime minister needs a speech. Can you help us?"

I readily agreed, amazed by this turn of events, and he asked for my phone extension at the Mission, and told me that he would call me back shortly.

"The only thing," he said, "is that for now you can't tell *anyone* but Dalia that you're working on this. Nobody at all. Do you understand?"

I told him that I did.

"I'm writing a speech for the prime minister?" I asked Dalia incredulously after I hung up the phone. She shrugged, as shocked as me.

I went back to my office and the speeches I had on my to-do list suddenly seemed a bit pathetic. I tried to concentrate on them, but it wasn't long before the prime minister's aide called me back. He told me that he was in the Knesset, the Israeli parliament, so he couldn't talk very long, but he wanted to give me a quick outline of the basic requirements of the speech. I closed my office door, and lowered my voice as I spoke with him.

We had a few of these secret phone meetings over the next few days. I would cloister myself in my office, speaking softly so that none of my U.N. Mission colleagues would hear me. I got more detail on what they wanted in the speech, and started sending drafts of it to Jerusalem, and then getting feedback by phone. It was difficult, not only because this was a prime-ministerial-level speech, but also because it was full of delicate, nuanced subject matter about the reasoning behind Sharon's withdrawal plan.

What made it even trickier was that I had to hide the fact that I was working on it from everyone around me, which was hard when they were themselves giving me work to do, and I was taking far longer than I normally would to complete it. At one point, the new deputy ambassador, who had replaced Ambassador Mekel, called me into his office to ask about the progress of something I had been working on for him.

"Are you almost done with that speech?" he asked, knowing that I didn't have too much other work at the Mission at the moment.

"Well," I began, trying to figure out how to explain that I hadn't even started it yet. "Not quite."

"You've had a while," he told me, "you should be able to be done with it pretty soon."

Listen, I wanted to say, *I'm writing a speech for the PRIME MINISTER right now, so I'd appreciate it if you just got off my back.*

But I said, "Absolutely," and went back to my office to work on Ariel Sharon's speech instead. When I had written several more drafts, revising on the advice of the prime minister's aide, I sent what would be my final version, and told Dalia that I had done so.

"Great," she said. "I'll make sure that you'll be able to be there when he delivers the speech."

When that day came, I was just a week or so away from finishing my time at the Mission. I had long since told my superiors that I was leaving, and they were in the process of finding a replacement. I would finish work, spend just a couple weeks finishing up law school, and then move to Washington, D.C., to be near Abby. I didn't have a job lined up there yet, but figured that my soon-to-be-completed law degree and the past year and a half of interesting work would help me find something. It had been a remarkable experience, and I was in many ways sad to be leaving the U.N. Mission and New York, but I was also ready to move on. And writing a speech for the prime minister, I thought, was a good way to end my time there.

The speech was at New York's Baruch College, on the east side of Manhattan. There were NYPD roadblocks everywhere and, of course, protests. I counted three of the latter, though all were Jewish and not, as one might expect, Arab. The first was a small group of secular, left-wing Jews protesting the occupation, but they were completely overwhelmed by the two other protests. One was a large group of "Satmar" ultra-orthodox Jews, who object to the very idea of a Jewish state and often align themselves with the Palestinians. I recognized them from their frequent protests outside the consulate building, where on some occasions over three thousand people had shown up in ultra-orthodox garb, totally shutting down Second Avenue.

The third group of protesters was all dressed in orange, the color used as a sort of uniform by the right-wing settlers in Israel and their very vocal supporters in the United States. These were the people who had idolized Sharon for so many years, and had now turned against him as he planned to implement his "disengagement plan." I looked at them shouting angrily and waving banners condemning the prime minister and his plan. Before I had started working for the government and dealing directly with the facts of the Middle East, these sorts of people didn't really register on my radar. I would never have agreed with them, but if I'd thought of them at all, it would have been as some strange fringe element. Now, watching them seek to scuttle the best chance the Middle East had for peace, I had to choke back my disgust.

With these three groups of protesters—all of whom presumably also hated one another—and the mass of invited guests waiting to get in to see Sharon speak, not to mention the dozens of security people everywhere, the scene outside the college was pandemonium.

Inside, I made my way to the press area, where, Dalia had said, there was a seat for me. There were several dozen reporters there, from every major news organization. The room was at its capacity, about twelve hundred people, which included much of the leadership of America's wide array of Jewish organizations, as well as U.S. government officials. After being introduced, Prime Minister Sharon took the stage amid a torrent of cheers, mixed with a scattering of boos from protesters who had apparently made it inside. I watched as one of these, who was obviously seeking to disrupt the event, was quickly nabbed by security and manhandled out of the room.

When Sharon started speaking, I was shocked to hear that the speech was pretty much exactly as I had written it, with just a few changes here and there. I knew that he had committed some serious brutalities in the past, and was probably one of the people responsible for many of the ailments that plagued the region—the settlement enterprise, for example—but I also believed that he had turned a corner, and was trying to take Israel with him. If he had been a major part of the problems of the past, I thought, he was now the engine of their solutions. He seemed to me to be an epic, almost Shakespearean figure, and here he was delivering the speech I had written.

My reverie was broken by a person standing up in the middle of the audience, ripping off his shirt to reveal an orange undershirt—the color of the right-wing settlers—and hurling insults at the prime minister. Sharon stopped speaking for a moment, and another audience member pushed the heckler to the person beside him, who did the same thing. In this way, he was passed down to the aisle, where a security guard was waiting to carry him away, still screaming. The prime minister watched all this calmly, and then thanked the audience.

"Usually I handle these things myself," he quipped.

It turned out, in fact, that there was a collection of these under-cover protesters in the audience who periodically jumped up, revealed their orange shirts, and interrupted the speech with streams of loud vitriol. After one of these outbursts had distracted from something Sharon had said, the *New York Times* reporter beside me turned to me and asked, "Did you catch that?"

I actually hadn't, because of the protester, but after having labored over the prime minister's speech, I knew it very well.

"Yes," I said, and told him the sentence he had missed.

At one point during my last week at the Mission, when I had stepped out of the office at lunchtime to run an errand across town, my cell phone rang. It was Dalia.

"Greg," she said, "I got another call from the Prime Minister's Office."

What could it be now? I wondered.

"Well," she continued slowly, and I could tell by her voice that she was smiling. "The prime minister liked your speech, and so did his aides, and they want to know if you want to come work for him in Jerusalem."

I couldn't believe what I had just heard. I immediately felt exhilarated and confused. I was, of course, immensely flattered, and started wildly picturing where this unexpected turn could lead me—writing speeches and working for one of the most storied figures in international politics. Sharon was both hated and loved, but nobody denied his importance. The idea that I could work on his staff astounded me. And not just that, I thought, I could be doing this at a uniquely pivotal time in the Middle East's history, as he tried to implement the disengagement plan and move Israel forward. It was a time when real positive change could be brought about for both Israel and its neighbors, and my head spun with the possibilities of tangibly helping to make it happen.

But in the next second I started coming back to reality. It was one thing to do this strange job in New York, and another thing entirely to relocate to Israel. How could I reasonably pick up and go to the Middle East? I was about to move to Washington to be with Abby. I couldn't possibly leave her.

"Are you serious?" I sputtered.

"What should I tell them?" Dalia asked.

I decided that this probably wasn't the time for me to be deciding anything, and told her to hold off responding until I got back to the office. By the time I did, I had spoken on the phone to Abby, who was understandably unenthusiastic about the idea. She needed to finish school, and I wanted to live near her, or at least not an ocean away, and so we agreed that we would have to rule out this idea. But still, I had the lingering thought *How often do you get a job offer from a world leader?*

Conflicted about this new turn of events, I asked Dalia to tell the Prime Minister's Office that I would get back to them the next day. I went back to my office, which I was in the process of cleaning out, and found myself very preoccupied with the offer from Jerusalem. Ever since I had applied for an internship at the consulate, I had let myself be carried along with the flow. Why not continue? And since I was determined not to leave Abby behind, I thought, why not bring her with me?

I called her that night and found that she, too, had considered this possibility, realizing what an opportunity it was for me. Even so, she was leaning toward rejecting it. After living in Israel for a few months, she had decided that it wasn't for her, and now she was in school in Washington. On top of all that, we had only been dating for about six months, none of that time even living in the same city. It really didn't seem like a reasonable idea.

The next day I found out that we didn't have much time to make this potentially life-changing decision. I spoke to the prime minister's aide again, who told me that the position they were offering me would soon be opening up and they needed to fill it. It included English speechwriting for the prime minister, and a lot of work with the foreign media and other foreign organizations. The withdrawal from Gaza was coming, he said, and they needed all the help they could get. I would have to make the decision very soon so that they could begin the procedure of getting me on the prime minister's staff. He suggested that early the next morning I speak to Ra'anan Gissin, Prime Minister Sharon's English spokesman and foreign media adviser. If I took the job, he'd be one of my supervisors.

I woke up at six the next morning, and still lying in bed, I called the Prime Minister's Office. For several years now, beginning before I had become involved with the government, I had been watching Gissin on television. He was in his late fifties or early sixties, and in a fast, clipped, and heavily accented but fluent English, he had heatedly given the Israeli position in frequent appearances on all the major cable networks, always seeming particularly hawkish and angry, even for an Israeli.

"Yes, hello, hello," he snapped into the phone.

"Ra'anan," I said, "this is Gregory Levey, calling from New York."

"Yes; hello, Greg," he barked quickly, and I had to move the phone away from my ear a little. He was yelling, and I didn't know why. "You're gonna come work for us? Work with me? We need you. It's a very busy time here, and it's going to get busier. Are you coming? When are you coming?"

He was talking nonstop and rapid fire, and it was very difficult to get a word in.

"I've been watching you on television for years," I said, rather lamely, "and it would definitely be interesting to work with you."

"Yes, I'm on TV a lot. You know, let me tell you about this position. When I was in the paratroopers, we thought of ourselves as the advance guard, the guys who go in first, who don't wait, who don't take orders, who just go on ahead and look for dangers and opportunities. If you get injured, you deal with it, and you just go on. You know what I'm saying?"

I had absolutely no idea what he was saying, but that didn't matter because he didn't give me any time to respond anyway.

"That will be like you, Greg, in this position. You'll just march on ahead as my sort of front line, looking out for me and the prime minister, for information and news we might need. I don't need people who just want to take orders. I want them to take initiative, like a paratrooper."

I tried to say something, but there was still no room for me in the conversation.

"Greg," he continued at lightning speed. "There's a lot to do. A lot of things to do. News comes in, and we just move. We don't wait at all. If you wait, you get left behind. This is the Middle East. It's not New York. In fact, sometimes we don't even wait for news. We make it ourselves. Greg, I've got to go now, but we're looking forward to seeing you here soon. We need your help. There's a lot to do. Okay? Bye."

With that, he hung up the phone, and I lay there in my bed, going over what had just happened. I was considering saying to Abby that maybe we should go after all, despite everything. I knew that if I missed this chance, I would always wonder what might have been, but I didn't want to go without her.

But I was also aware that making the decision to go ahead with this crazy idea, and asking Abby to go with me, would mean more than just an adventure. To have her disrupt her life, leaving behind her studies, to say nothing of her family and friends, would certainly signal that our relationship had suddenly been upped more than just a few notches in seriousness. Besides leaving the United States to move to Israel, I wondered, was I really ready to so decisively leave behind bachelorhood? I lay there in bed for a long time, waiting for it to be late enough for me to call Abby to tell her about the strange one-sided conversation I'd had with Ra'anan, and the even stranger ideas it had triggered.

"Why don't we do it?" I said to her on the phone a bit later. "Jerusalem is like D.C., except not as dangerous or ethnically divided."

I told her what I was thinking, and by the time we had finished our phone call, I could tell that she was considering taking the plunge. By the end of the day, we had made our decision, just a few days after I had gotten the offer from the prime minister's aide. It was a gamble, and we knew it, but she would drop out of her program and go with me to Israel. Everything was suddenly moving very quickly.

I had a small going-away party on the patio just outside the room where Naoko had once lived, and I was relieved that I did not have to lie to her and tell her that I was now *moving* to "Belgium." My New York friends, meanwhile, didn't really know what to make of this sudden upheaval. Working for the prime minister? Moving to *Israel*? From a New York perspective, hadn't the idea of moving to Washington been bad enough? And when I told my colleagues at the Mission what my new plan was, they were all a bit stunned as well, having had no idea that I even had contact with the Prime Minister's Office.

"You're moving to Israel?" Ambassador Gillerman said, when I sat down with him in his office. Then he added drily, "You know, I can get you the name of a good psychiatrist."

They held a little going-away party for me, and for my new desk in the Prime Minister's Office, they gave me a collection of office accessories stamped with the U.N.'s seal. I looked around the table at the cast of characters I would be leaving behind, and felt a bit nostalgic for events over the past year and a half, most of which had been unbelievably frustrating at the time that they had actually occurred. It had been strange to arrive at the Mission in the first place, but now it was sad and unnerving to be leaving. Just a few weeks later, I knew, I would be on a plane to Israel, with no idea what lay in store.

"When you first meet the prime minister," Ambassador Mekel, who had returned to the Mission for my going-away party, said to me, "tell him I sent you."

11

Is *Plein* Even a Word?

As Abby and I prepared to uproot our lives, the Israeli bureaucracy did its best to make our move as frustrating as possible. Abby had dropped out of her program at school, and we were working on finding a job for her and an apartment for us in Israel. But suddenly there was the possibility that there would be no job for me in the Prime Minister's Office after all. I was speaking to Ezra, Prime Minister Sharon's personal assistant, who, I had been told, was just a few years older than me and one of Sharon's closest confidants. He was coordinating the process of my joining Sharon's staff, but now it seemed there was a snag.

"You see," he told me, "every time someone is hired, there is a committee that has to meet to decide if the job is necessary."

"I don't understand," I said. "There is someone in this job now who is leaving, right?"

"Yes."

"And you need to replace him?"

"That's right."

"So what exactly is this committee deciding?"

"They're deciding whether the position is necessary. If they decide not, then the prime minister can't hire you."

I asked him when the committee was meeting.

"That's the other thing," he said. "They haven't scheduled a date yet. Maybe very soon. Maybe not. It's hard to say. I'll contact you when I know."

After a week passed, I decided to call again.

"I haven't heard anything yet," he told me, sounding blasé, and apparently unaware that this situation could be distressing me at all. "I'll call you when I do."

"This is ridiculous," Abby fumed, after I had hung up the phone with Ezra. "Are we going or not?"

A few days later I called him yet again and got the same response. I waited and waited, hoping it was him each time the phone rang, and feeling increasingly bad about disrupting Abby's studies for what might have been just a waste of time. Even when the committee did meet, there was no guarantee that they would decide the job was needed. Although it seemed to me that the prime minister would need a speechwriter, I wasn't about to put any absurdity past these people. Then, one Sunday afternoon, Ezra finally called.

"Greg," he said. "I've got good news. The committee met and they decided that the position is needed. But we need someone to fill it soon, and I'm worried that if you don't come very quickly, they might give the job to someone else. Can you be here in a couple days to start the process?"

Afterward, my head spinning, I told Abby what Ezra had said.

"A *couple days*?" she asked. "They make you wait weeks to find out if there is even a job, and then ask you to be in Israel in a couple days? Are these people crazy?"

"Yes," I answered flatly. "These people are crazy."

Later that week I was at the airport, ready to find out just how crazy.

Because she still had some things to take care of in Washington, Abby planned to come to Israel a bit later in the summer; meanwhile, I started to prepare for my job. My first meeting was with Ra'anan, who would be one of my two supervisors. Ezra was going to be supervising my speechwriting, and Ra'anan my work in media relations. Ra'anan's secretary told me to meet him and Ben, the person I would be replacing, at one of the big, glitzy hotels along the Tel Aviv beachfront.

Ra'anan was wearing a suit and high-top sneakers. We sat in a lounge area in the lobby, and because Ra'anan was a semifamous person in Israel, people kept walking by and staring at him. He seemed oblivious to this. To me, he looked smaller than he did on television, but as soon as he started talking in his fiery style, he was just as overpowering.

"Greg," he said, "what happened? Why did it take so long? I thought you weren't coming, and I started looking around for other people for the job."

It had in fact been well over a month since I had spoken to him on the phone from New York, but I had naturally assumed that Ezra or someone else would have told Ra'anan that the committee had taken its time. The fact that Ra'anan had started looking for someone else to take the position told me that the Prime Minister's Office had a serious communication problem, which was especially troubling because my new job title was "Senior Foreign Communications Coordinator."

"Ezra told me that a committee had to meet to confirm my appointment," I said.

"You should have called to let me know," he said, but before I could respond to this, he was already speeding into a monologue. "Okay, so today I want to tell you about the job, about what you're going to have to do, and Ben here will tell you his side of things. Because I can't be expected to know everything. Some people think

I should know everything. But Ben's job, your job now, is to know things, and tell me those things."

Suddenly Ra'anan's cell phone rang, and he answered it.

"Get used to that," Ben said to me. "He's on the phone every two minutes. He's actually got three cell phones or something like that."

Ben was an American in his twenties who had moved to Israel about five years earlier. After serving in the military in the same unit as Ra'anan's son, he had ended up in this job. He was ready to move on to other things now, he told me, but it had certainly been interesting.

Ra'anan's call ended and he said, "What was I saying?"

I hadn't been clear on what he was telling me and was searching for the right way to say that when his phone rang again. "Hold on," he said. I looked at Ben, who just shrugged.

Ra'anan started yelling into the phone: "The prime minister's position is that we're not going to wait for a partner. We're going to move ahead, and shuffle the pieces on the board!"

"The job has its ups and downs," Ben told me calmly. "You get to do some very interesting things, and be in a very interesting place, that's for sure. The way things work is a bit insane, though, but you're probably used to that from the U.N."

I nodded, fully in agreement.

"You're going to share a very tiny office," Ben continued, "with a very large man."

But before I had a chance to ask who exactly this very large man was, Ra'anan was back in the conversation.

"Okay," he said. "So early every morning I wake up and call the prime minister and tell him what the important news in the world is. You have to scour the papers and find me that news. You have to be my advance party. You got it? And sometimes I'll ask you to write statements or letters on behalf of the prime minister. You understand? And you'll have to deal with the press a lot. And we'll be doing interviews all the time. You'll be helping me with that. And you'll write speeches for the prime minister sometimes. You know Ezra? Yes, of course, you said you know Ezra. You'll work with him on the speeches. Ben, I told Greg when I spoke to him that this job is kind of like when I was in the paratroopers, because—"

Thankfully, his phone rang again. He looked at it and said, "It's the prime minister."

Then he got up and walked a short distance away, speaking with Ariel Sharon in the same hyperanimated way as he'd spoken with Ben and me.

"Who is the big man I will be sharing an office with?" I asked Ben.

"His name is Alon. He's the director of the Situation Room, which is next door. He's a great guy, but it's a *tiny* room. You know, when I was in the army, some nights we had to share one sleeping bag for two guys. I think this is worse than that."

I had been keeping my eye on Ra'anan, who stood about twenty feet away from us. I was amazed that he was just chatting away with Prime Minister Sharon, and now I saw something even more amazing. Another cell phone rang, and Ra'anan reached into his pocket and produced a second phone. Then, as he took the other call, he seemed to ask the prime minister to hold.

"But don't worry," Ben continued. "Alon is a great guy. A lot of the people you'll work with are great. Ra'anan is great. Others, though . . ."

Here he trailed off for a moment, and I watched Ra'anan return sensibly to the phone call with the prime minister.

"There are some people at the Prime Minister's Office," Ben told me, "who will make you doubt your faith in humanity."

I stared at him to see if he was joking, and although he realized that he was being funny, he seemed at least partially serious.

"Eventually you'll meet a man in the Prime Minister's Office named Yaacov Yerushalmi," he said, and then added slowly, as if to underscore how serious he was, "He will be the worst person you have ever met in your life."

Ra'anan came back to us, holding both of his phones.

"I told the prime minister that I was talking to you," he said, "and that I had to come back to you now to continue my work in immigrant absorption."

I had been told to block off an entire day for my next meeting, which was with the Shabak, Israel's internal intelligence organization. Although my security clearance from the Mission apparently counted for something, I now had to undergo an even more rigorous process.

I was given a Tel Aviv address in an area that I knew was the hub of the Israeli security apparatus, just a few blocks from the headquarters of the military and of the Defense Ministry. I went into what seemed like a regular office building, and took the elevator to the floor I had been told. A middle-aged woman greeted me warmly and, after asking me to sit down in her office, offered me something to drink. The prospect of spending a day with the Shabak had been wholly intimidating, but she very quickly relaxed me.

Even so, despite her being kind and understanding—and allowing me to occasionally slip into English when I couldn't properly answer a question in Hebrew—she was clearly a professional, and this interrogation was far longer and more systematic than what I had experienced in New York. There were different sections, each focusing on a separate aspect of my background and taking between an hour and two; we took little breaks between sections. The whole thing took six hours, all of it, except for the breaks, in the little room with this woman. I wondered if it was the longest conversation I had ever had with anyone.

And the most intrusive. In addition to going over all the questions I had been asked by security in New York, only in even more detail, she asked me to list, year by year, what I had done with my life from the time I had been born.

"What were you like when you were five?" she asked.

"I was like a five-year-old," I told her.

And when we got to the third grade, she asked, "In third grade, were you a good boy?"

Was I a "good boy" in third grade? What does that even mean?

For each period of my life, she asked me for names and contact information for people who had known me, from the time I was an infant until that day. This made sense for my college professors, and maybe even for my high school friends, but she also asked for references from my early childhood, wanting to know phone numbers of my kindergarten teachers. We talked about my family in depth, of course, to the point that I was pretty sure that they would have been unhappy if they had known what I was revealing. When we got to my younger sister, the interviewer asked if she was dating anyone.

"Yes," I said, "but I've only met him a couple times."

"Tell me about him."

I really didn't know much. He was from Winnipeg. I was pretty sure his parents still lived there.

"What do they do?" she asked. "What is their last name? Have they ever been to Israel?"

I gave her the little information I had on these people, and she said, "Okay, we'll check them out."

Finally, when I was already very worn down by this inquisition, we got to the last hour-long section, the most abstract and strange part of the questioning. It began with religion.

"I'm an atheist," I told her when she asked about my beliefs, and she wrote that down.

"Is there any particular rabbi you follow?" she pushed on, which seemed like a pretty stupid question after what I had just said. She then moved on to ethics, morals, and philosophy, and she asked me hazy questions about my belief system, about where I thought morals came from, and other echoes of undergrad dorm conversation.

Finally it was over, and she told me that the Shabak would now investigate my story. I had given her the names, and to the extent possible, the addresses and phone numbers of dozens of people, and wondered if her shadowy associates were actually going to contact them.

They did contact Jacob, who was increasingly getting both amused and disturbed by the demands that my work made on him. Jacob worked at an American internet company based in Tel Aviv, and one day an agent from the Shabak called him at work and asked to meet with him. They arranged to meet at a café near Jacob's office, and Jacob went there at the appointed time. He waited for a while, and then the intelligence agent called him on his cell phone.

"Can you come out and meet me in the car instead?" he asked.

Jacob went outside, wondering what was in store for him. He got into the agent's car and underwent a round of questioning about my past, my interests, my affiliations, and my habits. Just like in New York, they seemed particularly interested in the possibility that I had once been somehow involved in a cult.

"That was pretty damn weird," Jacob said. "They asked about everything, but they asked a *lot* of questions about cults. They seem to think you might have been in one."

Although I still didn't have my new security clearance, I was told to go to the Prime Minister's Office itself for the first of a series of preliminary meetings. I didn't know where the Office was, but I figured any taxi driver would be able to get me there, so I flagged one down. He drove to a big collection of government buildings that all looked pretty similar, and pulled up in front of one of them.

"This might be it," he said.

"*Might* be?"

"Yes, it might be."

"You don't know which building is the Prime Minister's Office?"

"No."

I sat there, shaking my head. It seemed that every step of the way there had to be some stupid difficulty. He put the car in park and turned to look at me.

"Why do you want to go to the Prime Minister's Office anyway?" he asked.

"Because I'm starting a job there," I said, more than just an edge of irritation in my voice.

"Can you tell the prime minister something for me?"

"Sure." I shrugged.

"Tell the prime minister that I said that if he wants peace, he first has to crush his enemies completely."

"All right," I agreed. "I'll give him your advice."

"Good." He smiled, obviously pleased with himself and his insightful strategic thinking.

I made my way toward the building. The heavily armed guard at the gate scrutinized me warily and told me that I was at the Finance Ministry. The Prime Minister's Office was about a block away, and I trudged up the hill toward it in the hot sun. My first thought upon approaching it was that it was absolutely hideous. I had known not to expect the regal beauty of the White House, but I hadn't expected a building that looked like a run-down factory off the side of a highway either.

My next task was to figure out how to get inside. A fence surrounded the building, and I couldn't see an entrance. At the top of a little hill was something that looked like it might be a gate, but there wasn't a path. I stood there for a while, considering my options, and conscious of the fact that I was probably being watched by security cameras as I essentially lurked in the bushes outside the building. Indeed, after about thirty seconds, a guard appeared, barking at me not to move.

Great, I thought, *I'm going to be shot on my first day at the office.*

He approached me threateningly, a gun held firmly in one hand, and demanded to see my ID. I showed it to him, and he asked me what I was doing there. Then he led me down the little dirt hill and around the fence to the gate.

"Oh," I said, trying to sound as congenial as possible, *"that's* how you get in."

He eyed me with irritation and didn't answer, taking me to his colleagues at the entrance. There were a lot of them standing around with vicious-looking attack rifles. When I was finally inside I was passed on to one of the administrators, and shown around the building a bit. I saw the area where I would be working, the media wing, which buzzed with staffers running around urgently and computer monitors giving information in Hebrew, English, Russian, and Arabic. As advertised, my office was tiny, and my officemate, Alon, very large. He was the director of the Media Situation Room, a television-lined room right beside our office that was the hub of much of the chaos. He was very friendly and welcoming, and filled what would be our tiny shared space with warmth. We made small talk for a while, and he told me that he had come into the Prime Minister's Office at the same time as Prime Minister Sharon, and had since moved in ideological sync with his boss. Although he had leaned heavily rightward five years earlier and, he said, was still very proud to do regular reserve army service in the tank corps, he now firmly believed in what Sharon was doing—the disengagement from Gaza and, possibly, even further withdrawals.

After a while, Alon had to get back to work, and I spent the next hour filling out some necessary paperwork and meeting a few more people, but there wasn't much I could actually do until my security clearance came through, and soon I was told to go back home.

"Home" was the apartment we had found in Tel Aviv. Although the Prime Minister's Office was in Jerusalem, I was determined not to live there—perhaps because not having a religious bone in my body, I had never found it inspiring. To me it was tense, depressing, and despite its famously beautiful "Jerusalem stone," kind of ugly.

Tel Aviv, meanwhile, was modern and cosmopolitan, its residents seeming to strive to live as if they were somewhere other than the crazy Middle East. While Jerusalem was trapped in the suffocating Judean hills, Tel Aviv looked westward across the Mediterranean, toward the cities that I loved in Europe and America. There were cafés and sushi restaurants, theaters, and a thriving nightlife. For someone coming from New York, it was a place that I could actually see us living. Tel Aviv was a city with vibrancy and life, while Jerusalem felt like a memorial to endless generations of often pointless martyrdom. Making the decision even easier, Abby's internship was to be in Tel Aviv, and since she had made sacrifices to come with me, it seemed only fair not to burden her anymore. My commute would be about an hour each way, but it made sense.

Our place was very central, and looked out at the city's most famous square, Rabin Square, where former Prime Minister Yitzhak Rabin had been shot by a Jewish extremist ten years before for daring to try to give away land for peace. As Sharon's disengagement plan got under way, it was eerie to look out at the square and wonder what might have been, and what might now be.

As I settled in, I spent a lot of time watching the progress of the disengagement plan on television. Although I had been told that the reason I needed to rush to Israel was so that I could help the Prime Minister's Office during this pivotal time, all the bureaucracy had stood in the way and I sat in that apartment by Rabin Square for weeks. The news played footage of Israeli troops removing the Jewish settlers, kicking and screaming. At the same time, Sharon and his allies told the nation that we had to be sensitive to the suffering of these settlers, many of whom were in tears as they were pulled out of their houses, and some of whom referred to the Israeli soldiers as "Nazis." For my part, I could no longer really think of myself and the zealots among the settlers as being "on the same side." I felt strongly that the settlers shouldn't have been living there in the first place, and that they were among the many obstacles to peace. Perhaps I was being insensitive, but to me it all just seemed like needless melodrama.

Meanwhile, I waited to see which would come first, my security clearance or Abby's arrival. In the end, Abby's arrival did, and I went to meet her at the airport, excited that I wouldn't be alone anymore on this ridiculous adventure. She came off the plane looking tired and worn down but happy to see me. I hugged her and said, "It's so nice to have you here." She hugged me back, but her first words to me in Israel were "It's so horrible to be here."

Abby had some bad memories of Israel. The last time she had been there, she had been considering a longer-term move. She had worked several jobs she hadn't liked, and had wanted to take Hebrew classes but had only been able to afford them by living in an isolated kibbutz in the Negev desert.

This time, though, she actually settled in more quickly than I did. For starters, she found an internship at an engineering firm dealing with water scarcity issues, which was what she had been studying in school. In addition to starting Hebrew lessons, she began working at this firm shortly after she arrived, dealing with one of the most important issues in the Middle East. I, meanwhile, spent most of my time at home, waiting for my security clearance to come through.

It was during this uneventful period that I made the mistake of experimenting with Israeli alcohol, starting with a bottle of something called "Taco Taco." I bought it because the label said "with the taste of Mexican tequila," but I soon learned that this was very different from actually *being* Mexican tequila. In fact, instead of the "taste of Mexican tequila" that it promised, it had the taste of Mexican paint thinner. Still, I thought, at least it was something to do.

After a few weeks, the next stage, a "lie detector" test, finally arrived. Sent to a large office building on the outskirts of the city, I went into a suite that had the feel of a doctor's office. I told a receptionist in a white lab coat my name, and after she told me to sit down and wait, I flipped through the magazines and looked up at a television showing the latest news about the disengagement. There were some other people sitting in the waiting room, and we eyed one another curiously. Instead of thinking *I wonder what disease he has,* I thought, *I wonder what secret job he is trying to get.* Now and then a man in a white lab coat would emerge and call the next person in, and I marveled at the fact that the military and security complex in Israel was so big that there was an entire office—and probably, I thought, more than one—devoted to the lie detector.

When it was my turn, I was led into a little room and told to sit in a big leather chair. An attendant wordlessly strapped me in, putting bands tightly around my chest and some kind of sensor on my thumb. I sat there nervously, not because I had anything to hide, but because this was quite unlike anything I had ever experienced before. Then I was left alone, strapped in, for what seemed like a long time, before "the doctor," or whatever he was, came in, holding a clipboard.

"We're not going to do your polygraph test today," he said, "because of your friend in the FBI."

I closed my eyes in frustration. Before I had arrived in Israel to begin all these procedures, I had filled in and sent a very extensive, thirty-page questionnaire to the security agents in Israel. On it I had listed dozens of names and references they asked for, as well as the names of the various foreign governmental officials I had made contact with at the U.N. They were, of course, particularly interested in whether I had any contact with foreign intelligence agents, which I did not.

When I relocated to Israel, though, I sent out a group email to everyone on my email list to tell them about my new location. I received many congratulatory emails, as well as a fair number that seemed to question my sanity. And there was also one email that was a bit distressing. An acquaintance wished me congratulations and mentioned the fact that he had just started a job with American intelligence, as an analyst on Middle East issues. I knew that this would interest the Israelis tasked with granting me security clearance for the Prime Minister's Office, so I had mentioned it on my first visit to the PMO. Apparently, though, this wasn't enough.

"We need a week to investigate your friend and reformulate the polygraph questions," the man in the white lab coat told me, not explaining why they had strapped me in anyway. On that first visit to the PMO, I had been asked to sign off on the questions they were going to ask me on the polygraph, and one of them had been "Have you ever worked for a foreign intelligence agency?"

I returned to the little office after another week of waiting, and was again put in the chair and strapped in to the polygraph. The same man in the white lab coat came in and told me that they had investigated my acquaintance and determined how best to rephrase the question. He showed it to me on a piece of paper to see if I would agree to answer it.

It now said, "Have you ever *actually* worked for a foreign intelligence agency?"

That took a week? I thought. *To add the word* actually?

"Is the new wording okay with you?" he asked.

"Sure," I said, considering the meaningless change. "Whatever."

This question obviously didn't cause me trouble when we started the polygraph test, because I had never worked for a foreign intelligence agency, "actually" or not. But, oddly, another question turned out to be problematic. The test included questions about foreign intelligence, my psychological well-being, the ubiquitous concerns about my suspected involvement in cults, and all of these apparently caused no problems. Then he asked me, "Have you ever been involved in a major crime?"

I answered no, of course. This was one of the questions that I had been amused by when they had shown me the list. He stopped, and stared at the screen in front of him, his eyes narrowing in concern. He noted something down and then looked up at me.

"We're going to do that one again," he said, paused for a moment, and then asked again, "Have you ever been involved in a major crime?"

"No," I repeated.

Again there was a look of concern on his face, and he stared at the screen as he wrote something down. He paused again, sighed a little, and then looked up at me again, pursing his lips thoughtfully, as if trying to decide how to proceed.

"Gregory," he said, "when we say major crime we are referring to murder, rape, or armed robbery. If you've done something smaller, it is not part of this. Let me ask you again. Have you ever been involved in a major crime?"

I had no idea what his machine was telling him, but it didn't seem good. I had definitely not been involved in a major crime.

"No," I said again, and once more a look of concern flashed across his face. This time, though, he continued on with the other questions, while I wondered if any major crimes had somehow slipped my mind.

Only after several more weeks did I get a phone call to say that all the requisite parts of my security clearance had come through successfully. Since I had had nothing to do as I waited, and was not even being paid during this dead time, I was very relieved.

"Great," I said to the administrator who had called me. "Can I start work this week, then?"

"No!" he exclaimed, and laughed, as if this idea was completely preposterous and he was surprised that I would even suggest it. I wanted to reach through the phone and pummel him.

"What else is there?" I asked, as he himself had told me, just a few weeks before, that this was all that was needed.

"You just have to take a math test, and then you can start working."

I thought that I must have misheard him.

"A math test?"

"Yes, but don't worry, it's very easy math. You'll be fine, I'm sure."

The only problem, he told me, was that because the math test had to be in English so that it would be fair for me, it might take a while for them to find someone who could administer it. He said he'd let me know when that happened.

I hung up the phone, my severe frustration preventing me from seeing the absurd humor in all this. First of all, why the hell did I have to do a math test to be a speechwriter? Second, what did it even *mean* for a math test to be in English, or any language for that matter? And third, why did they need to find someone special to administer the math test—was this an oral test of mathematical ability?

The security check I had gone through had clearly been designed, in part, to make sure that I wasn't dangerous, an alcoholic, or unstable. But all these ridiculous bureaucratic hurdles seemed designed to make me into all three.

I reached for the bottle of Taco Taco.

A week passed before they had located someone capable of administering an English-language math test, and they gave me a time to come to the Prime Minister's Office to take it. I had never been good at math, and I was not amused by the possibility of not actually being able to start this job because of my poor abilities in long division.

"I told you that you should have studied math harder in high school," my mother told me on the phone.

When I got to the Prime Minister's Office on the day of the test, a woman took me up several flights, far from the area where I was going to be working. She led me into a small room cluttered with piles of books, papers, and magazines, and a little desk like the kind you have in grade school in the middle of this mess. I sat down, and she explained that there would be several sections on the test, and that she would come back after each section to give me the assignment for the next part. I noticed that her English was almost nonexistent, despite the fact that they had taken their time to supposedly find someone who could administer the test in English.

The test itself made even less sense. First of all, it was definitely not a math test, but was more like a badly written SAT test from 1951. The first parts appeared to be testing my English ability, but were themselves written in atrocious English, and I worried that I would fail this test of my English ability because I could not understand the incoherent questions. One of these, for example, relied on the word *plein,* and it was impossible to understand from the context if they were trying to write *plain* or *plane* or something else entirely.

Is plein *even a word?* I thought, and just guessed at the answer to the question.

There was also a section involving analogies, but they didn't seem to make sense either. After just finishing law school, and before that having taken the LSAT, the law school entrance exam, I was confident with analogies. But whoever had written the test definitely was not. "Seed is to blossom, as spark is to . . ." one of the questions began, and I looked for an answer that involved the fulfillment of a spark. "Fire," perhaps. Instead the available answers were "fireman," "extinguish," and other words that were related to fire, but that did not actually complete the analogy. I guessed again.

There was also a bit of general knowledge, including the question "How many agorot are in a lira?" I looked at this, dumbfounded. Agorot were the Israeli equivalent of cents, but the equivalent of dollars was shekels. The lira, Israel's former currency, had been abandoned a quarter of a century earlier. I had no idea how many agorot had been in a lira. The section ended with a relatively coherent question, and the instruction to put the answer "in the box." The only problem was that there was no box.

When I had completed this part of the test, the test administrator returned and took the pages in front of me. This time, though, she did not replace them with any new pages, as she had been doing up until now.

"Okay," she said, "I'll be right back and then we'll test how fast you are."

Then she walked quickly out the room, and closed the door behind her, leaving me to ponder what on earth she was talking about. *How fast I am? How fast I am at what?* Five minutes passed, then fifteen. After a full twenty minutes had gone by, I started to feel like I had been forgotten, and wasn't sure what I should have been doing.

"How fast you are?" What could that possibly mean?

I looked around the room and tried to determine if maybe I had misunderstood and there was something here I was supposed to be doing fast, but as far as I could tell, there was not. I imagined her coming back into the room with a stopwatch, looking at me, and saying, "And . . . stop!" She'd check the time on the watch, shake her head gravely, and say, "I'm sorry. Not fast enough."

Instead, when she came back, a little more than *forty-five minutes* after she had left me in the room doing nothing, she looked at me, seemed to suddenly realize that I had been waiting for her this whole time, and said, "Oh, I'm sorry. We went for lunch."

The last part of the test was just as stupid as the first parts. I was given a list of names and words and had to *quickly* rewrite them, as accurately as possible. When I had finished this last pointless exercise, I handed it back, relieved that this latest obstacle was over.

"How long will it take to grade it?" I asked the test supervisor.

"I have no idea," she said. "They have to now find someone else to do that, so it might take a while."

It was becoming obvious that I didn't actually have as high a tolerance for frustration as I had imagined. After having worked at the U.N. Mission, I didn't think this could possibly be the case, but I found myself dealing with a whole new realm of ridiculousness, the depths of which I couldn't have previously imagined. By this point, as I waited for the results of my "math test," it had been more than two months since I had first arrived in the country. And for all I knew, there could be more hurdles still to come.

Why stop at a math test? I thought. *Why not a Spanish exam? Or maybe a test of my vertical leaping ability?*

It was already becoming clear to me that I wasn't cut out for life in Israel and I hadn't even started work yet. Besides the bombings and the wars, the fanatics of all stripes, the hard living conditions that Israelis faced, and the dangers that they braved, I couldn't imagine ever getting used to the very foreign way that they treated one another. They just seemed so absurdly inconsiderate, and I wondered if what I was experiencing was merely a personal version of the same kind of behavior that sometimes torpedoed the country's diplomatic efforts.

Or maybe I was simply more Canadian than I had ever thought. I had always felt at best ambivalent about my Canadian upbringing, but as I got progressively more irritated with the way that Israel and Israelis functioned, I began to think that perhaps being Canadian wasn't so bad at all.

Abby, meanwhile, seemed happy enough with her internship, even though she had been the one much more hesitant to come in the first place. It was me who skulked around the apartment, occasionally checking the ticket prices on flights back to New York, while slowly making my way through that foul bottle of Taco Taco. It was awful, but it was still better than the taste the rest of this experience was leaving in my mouth.

And then one morning, after another week, the head administrator at the Prime Minister's Office called to tell me breezily that I had "passed the math test," and asked if I could be at the PMO in Jerusalem in just a few hours. It was time to start work at the Prime Minister's Office, and to *really* know frustration and absurdity.

12

Dancing Queen

I was considering getting a car for the daily trip to Jerusalem, but in the meantime, there were several other options available—a train, a bus, and a somewhat shady minibus usually filled with a collection of unsavory characters and driven by a madman. I didn't particularly relish the idea of being the victim of a bus bombing, and having taken the minibus a few times in the past and hating it, I was taking the train for now.

The train took a long, indirect route and ended in a spot in Jerusalem far from the Prime Minister's Office. From there I had to get a cab, which on that first day I shared with three strangers, none of whom knew one another. We told the driver our destinations, and almost immediately all of them started quizzing me about why I was going to the PMO. When I told them, they immediately launched into a loud argument about the direction in which Israeli politics were going; I stayed silent.

Ra'anan was nowhere to be found when I arrived, so I went to my office, where I greeted Alon and squeezed in next to him, our shoulders inches apart. Turning on my computer, I looked at the various files that Ben had left for me, scanned some newspapers, and wondered what I was supposed to be doing. After a while, though, I heard a familiar voice in the hallway outside. Ra'anan was out there yelling about something, and I went out to find him walking quickly toward his office.

"I started looking through the day's press," I told him. "Is there anything else I should be doing at the moment?"

"I've lost my phone," he said. "I need to find my phone. I can't work without this phone. I was just with the prime minister, and I realized I lost my phone."

He went into his office, seeming a bit frantic, and I decided perhaps this was not the time to talk to him. But after reading news reports for the next hour, I decided to venture back. As I came into his office, he was standing in the little area where his secretary sat and talking on two cell phones at one time. He had one in each hand and was alternating quickly between them, speaking in Hebrew too fast for me to fully understand. He seemed to be saying something about Sharon's Likud Party. Many prominent members of the party were, at this time, trying to launch a rebellion against the prime minister, in retaliation for his withdrawal from Gaza. I stood there watching Ra'anan yelling into both phones, until the two conversations ended about simultaneously.

"I see you found your phone," I said.

"No," he barked, holding his two cell phones. "That's a different phone, and it's still missing."

The next day a bald, pudgy little man in his late thirties, with a pretty close resemblance to Danny DeVito, suddenly burst into my office and exclaimed, "Let's play meet the press!"

He was talking to me, but it took me a moment to realize who he was. I had met him during my preliminary visits to the office, but had never really spoken with him much. His name was Isaac, and he had told me that he was from Queens, New York, but had moved to Israel more than twenty years ago. In the Prime Minister's Office, he was a spokesperson for the English-language press. He worked under Ra'anan, which seemed appropriate because he was bursting with a similar level of frenetic energy.

"Hey, Greggy!" he went on. "How you doing there? Hey, let's play meet the press, Greggy!"

"Excuse me?"

"We'll go into the briefing room, and pretend to be interviewing each other. It's good practice."

I really didn't have much to do, but this sounded horrible, so I demurred, explaining that I was still getting set up.

"So you worked at the U.N. Mission?" Isaac said. "Do you know Mekel? Do you know Gillerman? I was just at the U.N. Mission visiting a few weeks ago. Gillerman loves me! He just can't get enough of me, he loves me so much! Mekel, too. Just ask Mekel about me, and he'll tell you. But Gillerman! Gillerman goes nuts for me!"

I spent much of the rest of the day avoiding Isaac's requests to play "meet the press," but when he asked me what I was so busy with, I was at a loss to come up with much. Ra'anan still seemed distracted by his missing third cell phone, and I hadn't yet been able to connect with my other supervisor, Ezra. But instead of realizing I was just avoiding his media role-playing games with him, Isaac decided to give me some advice.

"See," he said, "you've got to think of your job here not as a daily grind, but more like a fireman's. You sit around the station, on call, and you don't have to do that much most of the time. But when something happens, pow, you move like crazy, and that's why you're paid the rest of the time. So, what I recommend is that you just enjoy the quiet times, put your feet up, put on the radio, and just relax—because it's not always going to be like that."

I was scouring the foreign press for relevant articles for Ra'anan to show to the prime minister, and meeting various staffers in the PMO, but after a few days I was finally given more of a concrete task. The prime minister was sending a statement of support and friendship to the Iranian Jewish community in the United States, and Ra'anan wanted me to write it. It wasn't quite the same sort of substantively high-level statement I had regularly written at the U.N., but just the fact that it would be in the prime minister's name made it significant.

I was also summoned to my first real meeting with Ezra, Sharon's personal assistant, who was, in effect, my other supervisor. This was particularly interesting because it would afford me the opportunity to go into the most hallowed parts of the Prime Minister's Office. The building as a whole was an enormous, ugly monolith, with four hundred employees spread over a slew of different divisions and floors. Many of them worked in areas that had nothing to do with the prime minister himself, but operated under the auspices of the Office. Some of these were involved in the sort of top-secret work that was only known about by an inner circle, while others worked in more mundane projects that just didn't have a natural home elsewhere in the government. I was part of a smaller unit called the Bureau of the Prime Minister, which was made up of the prime minister himself, his personal advisers, and their staffs.

Around the corner from the media wing, where I worked, was a long hallway called the Hall of the Advisers, where most of the prime minister's senior advisers worked. To get into this area, I had to swipe my security card and be buzzed in by a guard. Only a fraction of the people in the building had access to this area, including some who had been there for decades, but I was amused to learn that, as a member of the Bureau, I did.

I passed through the locked door and made my way down the long hallway, glancing into each office as I passed. The place was a hive of activity, with staffers scurrying in and out of the offices of their various bosses, the PM's advisers. I read the little plaques outside their doors, noting the advisers on military matters, foreign affairs, public relations, and a bunch of others whose functions I didn't really understand. It was in this hallway, I thought as I strolled along, that the bulk of Israel's real decision making took place.

At the end of the Hall of the Advisers was yet another security point, where I entered what was called the Aquarium, a sort of Holy of Holies, where even fewer people were allowed to enter. There was another security guard, who looked at me carefully to check that I was the same person pictured on my security card. A pair of doors separated and I went in.

Unlike the rest of the building, the Aquarium was well kept. That was because this was where foreign leaders visited, unaware that the rest of the PMO was more than a bit ragged. It had some very nice paintings and other decorations, and a little waiting area with plush chairs. There was an ornate conference room where some of the highest-level meetings were held. There was a small room in which some young female soldiers—serving their compulsory army service at the Prime Minister's Office instead of elsewhere in the military—were working with what looked like very high-tech equipment. I assumed that this was the minute-by-minute point of contact between the army and the prime minister. There was also an office where some of the prime minister's closest aides, including Ezra, were based. And, of course, there was the prime minister's own personal office, with a little anteroom where his personal secretary sat. I didn't know if he himself was in, but when I looked in at his secretary, she gave me a questioning smile.

I went into the office where Ezra worked. He greeted me and asked me to sit down, introducing me to those around him, among them a woman named Naomi, who was the prime minister's adviser on Diaspora affairs. I had been told earlier that she had been an assistant to Sharon for over ten years. She welcomed me warmly and told me that we would be working together a fair amount, as many of the speeches I would be doing fell under her portfolio.

Ezra was only a few years older than me, and it was astonishing that he had such a key position in the Sharon administration. He served as Sharon's right-hand man, and wrote many of his Hebrew speeches. I had been told that when Ezra was in his early twenties, at a time when nobody had thought that Sharon would ever make a successful comeback in Israeli politics, he had begun working for the old general as an assistant, and had stayed with him ever since. He looked fit and energetic, just a few years out of the army and into public service, and as I spoke to him I wondered if one day he would himself be part of the top echelon of Israel's leadership.

Ezra asked me how things had been going so far, and gave me a brief preview of some speeches I would be writing for the prime minister in the coming weeks. They were on low-level issues and were mostly ceremonial, but because they were for the prime minister, every word would be important. A couple of them were to be delivered by video conference to summits of American Jewish organizations, one for five thousand Jews who were meeting in Texas.

"Hi, Dubi," Ezra said suddenly, looking out to the hallway where a middle-aged man was standing outside the prime minister's door. I recognized him from the press as Dov Weisglass, one of Prime Minister Sharon's closest advisers. He was reputed to be the strategist behind a lot of Sharon's political maneuvering, and to have a heavy Machiavellian streak. He was also, I had been told, the main line of contact between Sharon and the White House, and supposedly spoke to Secretary of State Condoleezza Rice on his cell phone almost daily. In fact, as he waved back at Ezra, he was in the midst of making a call on his cell phone, and I wondered who he was calling.

Ezra finished telling me about the speeches, and said that he would give me more details soon. I could tell that he was very busy—the prime minister was now engaged in serious political battles with his rivals, and Ezra was surely working hard as a result—and soon I excused myself. But on my way back to my office, just outside the Aquarium, I was surprised to come across Isaac from my own department. He was holding a giant chunk of what appeared to be salami and gnawing on it roughly.

"Hey, Greggy," he said between bites. "Do you want some?"

There were bits of meat falling out of his mouth; I declined his offer. I tried to imagine a similar scene in the halls of the White House.

"They're feeding the prime minister this," he told me, his mouth still full, "and they had some extra."

I didn't know who "they" were, but his phrasing made it sound like the prime minister was some kind of caged beast, and that his keepers were throwing him hunks of meat.

Gradually, I started to feel more at home in the Office, and to better understand my role. I had been relatively involved in most of the Mission's operations, and was at least aware of almost all of them. Compared to the PMO, the U.N. Mission was just a tiny outpost. Here in Jerusalem, I was a small fish in a much bigger pond.

Each morning I went through about a dozen newspapers and websites, finding any articles that would be of particular interest to Ra'anan and the prime minister. I answered emails addressed to the prime minister, mostly from cranks, but sometimes from legitimate foreign lobbying organizations. I also answered questions from journalists who had not been able to reach Ra'anan or other senior officials, using the talking points I was provided, and I wrote statements that were released in the prime minister's name. And, of course, I worked on the little speeches that Ezra assigned me. I would talk with Ra'anan for the first time each day at around noon, when he would breeze into our section of the building. For no apparent reason, whenever Ra'anan arrived, Isaac always yelled, "DADDY'S HOME!," his voice booming through the halls.

I saw Sharon himself only a couple times each week. The first of these was at a party at the PMO for one of the Jewish holidays. There was a lot of food and drink, and a huge number of people I didn't know milling about in the courtyard outside the Office. When Sharon appeared, I was struck by how short and wide he was. He seemed about the same size side to side as up and down, and he walked in a manner that jibed perfectly with his reputation as an unstoppable bulldozer. Leaning forward in a way that suggested that gravity had no power over him, and that the idea that any obstacle could ever stop him was ridiculous, he pushed through space with the force of a truck.

I went up to him, introduced myself, and shook his hand. We exchanged a few quick pleasantries, even though he didn't actually know who I was, but since there were staffers mobbing him from all directions, I didn't get much time with him. One of his top advisers was standing next to him, and, gesturing at the long table of food, said to me, "Greg, you're new here. I recommend that you do *not* get used to all this."

After that, I would see Sharon at various press conferences and briefings, and occasionally in the Aquarium itself as he came in and out of his private office, always moving with that same forceful, determined gait. I never got a lot of face time with him. He knew I worked on his staff, but probably not exactly what my role was.

I also saw him at the weekly cabinet meetings, the first parts of which were open to non–cabinet members and select journalists. I started attending these, followed by a postmeeting briefing by the cabinet secretary, so that I could understand the week's talking points. Before the meetings, I would help escort some of the journalists to a waiting area near the Cabinet Room, where they stood while the cabinet ministers filed in, talking briefly with the press as they went. The prime minister usually entered last. I occasionally had the chance to speak briefly to a few of the ministers, shaking their hands and making a bit of small talk, among them the deputy prime minister, Ehud Olmert.

Once the cabinet ministers were all seated in the Cabinet Room, the journalists and I would go in. There would be some photo ops, and a few words from the prime minister. Sharon presided over these meetings from his chair, which was taller than all the others. He always seemed confident, cool, and in total control of the room, even though some of his most dangerous political rivals were usually present. He seemed like an invincible force of nature.

Another of my frequent duties was to go with Ra'anan to the large building on the edge of the city that housed all the foreign television networks and cable stations to help coordinate his constant interviews with CNN, BBC, and the rest of them.

On one of these trips, Ra'anan was driving, and Isaac was in the passenger seat. I was sitting in the back, hoping that we didn't get into an accident. Israel's roads were full of crazy drivers, and Ra'anan was decidedly one of them, swerving around in a kamikaze style. As we shot out of the Prime Minister's Office and toward the Studio Building, he put a CD in, taking his hands off the wheel for a scary moment. It was ABBA, the Swedish pop group, and he skipped ahead to the song he wanted.

It started playing: *YOU CAN DANCE, YOU CAN JIVE!* He raised the volume very high.

Isaac looked back at me and smiled, as if this was all quite normal.

"I love this song," Ra'anan said to me, "but it's before your time."

In fact, I was pretty sure I had heard the song "Dancing Queen" coming from behind Ra'anan's closed office door on at least a couple of occasions before.

HAVING THE TIME OF YOUR LIFE!

We sped through the twisty Jerusalem streets with our windows open and "Dancing Queen" blasting out. When the song ended, Ra'anan pressed the button to play it again, and the whole thing started once more. As we swerved through traffic to this improbable sound track, Ra'anan reached into the little compartment beside his seat where a collection of kumquats were rolling around with some loose change. I had noticed that he always seemed to have these around somewhere—in the drawers of his desk, or loose in his suit pockets. When I asked his secretary about them, she had nodded and told me they were really the only things she ever saw him consume.

He popped two of the kumquats into his mouth and then offered some to Isaac and me. We both declined, and he said, "These things are great. I get them every morning at the gas station near my house."

SEE THAT GIRL, WATCH THAT SCENE.

One of Ra'anan's many cell phones rang, and he answered it on speakerphone without turning off the music. It was CNN Radio calling from Atlanta and they wanted to do an interview with him. Instead of rescheduling it for a more convenient time, as I expected, he agreed to do the interview immediately. He turned the music's volume down, but didn't turn it off.

DIG IN THE DANCING QUEEN.

The interviewer in Atlanta, of course, had no idea that we were racing through Jerusalem as he calmly interviewed Ra'anan, but I wondered if he could hear the music in the background. Ra'anan answered each question in his usual unstoppable torrent of words.

"The prime minister believes that in order to move forward we need to shake things up, shuffle the cards, plunge ahead like he did in his days in the army, not looking back, not waiting, but just going on ahead courageously."

YOUNG AND SWEET, ONLY SEVENTEEN!

Suddenly, in the middle of answering a question, Ra'anan cut around a car in front of us that he judged to be going too slowly, and careened onto the sidewalk with a thud.

SEE THAT GIRL, WATCH THAT SCENE.

Rather than going back down into the road, he stayed on the sidewalk, still talking to the CNN interviewer, as he sped merrily along. We narrowly avoided hitting a man on the sidewalk; he leaped out of the way and swore loudly at us. As the CNN interviewer asked the next question, Ra'anan leaned toward the open window and shouted back at the pedestrian, angrily swearing at him that *he* was a lunatic.

DIG IN THE DANCING QUEEN!

The call from CNN completed, and no pedestrians dead, we arrived at the Studio Building and parked the car. Isaac got on his cell phone and started calling all the networks and cable stations arrayed inside to see who wanted to interview Ra'anan and when— CNN, BBC, Fox News, Reuters, and a half-dozen others.

"Daddy's home!" he told them triumphantly.

I, too, was supposed to deal with the press, sometimes giving them information, but also helping to coordinate their relations with Ra'anan and the rest of the media apparatus at the Prime Minister's Office. But I quickly ran into some major obstacles. First of all, I had no voice mail on my office telephone. I assumed this was a mistake, or that it simply had not been set up. But it turned out there was not meant to be a voice-mail system on my phone. If the journalists and foreign lobbying organizations whom we dealt with tried to reach me, or Isaac, or even Ra'anan, and we weren't in our offices, our phones would simply ring unanswered. Everything at the PMO, it seemed, worked on cell phones. But it turned out that getting one was not exactly easy.

"You have to make an official request for a cell phone and it has to be approved by the telephone committee," Alon told me.

"The telephone committee?"

"You fill out a request and explain why you need a cell phone," Alon told me, "and then you wait for the committee to meet and decide on the request. It takes about a month."

It was essentially impossible to do my job without a cell phone, and I had already received emails from a few fairly important American journalists based in Israel, and from outside organizations in the United States, asking me why I didn't have a cell phone or even voice mail on my office phone.

"The person who runs the committee," Alon told me, "is called Yaacov Yerushalmi."

As he said the name he shook his head with a look of disgust. The name was familiar, but it took me a moment to remember that Ben, my predecessor, had told me that I would eventually meet this Yaacov Yerushalmi and that, as he put it, he would be the worst person I ever met in my life. When I now mentioned to someone else in the Office that I was on my way to meet him, in fact, I was told that Yerushalmi was personally "what was wrong with Israel."

Yaacov Yerushalmi, it turned out, was one of dozens of people who worked in the bowels of the Prime Minister's Office doing somewhat unclear jobs concerning logistics. His particular role seemed mostly to involve electronic devices—cell phones, pagers, and the like—and he ruled this domain despotically.

A fat middle-aged man, he was sitting behind his desk when I found him, his shirt unbuttoned almost all the way down his chest; bountiful tufts of gray chest hair cascaded in all directions. Another middle-aged man sat on the other side of the desk with his feet up, but Yerushalmi beckoned me into the room anyway.

I stood there in front of them and self-consciously said in Hebrew, "My name is Gregory Levey. I work with Ra'anan Gissin in the Press Department."

Yerushalmi responded in the most guttural Hebrew I had yet heard, "I work with Ra'anan Gissin in the Press Department."

He flashed a toothy smile at his friend on the other side of the desk. It took me a moment to realize that he was mocking the way I spoke—not my actual Hebrew, but simply my accent. I decided to go on regardless.

"I need to get a cell phone, so I wanted to make a request for one."

"I need to get a cell phone, so I wanted to make a request for one," Yerushalmi repeated again, chortling a bit. His friend sputtered a laugh.

Eventually this routine stopped, and he told me that I would have to come back the next day to make the request, because he was just about to leave the office. When I came the next day, though, I was told by someone else in the basement hallway that he wasn't scheduled to be there that day or, probably, for the rest of the week.

When I showed up at his office the next week, I found him eating sunflower seeds from a giant bag. I asked him if I could now make the request, and he didn't respond for a moment, carefully shelling a seed inside his mouth. Then, to my shock, his spat the shell directly into my face. I couldn't understand his hostility, and told myself that this had to have been inadvertent. He didn't apologize, even when I wiped my face.

"You can fill out a request"—he shrugged, putting another seed into his mouth—"but the telephone committee will have to meet about it, and right now we don't even know when their next meeting will be."

He chuckled a bit, and once again spat a sunflower seed shell at me, catching me on the side of the face. *Ben was right*, I thought. *He really is the worst person I have ever met.*

"Fill out this form," Yerushalmi said, tossing me a sheet of paper and then putting another seed in his mouth.

I hurried to fill out the form before he had finished de-shelling the seed, and asked, "How long do you think it will take?"

"How long do you think it will take?" he repeated, mocking my accent again, like he had the first day I had met him. He then spat the next seed at me. It hit my shoulder and then fell into my lap, covered in little bubbles of saliva. Disgusted, I flicked it onto the floor.

"At least six weeks," he finally answered. "Maybe longer."

I was sitting in my office working on one of the speeches that Ezra had assigned me when my office phone rang. It was one of the multitudes of secretaries at the Office, with a request from Ra'anan. A Swedish undersecretary of state and the Swedish ambassador had just arrived at the prime minister's office and were being passed through security. They had a meeting set up with Ra'anan, but he was nowhere to be found, and when contacted, he had told the Office that he was delayed in traffic somewhere and wouldn't be back for about half an hour. He had asked that I welcome these dignitaries, show them into his quarters, and talk to them until he arrived. This seemed completely ridiculous to me, and more than a little intimidating. I was to play host, effectively as a representative of Ariel Sharon himself, to some very high-ranking diplomats.

I walked to the foyer and waited for them to get through security. They soon appeared, their Scandinavian looks unmistakable amid a sea of tanned Israelis. They were middle-aged, impeccably dressed, and seemed a bit frazzled by the level of security they had just been made to go through. I introduced myself and apologized for Ra'anan's tardiness, explaining that he was with the prime minister and would be along shortly. This white lie, I reasoned, seemed a bit less disrespectful to them than saying that Ra'anan was stuck in traffic, or was busy arguing with another motorist, or doing whatever it was he was actually doing.

I led them to the lounge area in Ra'anan's office, making small talk. Although they were unfailingly polite, I thought I sensed that perhaps they were slightly insulted that some very young person in the Office, who didn't actually seem to be Israeli at all, had been assigned to welcome them. I asked the undersecretary how his trip had been, and how he was enjoying Israel so far, and asked the ambassador how long he had been posted there. Soon, though, I was running out of things to say, trying to draw out this inane conversation without embarrassing both myself and the Israeli government.

They took pity on me and tried to make conversation themselves, asking why Ra'anan's office looked less like an office and more like a movie-set version of one. The books on the shelf behind the desk were arranged with obvious precision, as was an artfully arranged Israeli flag. Also, along with regular lights, the ceiling was equipped with the giant stage lights used in television studios. I explained that when Benjamin Netanyahu had been prime minister in the late 1990s, one of his greatest pleasures had been to give television interviews. But because it took a tremendous amount of time and effort to get TV crews through the security all the way to the prime minister's personal office, he had requested that this mock-up of the Office be built for his interviews. Prime Minister Sharon was more reluctant to speak to the media, so when he had moved into the Prime Minister's Office, there had been little need for him to use this mock office for his very occasional interviews. But Ra'anan, who *loved* to talk to the press, was more than happy to take it as his own.

At this point, about half an hour late for his meeting, Ra'anan himself slid into the room, a characteristic whirlwind of energy. He apologized to the Swedish diplomats, thanked me, closed the door behind us, and very carefully put some kind of little package on his desk, all within about three seconds. I could tell that our visitors had been almost violently jolted from our calm small talk by his manic vigor.

"I'm sorry for being late," he repeated, shaking their hands, and I suddenly realized with a bit of horror that he might contradict my story that he had been with the prime minister. "This new pen I ordered just arrived, and I stopped to pick it up at the post office."

I cringed, embarrassed, and didn't look at the Swedish diplomats. *Of all the possible explanations,* I thought, *why did it have to be such a silly one?* Ra'anan, I had recently found out, collected pens. He had all kinds of fancy and expensive ones, and also ones that did little tricks like lighting up or folding in intricate ways. He had apparently exhausted the supply of interesting pens available in Israel, and had taken to sending away for foreign novelty pens. I had no problem with any of this, but was it really a reason to delay a meeting with foreign diplomats? And was it really necessary to *tell* them that that was the reason?

"Look at this pen," Ra'anan said, taking a little folding pen out of the package and demonstrating to the Swedes how it worked. They looked on, obviously perplexed by this whole scene, but feigning interest.

"You can't buy this in Israel," Ra'anan added proudly, as if they might be in Israel looking to buy stationery.

The Swedes just nodded politely.

13

And Still Nothing

I got back to my desk after the meeting with the Swedes and collapsed into my chair. I wasn't sure how much more of this I could take. I was trying my best to behave professionally, but everyone around me acted like we were in some government satire. I was frustrated.

Besides the sort of unintentional silliness I had just witnessed with Ra'anan and the visiting diplomats, there was also a good deal of wholly intentional comedy in the Prime Minister's Office. One official who dealt with quite serious issues often sang his status reports to his supervisor, loudly, rather than just speak. Another one routinely amused himself by giving cryptic but meaningless information to print and television reporters, who eagerly tried to decipher it. Like at the U.N. Mission, many of the people around me seemed to deal with the intensity and gravity of their work by engaging in mostly harmless comic relief.

So, I thought, *why not join them?*

For some time I'd been entertaining fantasies about committing minor acts of harmless sabotage, and now, I realized, was the time to act. I looked down at the speech I was currently writing for Sharon. Since almost nobody around me spoke perfect English, and half the time they didn't even seem to read things too carefully, I thought I'd be able to insert hidden references into the speeches. The government's overt intended messages would still be conveyed, and nobody would be the wiser. And so I decided that I would put covert references to *Seinfeld* into the speeches of the prime minister of Israel.

I knew I might be heading down a slippery slope of irresponsibility, but it seemed like everyone else was already way down the hill. I also realized that my commitment to my work was taking something of a turn for the worse.

I had to be careful. I couldn't make obvious references that would embarrass the prime minister, or be recognized by those vetting my speeches and removed. Also, in order to make my task more challenging and the project cleaner, I decided only to include references to a specific episode, the one about the imaginary holiday of "Festivus."

"You're not *really* going to do that?" one of my new friends in Israel asked me. "Are you?"

I nodded. "I'm afraid so."

My goal was to insert the references in a way that seemed natural and flowed with the rest of the speech and its message. The *Seinfeld* characters said, about Festivus, "It's your heritage. It's part of who you are," which seemed like an easy phrase to get into Sharon's small speech to a group of young Diaspora Jews he was encouraging to immigrate to Israel.

Seinfeld and company also talk about the Festivus "feats of strength" ritual. This was a bit trickier, but since it would be coming from the strongman, Sharon, it seemed doable. So, in a speech touching on the prospects for peace, I wrote, "There is a time for feats of strength, and a time for feats of reconciliation."

A third reference, and the hardest to incorporate, was the other ritual of Festivus, the "airing of grievances." It was a stretch, but in a speech about the future of Israel, I wrote that Israelis had "to choose between the pessimism of airing of grievances and the optimism of moving forward."

Every speech I wrote for the prime minister had to pass through a few people, and each of my first three attempts, somewhere along the way, was cut out. It wasn't that they recognized the *Seinfeld* references. They just didn't think it was the right wording for the particular speech. This was reassuring, because it meant that eventually one of the references would slip through.

There was other humor in the Prime Minister's Office as well. Around this time, a video started circulating in the Office that repeatedly reduced us all to fits of laughter. The video was of an interview Sharon had recently given to a pair of Japanese reporters. During the interview, Sharon's cell phone rang—his ring was a Mozart melody—and he stopped to answer it.

"Yes," he said in Hebrew while the journalists waited. And then, after a moment, "Wrong number."

The Japanese journalists, of course, were totally unaware that someone had just dialed a wrong number and accidentally called Ariel Sharon's cell phone.

The comic relief felt necessary, because life in Israel was difficult: I was sure there were many wonderful, kind, and caring Israelis, but they all seemed to be on vacation.

"The customer service alone is enough to make you want to start an intifada," an American I met quipped, and I thought that there was something to this. In fact, in Tel Aviv I discovered a little community of Americans, Canadians, and British expatriates who seemed to spend most of their time complaining about the Israelis they lived among.

"At a bar, you order nachos and salsa," Jacob said, "and they bring you Doritos and ketchup. And if you point out that it's not really the same thing, they call you a snob."

A Scottish friend, Mark, was particularly annoyed by the banks, which not only operated incredibly inefficiently but also stayed open for only about half the day. He once yelled in his thick Scottish accent, "I just want to say to these people, so, like, do you have a second job, or are you just INCREDIBLY lazy?"

A Canadian named Dan told me that he had been trying to convert his foreign driver's license to an Israeli one. At the government office that dealt with licenses, they told him that there was one person whose entire job was to do this, but that she only came in once a week. For several weeks in a row he arrived on the day she was supposed to be working, only to find that she wasn't there. Then when he finally found her and told her what he wanted, she looked at him blankly and said that she'd have to check on how to do that.

All this, I reasoned, was just culture clash—the kind of frustrations you encounter in many foreign countries. Once, though, the culture clash became physical. Abby and I had been at a party in Jerusalem late one night, and had taken the minibus back to Tel Aviv with a friend of ours. When we got out of the bus, we hailed a taxi to take us to our apartment. We told the driver our destination, perhaps the most central part of the whole city, and he told us that since he didn't know how to get there, he would have to charge us an exorbitant flat fare instead of using the meter. When I said that didn't make any sense, he said that he was not from Tel Aviv, but from the city of Ashdod, and so he didn't know the city. I couldn't understand why this justified the flat fee, and since we had all grown tired of being ripped off by crooked cabdrivers—the law was that they *had* to use the meter—we decided to get out of the taxi and find a different driver.

We walked to the little group of drivers that was standing nearby waiting for customers and asked a different one for a ride. Just then, the first driver came charging toward us aggressively, yelling angrily and swearing. I was more than a little exasperated with him, and I yelled back, swearing myself, saying that we wanted to find a driver who actually knew the city. My Hebrew came out a bit garbled in my frustration, and he seemed to think that I was insulting Ashdod, his hometown, when I really just wanted him to leave us alone so that we could get home.

He yelled something that I couldn't make out about me insulting Ashdod, and suddenly threw a wide, looping punch at my head. I managed to get an elbow up to block it, and he yelled something unintelligible and grabbed my hair with his other hand. He was about to throw another punch, but I managed to pull free and push him away. In a bit of a daze, we walked away from the taxis. There had to be better ways to get home.

That night I had a fitful sleep, waking periodically. What had happened with the cabdriver was just one incident, I knew, but it somehow seemed emblematic of larger issues. The more I got to know the different facets of Israeli society, from senior government officials to night-shift cabdrivers, the more I began to feel a constant sense of coiled tension and hostility just below the surface, ready to explode at any moment. I knew that it wasn't wholly their fault, that it was largely a product of their perpetually dangerous situation, but it still didn't feel at all healthy—and I didn't feel like I belonged. Each time I drifted toward sleep, an image of the cabdriver trying to punch me startled me awake.

But even with the actual physical violence, that still wasn't the worst experience I had with Israeli cabdrivers. On one of my earlier visits to Israel, I was in a taxi driven by the Middle East's version of a burned-out hippie. He was in his forties, but his clothes looked like he had been wearing them since his early twenties. His long hair was matted and visibly filthy, and his body odor suffused the car's interior. His English was very poor, but by that point I was sufficiently competent in Hebrew to deal with most things that came up in daily life. He refused to speak Hebrew with me, though, believing his English was better than my Hebrew. And he insisted on telling me a long, involved joke in English.

"There is Israeli woman," he began, "who tell husband, 'Put Mercedes in driveway,' and so he put Mercedes in driveway. And still nothing!"

He paused for effect at this line, and looked at me to see if I was amused. I gave him a polite smile.

"So she says, 'Put BMW in driveway,' and so he put BMW in driveway," he continued, then paused dramatically again for a second, looking at me and not at the road in a way that was making me nervous. "And still nothing!"

I had no idea what this joke was about, or what this nonsensical refrain was referring to, and I was hoping he would start looking at the road more as he raced through the swerving traffic.

But he just nodded at me, one side of his mouth curving up into a half grin, as he said, "And so husband went up to roof and paint a gold letter *M* and a gold letter *G* on roof."

Again a long pause, his smile growing, and I could tell the punch line was coming now. He turned to me and, with eyes wide with delight, roared, "And so neighbor looks out his window, sees gold letter *M* and gold letter *G*, and yells at man and woman, 'Fuck you one and one!'"

With this, he cackled loudly, smacking the steering wheel with one hand repeatedly as he convulsed with laughter. Only after about ten seconds of this did he turn to look at me, apparently expecting me to be laughing with equal vigor. I had to assume that this joke was losing something in translation. When he saw that I was just looking at him, perplexed, and wishing this ride was over, a look of hurt passed over his face.

"You no like?" he asked, wounded.

"I just don't understand it," I said. "Maybe if you told it to me in Hebrew . . ."

"Okay," he said. "I tell again. I tell again."

Now I saw that we were passing by the turnoff to our destination, and I alerted him.

"We come back," he said. "I tell again joke."

And so he started again, with me as his captive audience, but once more he insisted on telling it in English, and with the exact same wording. This time he slowed down toward the end, and tried to articulate the words carefully, as if the problem was my understanding of English.

"Fuck. You. One. And. One!" he whooped, and broke down into laughter again, his eyes tearing up as he smacked the steering wheel once more. I strained to decipher the meaning of this joke—but, well, still nothing. So I forced a smile so that I would not have to hear it again, and so maybe he would actually drop me off at my destination. But when his laughing fit had subsided and he turned to see my reaction, he apparently saw through my fake smile.

"You no like?"

"I like, I like! I just don't *totally* understand it."

At this, insulted or hurt or just plain crazy, his smile disappeared and he immediately pulled over into a gas-station parking lot and stopped the car.

"Okay," he said, leaning over me and opening my door. "You walk from here."

Transportation was an endless problem. One day after work I boarded the minibus from Jerusalem to Tel Aviv and found it full of Palestinian laborers, which didn't bother me in the least until Israeli soldiers suddenly swarmed the bus and ordered us all off. They demanded to see our identity papers, and then escorted away a couple of my bus mates because, apparently, they didn't have the right papers to be in Israel. I started to think that this might not be the best way to get home from work.

And every time I would use a cab to get to the Prime Minister's Office from elsewhere in Jerusalem, the driver would insist that I tell the prime minister something for him.

"Tell the prime minister," he'd say casually, "that he needs to deal more harshly with the religious people."

Or: "Tell the prime minister that he must remember that this is a *Jewish* country."

Or: "Tell the prime minister that he must not trust Egypt."

And on and on, as if I would just walk into Sharon's office and give him the latest wisdom from the crazy cabdrivers outside. Eventually this constant advice, the threat of being punched, the danger of being told another endless and inscrutable joke, and the worry that I was getting ripped off—to say nothing of the seemingly real possibility of being arrested as a suspected Palestinian terrorist—convinced me that I needed my own car.

I got a long-term rental that immediately started breaking down all the time. Many evenings after work, anxious to get back to Tel Aviv, I would sit in the car outside the Prime Minister's Office, waiting for the car company to come fix the problem, only to have the same thing happen the next morning as I tried to get to work.

"You should never expect anything to work here," Isaac told me sagely.

Indeed, the car seemed of a piece with everything else we were experiencing in Israel.

In many ways, things were harder for Abby than they were for me. She hadn't learned as much Hebrew as I had, which could make things pretty tough for her. And while I was busy at the Prime Minister's Office, she had to deal with the more mundane aspects of living in Israel, which were often infuriating.

Because of her less-than-perfect Hebrew, she didn't feel as productive at her internship as she wanted to be, and would often come home frustrated. But she would get even more upset by other aspects of everyday life. The inability of Israelis to line up or wait their turn, the pushing and shoving, the rudeness, and the way they had managed to make being inconsiderate into an art form all took their toll on her, as they did on me. Buying groceries, going to the gym, even just walking down the street turned into grueling exercises in Middle Eastern warfare.

As one foreign journalist put it to me, "I came to Israel because I liked the Jews who I knew growing up and I was fascinated by Jewish culture, but living in Israel is making me into an anti-Semite."

This was definitely not home.

Once, during a weekend afternoon on the beach in Tel Aviv, Abby went to the food stand to get some french fries while I stayed to guard our beach chairs and possessions. It should have been a five-minute trip, but she didn't come back for forty-five minutes, and when she did, she was somewhere between sobbing and screaming. She had stood by the counter waiting to get served and trying to use her broken Hebrew to order, but people had continually come in and cut in front of her, yelling their orders in Hebrew. A group of teenage boys had come in and actually physically shoved her to the side in their haste. The counter staff had completely ignored her. Now, back on the beach, she was practically hyperventilating from frustration. I put my arm around her and tried to comfort her, but it was to no avail. I had never seen her like this before, and I thought that it wasn't just this incident that had gotten her so riled up.

"I hate this country!" she yelled in frustration, and I looked around sheepishly to see who was listening. "I hate it!"

I soon realized that if I had any chance of convincing Abby to stay—and I certainly didn't want to be there without her—there was really only one way to do it. For some time now, I'd known I would ask her to marry me one day. I decided that now was the time, and so I started to plan my move.

Soon after the beach incident, we took a short vacation to Scotland—one of the advantages of living in Israel, we'd discovered, was the relative ease of trips to Europe—and I snuck along a ring I'd purchased. At a restaurant in Glasgow, on our first night in Scotland, I employed whatever speechmaking skills I had gathered over the past couple years and proposed. She said yes, and the next day, delighted and amazed, we took off for the Scottish Highlands for a few days, losing touch with the world. Israel and its problems felt so far away, like a fading dream.

But at the conclusion of our brief Scottish sojourn, we had to head back. Now an engaged couple, we agreed to tough it out in Israel together a bit longer, for better or for worse.

Israel itself was going through profound changes as it looked toward its own future. At almost the exact same time that Abby and I got engaged, Ariel Sharon decided to turn his back on the Likud Party, which he had himself founded decades before, because it was now rebelling against him as a result of the disengagement. Within just a few days he formed a new party called Kadima, taking his allies from the Likud with him, as well as friends from Israel's Labor Party like former Prime Minister Shimon Peres. *Kadima,* meaning "forward" or "onward," had an optimistic ring to it. The idea was to leave all of Israel's troubles behind and move confidently into tomorrow.

Like the disengagement itself, Kadima felt to me like the only hope for the country. Sharon's old Likud Party was corrupt and inexorably tied to the settler movement's dogmatism. The other parties lacked any momentum, and except for Sharon, the country's leadership seemed scared or unable to part ways with the depressing status quo. With Arafat gone, the disengagement complete, and Sharon moving "forward," it seemed possible that the future would not be as dark as the past.

I hoped that both the Kadima Party and our engagement would meet with success.

When Abby and I arrived back from Scotland, I thought it would be appropriate at least to tell the people I worked with my good news. This was easier said than done.

"You're back," Ra'anan said. "How was your flight?"

Before I could answer or tell him I'd gotten engaged, he launched into one of his routines.

"You know," he said, "a few weeks ago, I flew into the airport here, and from the time we landed to the time I was in my car, it was only twenty-eight minutes!"

"Actually," I said, trying to break in, but I was interrupted again. Isaac had come into Ra'anan's office behind me, and had heard Ra'anan's story.

"Speaking of planes," he chimed in, "I was on a plane a little while ago in the U.S. that was tinier than any I've ever been on!"

"It took me just twenty-eight minutes!" Ra'anan said again, now yelling above Isaac. "Twenty-eight minutes!"

"I mean," Isaac continued, his voice raising in turn, "I've flown on a *lot* of planes in the past, but never one this small for a regular flight."

"Twenty-eight minutes is a very short time!" Ra'anan yelled back. "Twenty-eight minutes for all that!"

"It was like flying in a small bus, and I tell you, I was getting nervous!"

"I've never gotten through the airport that quickly! That's pretty amazing!"

Okay, I thought, *I'm going to go now*, backing out of the room, where they continued to yell at each other.

"Twenty-eight minutes!" I heard Ra'anan say one more time as I made my way back to my office.

But I wasn't the only one who had trouble getting a word in. Ra'anan, and to a somewhat lesser extent, Isaac, were famous among Western journalists, diplomats, and lobbying organizations for their verbosity and loud bluster. Their rapid-fire, high-octane manner of speaking must have seemed the expected governmental counterpart to the famous intensity of the Israeli military.

A little while before I had transferred from the U.N. Mission, in fact, an astounding incident involving Ra'anan had taken place. He was frequently sent on tours of the United States and elsewhere to speak to journalists, college students, and community leaders on behalf of the prime minister. At one of his talks he had been confronted by an anti-Israel comment, and responded simply by loudly squawking "Shut up!" into the microphone. Apparently, this stunned the audience into submission, allowing Ra'anan to continue, but it didn't make the Israeli government look particularly diplomatic or professional. I tried to imagine Ra'anan's American equivalent, the White House spokesperson, telling journalists to "shut up." But after what I was seeing at the Prime Minister's Office on a regular basis, this story really shouldn't have surprised me.

I'd arranged a meeting for Ra'anan with a delegation from a small but active lobbying and educational organization from New York that wanted to explore possibilities for cooperation with the Israeli government. It was not earth-shattering stuff, but had the potential to be quite important. When they arrived, I brought them to Ra'anan, and took a seat to the side of his large desk. I was a bit nervous because I had made the connection and set up the meeting. One of the New Yorkers was an older rabbi with a long white beard, and he began explaining to Ra'anan what his organization did, what their plans were, and how they wanted to work with the Israeli government to forward their mutual goals. It was all fairly interesting, and I was happy that, at least so far, it was all going well.

But then I noticed that Ra'anan was clearly not paying attention at all. Instead, he was fidgeting in his chair and looking rapidly around, as if trying to take in the room, which made very little sense, since it was his own office. I knew that it was equally clear to the man speaking that Ra'anan was not paying attention, but there was really nothing I could do. Then I saw Ra'anan open one of his desk drawers, which immediately made me nervous. He reached in and pulled out a little black leather case, and I thought, *What the hell is that?*

Just under the desk, as the rabbi continued speaking, Ra'anan opened the case and pulled out a little Swiss Army knife, and extended one of his fingers. I noticed for the first time that this one finger had a very long nail, much longer than those on his other fingers, for some reason I didn't grasp. Then, from the little Swiss Army knife, he uncurled the nail clipper.

No! I thought. *You clearly haven't cut that nail in months! Why NOW?*

And instead of cutting the nail under the table, which would have been inappropriate enough, he brought the nail clipper and his weird, long-nailed finger to the top of the desk. The rabbi's eyes widened for a moment, but he continued on valiantly. Then Ra'anan began to cut his nail, and I cringed at the awkwardness of it all, especially as I noticed that he wasn't even aiming his hand down at the desk, but was aiming it more or less at the visiting New Yorkers. With a snapping sound, he clipped the giant nail, and as if in slow motion, I watched it fly slowly and steadily across the top of the desk and, to my horror, hit the man speaking on the side of the face, and then tumble down his neck.

The man stopped talking, surprise and disgust mingling on his face. He was apparently waiting for an apology, but none was forthcoming. Ra'anan simply folded the nail clipper, put it in the little leather case and back in the drawer, and then closed the drawer. Flustered, the New Yorkers pressed on with their presentation.

When they were finished, Ra'anan said, "Okay, here's what you should do," and proceeded to give his opinion on matters only tangentially connected to anything that had been mentioned in the previous ten minutes. It was quite clear to everyone in the room that he hadn't listened to anything that had been said.

One day Ra'anan came into my office and casually told me that I would soon be working on coordinating a "paratrooper jump" with the Defense Ministry. I had heard something about a paratrooper jump at some point earlier, but had no idea what it meant. Before I could procure any more details about this, Ra'anan was storming down the hall, talking on one of his many cell phones.

I was already occupied with another issue that seemed to involve the Defense Ministry, and that I also didn't really understand. I had received a phone call from a man who spoke very quickly and with a thick accent.

"Who are you?" he asked me.

"Greg."

"Who do you work with?"

"Who is this?" I asked.

"Racham," he said, as if this explained anything.

"Hi, Racham," I said.

"Who do you work with?"

"I work with Ra'anan Gissin."

"I need to set up a meeting with you."

"With me?"

"Yes, with you and, if possible, with Ra'anan."

It was sounding more and more like he didn't work in the Prime Minister's Office, as I had at first thought.

"About what?"

At this point he rambled for a very long time about how he had discovered some information that the government needed to know about the origins of the Second Palestinian Intifada, and gave me all kinds of details that sounded like a conspiracy theory. He was clearly connected to the government, but I didn't understand in what capacity. I told him I would get back to him, and took his phone number.

"Can I have your phone number, too?" he asked, which I thought was strange, since he had just called me.

"But you have it."

"No"—he laughed—"your cell-phone number."

Since I still hadn't received an office cell phone, I gave him my personal one.

"And your home number?"

My home number?

And that's when I made a huge mistake. Maybe because it was still sometimes hard for me to think quickly or clearly when trying to carry on a conversation in Hebrew, I gave it to him. After I got off the phone, I asked one of my colleagues about this strange character. He shook his head ominously and said, "I try to stay away from that guy. I think of him as 'the mad scientist of the Israeli government.' He's definitely got some interesting ideas, and he's smart as hell, but the guy is totally crazy."

He explained that Racham was some kind of freelance defense analyst who consulted for the Defense Ministry and other organs of the government. He was a physicist by training, and was well respected by some in the government, even though he was more than a little eccentric. My colleague then gave me the number of a high-ranking figure elsewhere in the government to call if I wanted to know more. When I called him, he, too, referred to Racham as "the mad scientist of the Israeli government."

He also told me that I should try to connect a bit more with Racham and hear him out, but that my role was to keep him from getting too much access to high-ranking figures in the Prime Minister's Office, because he had "a way of monopolizing people's time."

I soon found out how true that was. I called Racham back and got his voice mail, which had a recording that said just "Racham" and then beeped. I left him a message and said that I would be willing to meet with him. He called me back almost immediately and asked to meet with me the next day. I assumed it would be at or near the Defense Ministry in Tel Aviv, which was actually close to my apartment, and I agreed. But when I called him the next morning to get the exact location, he gave me an address in a residential suburb on the outskirts of Tel Aviv.

"Is that your office?" I asked.

"No, no," he said. "It's my home."

"Your home?"

"Yes, I've got everything set up here for you to see."

"All right," I said, and ended the conversation with the promise that I would be there. I then called someone from the PMO to ask about this strange invitation.

"His *home*?" he asked. "Why?"

"I have no idea."

"That seems kind of strange. Don't feel any obligation to go to that nutcase's home."

Someone else told me that Racham had set up an entire audio-video laboratory in his house, where he worked on his theories and investigations. But he also said that there was no reason for me to feel the need to go there. Never one for conspiracy theories or "mad scientists" with laboratories in their homes, I decided not to go. I called Racham back, got the one-word recording "Racham" and left a message telling him that something had come up and I couldn't make it. I was hoping that this would all start to dissolve on its own.

It didn't. Racham started calling me several times a day. I told him that I didn't have time to get into this at the moment, but he would not take no for an answer. When I was at work, he would call on my office phone and I would avoid the call or make some excuse why I could not talk. At other times he would call me on my cell phone, and in the evenings, and sometimes even late at night, he would call me at home.

"It's that weirdo again," Abby would say if she answered, handing me the phone.

Once he called when we were out to dinner with some of our Tel Aviv friends.

"I can't talk now, Racham," I said to him. "I'm at dinner."

But he wouldn't really listen, and prattled on for a while about something to do with videos and time signatures.

"Yeah," I said, "I can't really get into this now."

"Who was that?" my friends asked after I finally got him off the phone.

"The mad scientist of the Israeli government," I told them.

He called me at home later that night, and again over the weekend. As the calls continued, I just tried to avoid the home phone entirely, and to screen all calls on my cell phone, but he continued to leave detailed message after detailed message, all starting with his growl, "This is Racham."

Recently, he had been pestering other people at the Prime Minister's Office as well, and nobody seemed to want to get involved. The Defense Ministry was apparently interested enough in his findings and research to keep him around, but it was all a bit too weird, even for my colleagues. One of them told me, though, that Racham was actually his last name. At first I felt rude for calling him Racham when I was talking directly to him, but then I remembered that he kept introducing himself as that.

"You gave Racham your *home phone number,*" one of my colleagues said. "Big mistake."

"I noticed," I replied.

And the calls kept coming, filled with weird hints of conspiracy theory, until both Abby and I were at the end of our ropes. Very late one night, the phone rang and I knew it was him. I let it ring. On the advice of several people at the PMO, I had decided to ignore this madness, and wait for it to end.

"When will this stop?" Abby asked.

"Soon, I hope," I answered as the phone continued ringing.

And as the weeks went by, we waited for Racham to leave me alone, and for life in Israel to become a bit less strange. But as the cabdriver had said: still nothing.

14

A Prime Minister's Office Without a Prime Minister

What's wrong with the prime minister?"

I had just gotten home to Tel Aviv—a little late, because my car had had its daily breakdown in Jerusalem—and a journalist was calling me on my cell phone with this question.

Nothing was wrong with the prime minister as far as I knew, but it had been a couple hours now since I had left the Prime Minister's Office. The journalist told me that she had heard that the prime minister had collapsed, and that something serious had happened to him. I told her that I would get back to her.

Almost immediately, I got a call from Ra'anan to ask for the correct English translation of a particular medical condition that he knew the word for only in Hebrew. Something had indeed happened to the prime minister, and Ra'anan was being besieged by inquiries from the foreign media. I was unwilling to try my luck at translating it on the spot, to just guess at what might be the correct English term for the condition he was describing. Almost causing an international incident at the U.N. with my faulty French skills had been bad enough. I didn't even want to think about the possible fallout of me labeling Ariel Sharon's condition incorrectly to the foreign media, and I told Ra'anan that I didn't know the term.

The term that the Office started using was *minor brain event*, but soon it became clear that what he had suffered just after leaving work in his motorcade was a relatively small stroke. He briefly lost consciousness, and was then disoriented and unable to speak, but by the next morning, he was apparently already well on the way to recovery. According to the doctors, his prospects looked good.

That morning I had a long conversation with an Israeli journalist about how relieved everyone was that nothing more serious had befallen the prime minister. It had just been a couple months since he had formed his new political party, and the country was going through a time of profound political change. In a few months there would be an election, where the new party would be tested against the Labor Party and Sharon's old Likud Party. Right now Sharon was soaring in his popularity and there seemed little doubt that he would triumph, paving the way for him to proceed with more of the radical moves he was making—including, many hoped, further withdrawals from the Palestinian territories. With increasing belligerency from Iran toward Israel, the United States embroiled in Iraq, and Hamas growing in popularity among the Palestinians, in addition to the currents of domestic change in Israel itself, it seemed crucial to most of the country that Sharon remain at the helm. If something were to happen to him, it was totally unclear in what direction Israel, or the Middle East as a whole, would go.

But, despite the scare to the Prime Minister's Office and to the country, everything seemed to right itself. Sharon was only in the hospital for a few days, and our office did not allow the press to have contact with him during this time because we didn't want him to look old, feeble, or sick. We did our best to maintain the mystique of the invincible Ariel Sharon, which many Israelis seemed to hold as utter truth. It was a short time for a stroke victim to be hospitalized, even if it was a minor stroke, but the prime minister and his political advisers thought that it was strategically important for him to get back to work as soon as possible so as not to show weakness to any of his opponents, domestic or foreign, or undermine his image in the mind of the Israeli voter. Still lying in bed, Sharon even called up some of the major newspapers and media organizations and said whimsically, "I guess I overdid it. Apparently I should have taken a few days off."

When he did reappear in front of the camera, it was on his exit from the hospital, in a short, carefully crafted appearance. He wore a suit, not a hospital gown or casual clothes, and was neatly groomed. All this was artfully arranged, of course, to present the right image, and he stepped out energetically in front of the cameras and seemed to laugh off the whole episode as almost inconsequential. It was a good performance. Nothing, it seemed, could stop Prime Minister Ariel Sharon.

Back in the office, Sharon returned to his very busy schedule, and everyone breathed a sigh of relief. Despite his controversial past, many Israelis, even on the left, had come to see him as a father figure, and they now felt like a steady hand was back at the wheel after a brief but scary absence. Very quickly he was back up to speed at the Office, and because every week I received a copy of the classified document that showed the prime minister's schedule, I was able to see that he had perhaps even ramped up his activities to make up for the lost time, but at very least had certainly not diminished them as much as one would expect of someone who had recently suffered a stroke. His long daily schedule was unbelievably grueling. I also knew that he didn't eat particularly well—his favorite foods, some of his close advisers had told me, included falafel, of which he ate copious amounts—and didn't really have the time to exercise. And, of course, he was almost eighty years old and very overweight.

But maybe it really is true, I thought. *Maybe Ariel Sharon is invincible.*

Soon after the prime minister's return to the Office, he was due to give a short English speech for several thousand young people visiting from all over the world. Ezra called me in to the Aquarium to discuss our plans for it, and he also suggested I consult with Naomi, the prime minister's Diaspora affairs adviser. I arranged a meeting with her a few days later.

We met in the conference room in the Aquarium, sitting in the plush leather chairs where cabinet members, security chiefs, and the prime minister himself sat for the meetings of Israel's inner sanctum. I had spoken to Naomi many times, but now we actually had an in-depth discussion about my role in the Office, and how I could get further involved in helping her and the prime minister. She asked me how I had ended up in the Prime Minister's Office, and in the U.N. Mission before that, and was as surprised and amused by the whole thing as I was. She said that it was time that I had a personal meeting with Prime Minister Sharon, because she thought that he would like to get to know me more. I assumed she was just being polite. At the moment, she said, pointing to his office next door, he was at his desk working on something, but said that we would soon find time to arrange that meeting.

She also had another idea, which sounded even more improbable than the one about Ariel Sharon wanting to get to know me. Since this speech was about immigration, and about encouraging young people from around the world to consider moving to Israel, she suggested that we have Prime Minister Sharon mention *me* personally as a "successful immigrant to Israel."

A successful immigrant? I winced a bit, thinking of getting punched by cabdrivers, driving around in a constantly breaking-down car, being spat at by government officials, getting so frustrated by work that I was secretly putting *Seinfeld* references into the prime minister's speeches, being driven around by the prime minister's adviser who almost ran people over, struggling to keep my fiancée from killing waiters in restaurants because of the atrocious customer service, and getting progressively more disillusioned with the country that claimed to be my second homeland. *This is success?*

But Naomi seemed very excited about the idea, and assured me that the prime minister would be as well. She told me that when I wrote the speech I should have the prime minister say that not only was immigration to Israel possible for young people around the world, but that as a matter of fact, a member of his own personal staff, named Greg, had recently moved to Israel from New York. This seemed completely ridiculous to me, but Naomi was set on it.

"Just write it that way," she insisted, "and we'll see if the prime minister is happy with it. I'm sure he will be."

And, in fact, once I had finished writing the speech, including the bit about me, it was vetted and approved. My discomfort at including myself in his talk was outweighed by something far more important to me—my references to *Seinfeld* had survived the vetting for the first time. It seemed certain that when the speech was delivered just a few weeks later, Prime Minister Sharon would be unknowingly alluding to the sitcom. I was especially excited since I was actually going to be present to hear this speech. In the meantime, though, I was leaving Israel for a couple weeks. My parents were taking Abby and me on a trip to South Africa so that they could get to know my new fiancée better and show us both the country of my birth.

Just before we left for the trip, I went to observe one more cabinet meeting, escorting in a few members of the press and standing with them on the side of the room as the meeting got under way. Arrayed around the table were all the cabinet ministers and intelligence chiefs who ran the country, with Prime Minister Sharon at a central spot at the table. On the long cabinet table there was a very large spread of food and drink. It was the beginning of Hanukkah, and so it included two heaping piles of sugarcoated jelly doughnuts, a food traditionally eaten on the holiday.

Prime Minister Sharon welcomed everyone to the meeting, first the cabinet members around the table and then the handful of reporters and political aides standing alongside. He looked healthy and in good spirits, and I knew the reporters were all taking note of that—and that he was also aware of them doing so. He wished us a Happy Hanukkah, and told us all to make sure we celebrated it properly.

"Eat some jelly doughnuts," he said, his plump hands sweeping over the mounds of food in front of him. And then, indirectly winking at his recent health scare that had likely been brought on by his weight and lifestyle, added, "But make sure you don't eat too many!"

But that was the last time I would see Ariel Sharon, and he never did deliver the speech with the references to *Seinfeld*, and to me, in it. A little while into my trip to South Africa, I heard on the news that Prime Minister Sharon had suffered a second, much more major stroke, and that he was unconscious. I contacted my office and was told that everything was in disarray, but there was nothing I could do to help from all the way in South Africa. For the next few days, I was glued to the news and my email contacts with my office, following each development closely, as Israel and the Israeli government struggled to get through this traumatic time. This time it really did not look like he would make it through.

When I got back to Israel, the scene at the PMO was as bleak as I'd imagined. The optimism that had followed Sharon's formation of the new Kadima Party was gone, replaced by a palpable sense of gloom in the halls of the Office, and a numbness in the rest of the country. On my first day back, everything seemed quieter and more sedate, like we were working at a wake or a funeral.

Alon greeted me wearily—there were rings under his eyes and he looked exhausted—and told me in a hushed tone that the past few days had been the worst he had experienced in his many years at the PMO. Others seemed to have the same feeling. Everyone was tired and drained, their motions slow and full of effort. The usual constant chatter in the media wing was subdued, and sometimes entirely absent.

Even Isaac and Ra'anan were less energetic than usual. Isaac looked shell-shocked, and told me that he had been at the hospital almost constantly, standing outside in the cold—Jerusalem, I had been surprised to learn, actually got fairly cold in the winter—speaking to the vast number of journalists who had descended on Israel and camped out outside the hospital. In the next few days I went there to help out however I could, and saw the media pandemonium for myself.

While Ra'anan also seemed deflated, he was stubbornly maintaining that Sharon would recover and return to work.

"If anyone can do it," Ra'anan said repeatedly, "he can."

But it didn't really seem like anyone could do it, and more than one person in the Office told me that they thought Ra'anan was in a sad state of denial. His life had largely revolved around Sharon for so long that losing his boss must have been inconceivable. But there were hints that, beneath the surface, his heart was breaking with the realization that "Arik" was probably not coming back to the Prime Minister's Office. In an interview on Israeli radio that seemed to sum up everyone's mood and was floated widely around the Prime Minister's Office, Ra'anan said, "I still wake up at four in the morning and read the news every day, just out of habit, but now I don't have anyone to tell it to anymore."

Somewhat apprehensively, I made my way to the Aquarium to see how Ezra and Naomi, two of the people closest to the prime minister, were handling the situation. The staffers who worked in the Aquarium had constant contact with the prime minister, and were very close to him, and the mood there was even more somber than in the rest of the PMO. I found Ezra coming out of a meeting with a group of Sharon's other high-level advisers. All of them looked like zombies, walking in quiet, trancelike states down the hall, shuffling instead of stepping, as if they lacked the energy to raise their legs any higher. Ezra's face was pallid and his eyes looked red and sore. He stared at me blankly for a moment, before forcing a slow half smile.

"Are you okay?" I asked, patting him on the shoulder. "Staying strong?"

"It's a hard time," he answered stoically. Then, with a rueful smile, he added, "I don't think he's going to be doing your new speech."

Many of Prime Minister Sharon's closest advisers, including Ezra, Naomi, and Ra'anan, were spending hours by his side at the hospital, along with Sharon's two sons, Gilad and Omri. There was a twenty-four-hour-a-day schedule drawn up indicating who should be there when, in order to ensure that one of them was always present.

Some of those spending time at Sharon's bedside told me that they were playing Mozart in his hospital room much of the time, because that had always been his favorite music, and they were hoping that if it didn't rouse him, it would at least comfort him. His sons also brought one of his very young grandchildren to visit. The little boy spoke to his unconscious grandfather, and the story went around the Prime Minister's Office and the Israeli media that at the sound of the child's voice, Sharon had shed a lone tear, which trailed slowly down his cheek.

There was an Ariel Sharon–shaped hole seared in the Israeli consciousness. As the country began to grieve about what seemed inevitable, the reins of government were handed over to Ehud Olmert, one of Sharon's confidants and political protégés, who became acting prime minister. Olmert, whom I had sometimes seen on his way to cabinet meetings and in the meetings themselves, could not have been more different from Sharon. As the Israeli media constantly pointed out, he wore fine suits, smoked expensive cigars, and had spent a good deal of his adult life jetting around the world. Sharon, by contrast, had always claimed that if circumstances had not forced him to be a warrior—and a notoriously merciless one at that—he would have been a farmer. He hadn't particularly ever liked being away from his country, and preferred life on his ranch in southern Israel to trips abroad to foreign capitals. There was also a generational difference between them. Sharon was among the very last of the founding generation of Israelis, those who had been born before the state and struggled for its establishment. Olmert was of the next generation, which had grown up with the state and never known anything else.

But Olmert was consciously acting as a caretaker prime minister. He immediately did his best not to impose his own personality or style on the country's governance, instead endeavoring as much as possible to act as a place keeper for Sharon, trying to fill his shoes without the public really noticing that a very different person was now in charge. And the Israeli public seemed not to notice. In fact, it seemed a bit comatose itself, uncharacteristic for a populace that was usually at least as independent-minded as the officials who governed it. Perhaps, a few of my colleagues in the Office said, Israel was in shock.

Olmert started giving speeches to reassure the public that he was following in Sharon's footsteps as prime minister, and that a level head was running the country. I was walking down one of Tel Aviv's main streets one afternoon and saw that the little television at a corner falafel stand was showing a live feed of the acting prime minister making a speech at the Knesset. I stopped to watch, and the man working at the counter looked up at the screen to see what had interested me. He watched Olmert for a second, before looking back at me.

"What do you care?" he said to me. "He's just another dick."

In general, though, Israelis were mostly falling quietly behind Olmert as Sharon's successor. This was not necessarily the case inside the PMO, where things were very confusing. Unwilling to make the political mistake of jumping too eagerly into Sharon's place, Olmert would only come to the PMO for the occasional press conference and the weekly cabinet meetings, at which he made a point of sitting in his old seat, leaving the taller, prime minister's seat conspicuously and symbolically empty. He did all his other business as acting prime minister from his own office in the Ministry of Industry and Trade. This meant, in effect, that we were a Prime Minister's Office without a prime minister, a fact brought home in a somewhat spooky manner whenever I walked by Prime Minister Sharon's personal office, where his papers and belongings still lay, untouched.

The vague sense of emptiness was felt in all aspects of life at the PMO, even the most mundane ones. Olmert had some of his own media people, and a collection of his own personal advisers, and so in this weird twilight time, it put many of the officials in our office in a bit of a peculiar position, where we worked for the PMO—which effectively worked for Olmert—but didn't exactly work for Olmert himself. As one of those closest to Sharon said, although his team would do whatever they could to help Olmert, they would always be "Arik's children."

I felt at a loss as to what to do with myself. I wouldn't really have believed that things in the Israeli government could feel like they were *more* in disarray than before, but clearly anything was possible. One afternoon in the hallway right outside my office, one of the janitors stopped and stared down at a large garbage can that had been placed in the hallway. His face lit up with anger.

"Who put this here?" he yelled. "Who did this?"

One of the administrative workers appeared from a nearby office and said, "I did. What's the problem?"

"What's the problem? What's the problem?" the janitor raged. "What do you mean, what's the problem? There's going to be a press conference here in twenty minutes, and I moved all the garbage cans away. Now you move one back!"

"We're cleaning out files," the administrator responded. "We need to put this here!"

They were both yelling, and a senior official who worked with the administrative aide appeared to see what the commotion was.

"You can't put this here," the janitor yelled at the senior official, which seemed pretty jarring to me, given their two different stations at the PMO. "The prime minister will be here in fifteen minutes to do a press conference, and you want him to have to push this garbage can out of the way to get into the briefing room?"

"First of all," the senior official yelled back, "he's NOT the prime minister! The prime minister is in a coma."

"MAYBE *YOU'RE* IN A COMA!" the janitor screamed at the top of his lungs. "IT'S NOT YOUR JOB TO SAY WHO THE PRIME MINISTER IS!"

Now everyone was coming out of their offices to see what was going on. This strange, confusing face-off was clearly about issues bigger than the garbage can.

"HE'S THE *ACTING* PRIME MINISTER!" another official interjected as he came out of his own office, even though he had had nothing to do with the original dispute. "*ACTING* PRIME MINISTER!"

"THAT MAKES NO DIFFERENCE," the janitor screamed back, turning to face this new opponent. "HE'S THE PRIME MINISTER TO *YOU*!"

"*YOU* DON'T KNOW WHO THE PRIME MINISTER IS!" the senior official responded.

"NO, *YOU* DON'T KNOW WHO THE PRIME MINISTER IS!"

Here at the heart of the Israeli government, the center didn't seem to be holding. We were falling apart.

15

Pretty Woman and the
Prime Minister of Israel

Ariel Sharon was still in his coma and was surely not coming back, Ehud Olmert was struggling to establish the country's trust; the president of Iran was making increasingly threatening statements about Israel; the Palestinians had just recently elected their first Hamas government; and in the halls of the Prime Minister's Office, Isaac was angrily yelling something about a baked potato.

He had been in the United States for several weeks, on one of the periodic speaking tours he was sent on, and had just come back that morning. I hadn't seem him since his return, but I could hear him out there, haranguing someone furiously about, of all things, a baked potato.

"So I told him that baked potatoes can be had at any time of the day!" Isaac raged, his voice booming through the building. "At any time of the day! *Any* time! But that guy was crazy. Wasn't he crazy?"

I had no idea what Isaac was going on about, and I wasn't in the mood to find out. There were plenty of other things to worry about.

The United States had been pushing for a democratic election among the Palestinians for some time, but didn't quite expect that the result would be a Hamas government. Although Israel had been more reluctant to support the election in the first place, it, too, had been surprised by the results, its vaunted intelligence services embarrassed by their lack of foresight. Now a militant Islamic group that denied Israel's right to exist was in charge, and nobody seemed to know what to do. Israel, the United States, and even the Europeans were refusing to have any contact with Hamas until it agreed to a number of conditions. But inside the Israeli government, there still seemed to be a great deal of uncertainty about what this development meant for the country.

It was at this time that the recurring question "What would Sharon do?" began to plague Olmert's leadership and seemed likely to persist into the foreseeable future. Nobody, of course, knew for sure what the answer was, but even in the halls of the Prime Minister's Office, the question was bandied about. Over the two years I'd been working for the government, there had been a few dramatic shifts. When Yasser Arafat had died, it had seemed possible that a new, positive era had dawned. In fact, on instructions from my superiors, my speeches at the U.N. after that had been filled with the phrase *a window of opportunity*. But now, following Prime Minister Sharon's incapacitation and the election of a Hamas government, that sort of hopeful rhetoric was gone from all our statements, both at the Prime Minister's Office and, I saw, at the U.N. Mission. It felt like that window of opportunity had slammed violently shut and we were tapping hopelessly on the glass.

I had really believed that the momentum that had been built by Sharon and the formation of the Kadima Party might offer some reason for optimism. But in the wake of his stroke, and now this new development, my hopes had been all but dashed. As much as

I disliked the attitudes of the hard-line religious settlers, I hated the fanaticism and violence of Hamas much more. Inevitably, the settler movement and its allies blamed the disengagement from Gaza for the Hamas victory. I supposed that this may have had some truth to it, but at the same time, I couldn't help thinking that maybe Hamas's popularity was due more to aggressive Israeli actions, like the assassinations of Ahmed Yassin and Abdel Rantisi and the other heavy-handed moves I had defended at the U.N. and the Prime Minister's Office.

I was invited to a conference hosted by the Foreign Ministry, and attended by officials from a wide array of government ministries, to discuss Israel's PR strategies in the wake of the Hamas victory. I walked over to the Foreign Ministry, which was very close to the Prime Minister's Office, but had a beautiful modern design, in contrast to the Prime Minister's Office's faux-third-world aesthetic. Some of Israel's most important spokespeople were there, as well as some outside media consultants brought in from the United States. We held a discussion about what could be done from a media perspective, and received guidance from the U.S. consultants. Afterward, though, it didn't really feel like any of us had any better idea of how to deal with the situation. It was a mess.

And on my way out of the building I ran into someone who, I had no doubt, would only make things worse.

"Hey!" a tall, lanky man with disheveled clothes said, running into me in one of the halls of the ministry. I knew I recognized him, but couldn't place him. The fact that he was speaking English to me tipped me off that I must have met him in my time at the U.N. Mission.

"How are you?" he asked, swinging a very sweaty arm around my shoulders.

Something about that gesture, and the moistness I felt on my neck, suddenly reminded me who he was. He was the computer technician at the U.N. Mission who had once come into my office just minutes before a Security Council speech was due and insisted on taking my computer away from me to "check something." I asked him what he was doing in Jerusalem.

"I got transferred back to headquarters," he told me, sweeping his arm grandly to indicate the large, busy Foreign Ministry building. "Now I'm working on the computer systems here."

We really are all doomed, I thought.

In addition to the Foreign Ministry, I was also now spending time at the Ministry of Defense. Ra'anan's offhand remark some months before about me coordinating a paratrooper jump with the Ministry of Defense had actually materialized. The fiftieth anniversary of the 1956 war, in which Israel, France, and the UK had fought against Egypt, was being commemorated with a joint jump by the three countries' paratroopers. It would be taking place in Israel, and was meant to highlight the countries' continued friendship. British and French paratroopers were coming in for the jump, and were being joined by Americans, Canadians, and others. I had received a phone call from a woman at the Ministry of Defense who was coordinating what would be the first of a series of meetings about the event, and was told to come to the Defense Ministry in Tel Aviv to discuss it.

Passing by the modest, unmarked building that had been quietly pointed out to me as the quasi-secret headquarters of the Mossad, I walked on toward the Kirya, the sprawling compound in the center of Tel Aviv that served as the headquarters of the whole Israeli military apparatus. Instead of the professional security agents that were usually posted outside the Prime Minister's Office, the Foreign Ministry, and most of the other government buildings, here there were armed and uniformed soldiers standing guard outside. I showed them my Prime Minister's Office pass and they waved me in.

Inside, there were hundreds of soldiers walking around, military jeeps periodically passing by, and trucks moving different kinds of equipment. On one side of the compound was the massive Defense Ministry, a giant, sparkling new facility that towered above everything else and was capped by a huge helicopter pad. I made my way toward it.

I went to a conference room near the top of the building, where a group of military and Defense Ministry officials, most of them in army uniforms, were waiting. Also at the meeting were Ra'anan and a couple of other people from the PMO, and some PR and journalistic professionals. Among the latter was the Israeli journalist Uri Dan, one of Ariel Sharon's longtime best friends, who, when Sharon was forced to resign from the Defense Ministry in 1983, had famously proclaimed, "Those who didn't want Sharon as defense minister will get him as prime minister!"

At this first discussion, the general contours of the jump were sketched out, with everyone brainstorming and contributing. I attended several other meetings afterward, in which the details became somewhat more focused and established, though nothing was ever exactly orderly. The jump was going to be a giant undertaking, both in its PR dimension, which was the main impetus for it, and in its actual logistical aspects, like the mechanics of using giant transport planes for the paratroopers. To me, it seemed like a lot of expenditure of time and money for a fairly abstract reward.

In my core work at the PMO, I was still working with Ra'anan and Isaac on relations with the press about day-to-day events in Israel, even though it had become clear that the media center of gravity was now around Olmert himself and not the staffers in the PMO. I was occasionally asked to write short English statements for Olmert when he was addressing foreign groups. I wrote these, pleased with the fact that he was capable enough in English that I could pretty well write freely. But he never seemed to actually use any of them, and I started to think that his personal aides weren't even giving them to him. After I had written one, the liaison with Olmert in our office told me that the speech was "excellent"—but it wasn't used either.

The fact was, I realized, that Olmert's English ability and knowledge of the world outside Israel was such that he really didn't need someone to write these simple statements for him. He was able to speak breezily and confidently, off-the-cuff, in English or Hebrew. In this way he differed sharply from Sharon, who had nervously read my words straight from the page, not confident with his English and often stricken with mild stage fright.

The many ways in which Olmert and Sharon were different sorts of leaders were becoming more and more apparent. Besides Olmert's fancy cigars and suits, and his jet-setting life—he had stayed in the country for the past six months, and it was reportedly the only time in his adult life he had been there for so long—he was also much more thoroughly attuned to the modern world than was his predecessor. By the time he had his first contact with anyone in the morning, he had already done his daily workout and read all the foreign and Israeli press himself, making some press aides redundant. He was also comfortable addressing the foreign media in a way Sharon had never been.

I was shocked when someone in the office who knew Olmert quite well told me that he had named the 1990 movie *Pretty Woman*. It seemed wholly unlikely, but shortly afterward, an Israeli paper published a story saying the same thing, and my colleague in the Office explained that the high-flying acting prime minister had friends all over the world, including some big names in Hollywood.

He was also very technologically savvy. One day, weeks into his tenure as acting PM, Olmert was interviewed by a very prominent American journalist about the plan he had floated to continue Sharon's path of withdrawing unilaterally from Palestinian territory. He had already come up with an official Hebrew name for the plan, but the English translation had not yet been decided upon; we had been arguing about it in my office and the Foreign Ministry for a while. During this interview, Olmert forgot the English word that we were tentatively using, and, somehow, he—or perhaps his right-hand man, improbably nicknamed "Turbo," or one of his other close aides—managed to secretly send a text message to one of my colleagues asking for the word.

Olmert's dramatically different leadership style was very apparent to the Israeli public, including the taxi drivers, whose services I still had to use when my car broke down. As always happened when they dropped me off at the PMO, one driver asked me why I was going there, and then if I could tell the PM something for him.

"Okay," I said wearily, opening my door to get out.

"Tell him," the driver said, "that he needs to do something about his hair. That comb-over is just not working."

Although I sometimes found the extreme informality of Israeli society and the Israeli government off-putting and irritating, I had to admit that it was occasionally endearing. Once, for example, a woman I'd never seen before dropped in to my office to tell me that another person I didn't know who worked in the PMO was having trouble paying for the cancer treatments she needed.

"Would you mind helping to pay?" she asked.

She then explained that dozens of staffers in the building, most of whom didn't even know the ill woman, had volunteered to have their monthly salaries automatically docked a small amount to help her pay for her treatments. I happily agreed, of course, as did many people in my department, banding together for a stranger in a way I couldn't imagine happening back in North America. I was touched by the whole thing.

"That's Israelis," Abby said that evening when I told her the story. We were sharing a bottle of wine in a little café around the corner from our apartment, and she looked around at the Israelis sitting nearby as she spoke. "They're a bunch of jerks until you need them. Then they're there to help."

Abby and I took regular turns trying to calm each other down about life in Israel. But although she still wasn't particularly enjoying living there, and occasionally still vented about it, for the most part she was more stoic than me—perhaps because she didn't have to deal with the country's actual day-to-day politics. Often, in that little café, on walks around Tel Aviv, or in our apartment, she would try to soothe me as I complained about the various frustrations at the Prime Minister's Office and in the country in general.

"You have to think of Israel as a family," she said.

"Yeah," I told her. "A dangerously dysfunctional family."

But I had to admit that at times of emergency, the country did seem to come together like families do. Around this time, in fact, I saw this phenomenon firsthand. I was sitting at my desk in the middle of the day, lazily scanning various news sources, when I heard something alarming from one of the dozens of monitors and radios in the Media Situation Room, which constantly broadcast Israeli news, foreign news, and feeds from police, ambulance, and other emergency departments. Someone from Israel's ambulance service was saying that there had just been a suicide bombing at the bus station in Tel Aviv. Everyone sprang into action in their various roles, creating a hive of activity with an unmistakable feeling of familial unity and solidarity. I called Ra'anan to let him know what had happened and to get instructions that, I assumed, would involve setting up a flurry of appearances in the foreign media.

After speaking to him, I suddenly recalled with a jolt that Abby had been meeting a friend at the Tel Aviv bus station that morning. I was quite sure that she had actually been at the *other* Tel Aviv station, and that she would have left several hours before anyway, but that didn't fully assuage my instinctive fears. Life in Israel had suddenly become real for me.

Before I even had a chance to phone her to confirm that she was okay, though, I got a call from the BBC. They had been unable to reach Ra'anan or any of the other high-ranking media relations people, and were scrambling to get some information about the bombing so that they could put out a report as soon as possible. Specifically, they wanted to know which Palestinian group the Israeli government was pointing its finger at as the perpetrators of the attack. I told the BBC that I would get back to them right away, and rushed off to ask superiors in the Prime Minister's Office if we had answers to that question yet. They told me to call the Shabak, the famed and feared internal intelligence organization that dealt with Palestinian terrorism and other threats, and that I could pass the information I received on to the BBC. It would be one of the first times I had spoken directly to Israeli intelligence, other than when I was being grilled by them for my security clearance.

"Uh, yeah," I said awkwardly to the woman who answered the phone at the headquarters of the Shabak. "This is Greg from the Prime Minister's Office. I need to know if you can tell me who is responsible for this bombing."

I expected them to balk, hearing my accent and my ten-year-old's grasp of Hebrew. But to my surprise, they took me seriously as an official at the PMO, and gave me the information I needed. I thanked them and called the BBC back.

"Can you help us?" their reporter asked hopefully.

"We believe," I said, trying to sound authoritative and governmental, "that the perpetrators are members of Islamic Jihad."

As soon as I hung up the phone, the BBC began airing this information and ascribing it to "sources in the Israeli Prime Minister's Office."

Meanwhile, I raced back to my desk to call Abby with a kind of numb anxiety, which I knew was largely unfounded. As we began to receive reports about the number of dead and injured at the scene of the bombing, I dialed her number, and was relieved when she answered. She had been nowhere near the bus station, and hadn't even heard that there had been a bombing, but it was a moment that made me wonder how long we could possibly stay in Israel.

"I'm fine," she said. "You're paranoid."

The Kadima Party, with Ehud Olmert as its leader, was victorious in the election, although with a significantly smaller mandate than had been predicted had Sharon been leading it. Because Olmert had not yet accomplished all the political wrangling necessary to unite various disparate parliamentary factions into a ruling coalition, though, he had not yet officially become prime minister. It was only a matter of time, but he had not formally relocated to the Prime Minister's Office. I watched as Sharon's personal papers and effects were carted out of the Office, but for now, his seat was empty. Olmert was dealing with the demands of domestic politics, and running the country, from down the street.

But while all this happened around us—the political maneuvering, the suicide bombings, the threats from Iran, the nearby war in Iraq, and the frightening Hamas government—on that first morning back from his speaking trip in the United States, Isaac continued to seem mostly interested in some injustice involving a baked potato. For the second time that morning, I sat in my office and listened to him shout about it to someone out in the hall.

"Isaac's back," Alon said almost grimly, and I nodded. "He's yelling about a potato."

Then Isaac burst into the media wing and, with barely a break in his monologue, said to me, "Greggy, how are ya?"

"Fine," I answered. "How was your trip?"

He went into his rant about the baked potato, now in English. After hearing it no fewer than a dozen times over the next several days, here's as best as I can reconstruct it: Isaac had gone with his elderly mother to a diner in Queens to have lunch. He had ordered a baked potato, but the waiter had informed him that this was only available at dinnertime.

"I don't understand," Isaac said. "You have the potato?"

"Yes."

"So just put it in the microwave for me."

"I'm sorry," the waiter said. "We only do that at night."

"That doesn't make any sense. You can put it in at lunch, too."

Again the waiter demurred, saying that the manager didn't allow it, and Isaac asked to see the manager. Now things really escalated. When the manager also refused, Isaac started yelling, bringing some of his Prime Minister's Office spirit to the situation.

"If you have it, and a customer orders it," Isaac yelled, "I don't understand why you can't serve it at lunch!"

"Sir," the manager responded, "in thirty-two years in the restaurant business, I have never had a customer request a baked potato *at lunch*!"

Isaac continued to make a big fuss, but he never did get his baked potato. When the meal was over he refused to leave a tip.

"Can you believe that?" he asked me. "Can you believe how *crazy* that is?"

It did seem crazy, I admitted, but didn't add that Isaac's reaction to it seemed not much less so, especially since it was now days later.

"I mean," he went on, "what should I have done? What would you have done?"

"I guess just not have had a baked potato."

"But I wanted a baked potato! Why do I have to suffer because of his crazy rules?"

He stomped off, and I could hear him telling the story in Hebrew to all the staffers in the Situation Room. I had work to do, so I closed the door, muffling his booming voice only a little.

For most of the week, Isaac pestered everyone who would listen, in Hebrew and English, about the incident. I even heard him on the phone, talking heatedly about it to several journalists, who must have been less than pleased at this scoop. One afternoon late in the week, when I thought it had finally been forgotten, Isaac came back into my office.

"I'm still mad about this whole thing," he said immediately. "I mean, can you believe it? They had the damn potato and wouldn't give it to me? Is that right? No, that's not right!"

I looked straight at him silently.

"What time is it in New York?" he asked. "You know what? You know what I'm going to do? I'm going to call them right now, and ask to speak to that manager. That guy is not going to get away with this." And he stormed back to his own office.

But maybe it wasn't so crazy to obsess over baked potatoes when it felt like everything was falling apart anyway. One day I was called to the Aquarium, which was still without a prime minister, in order to be given some information for a statement Olmert's people had requested, and that I was confident would just be ignored like the others. I went out of the media wing, through the lobby, and toward the Hall of Advisers. I swiped my card as usual, but the door didn't slide open, and I noticed that it was off its rail and slightly ajar. I tried to push it open, but found it would not move, which meant that not only was I unable to get into the Hall of Advisers, but also that all those advisers and their staffs presumably had no way to get out. I went off to tell someone about this problem, wondering what could have rammed that very heavy door off its tracks.

Out in the lobby I saw Dov Weisglass, Prime Minister Sharon's former chief strategist, who I had been told was now acting as an adviser to Olmert, but with a greatly reduced level of influence. Weisglass was standing there with his chin up in the air and blood pouring from his nose, and there were two medics treating him. Either he had forgotten that the glass door was there, or it had not opened when he swiped his card, and he had smashed into it, somehow flinging it off the rails with a stubborn force appropriate for one of Sharon's closest aides. Apparently, the doors of the Prime Minister's Office didn't open nearly as readily for him anymore.

And this wasn't the only injury to befall the people of the Prime Minister's Office. In just *one week* there were four car accidents involving staffers from the Office, as if the political weariness around us were manifesting itself physically. One of them was a pregnant woman. Another was an already disabled woman. Both of them came out relatively unscathed, but the third, a staffer whom I had met once or twice, was not nearly as lucky. He had been riding his motorcycle, got in an accident, and been in a coma for a few days before passing away. At this news, Alon reminded me of a sad and ridiculous fact I had heard a few times before. In the history of the State of Israel, more Israelis had died on the country's murderous roads than in all the wars and terrorism combined.

The fourth staffer in a car accident that week was me. Not long before, I had finally gotten fed up with the car that constantly broke down and demanded a new one from the rental company. After some reluctance to admit there was anything wrong with my car, and some to-be-expected bureaucracy, they finally gave in. On the day of my accident, I had driven my new car all the way from Tel Aviv to Jerusalem, and then through a part of the city to the Prime Minister's Office. Just a block away from the tall, ugly building, I started looking for parking, driving for a while before deciding to do a U-turn. I slowed down and signaled, noted that the car behind me slowed down a little in response, and assumed that the driver would be rational and wait for me to complete the turn. Instead, he decided that he had no time for this and would pull around me quickly so that he didn't have to stop. Even this would have been okay, if still a bit dangerous, if he had decided to do it on my right side. Instead he tried to shoot by me on the left before I made the leftward U-turn.

The impact was thunderous, and my car spun out, the other driver having careened full force into the side of the back end as I was halfway through my intended turnaround. I had my seat belt on, but my face hit squarely and solidly into the side window with a thud. I felt my teeth cut into the side of my mouth and blood begin spurting out.

I stumbled out of the car, dizzy and disoriented, and found a short, unshaven middle-aged man a few feet away from me, pointing at our two cars and yelling at me in Hebrew. His car was lightly damaged, but mine was essentially destroyed. Most of the back was crushed inward and the left rear wheel was at a diagonal. I was not sure if I would even be able to drive it over to the curb to get it out of the way of traffic.

I said something in English, but he didn't seem to understand at all, and I tried to switch to Hebrew, but found that I couldn't really manage it with my suddenly pounding headache. My vision was a bit blurry and my back was starting to hurt. In order to even try to speak, I had to spit little globs of blood out of my mouth.

A tall young man who had been walking by decided for some reason to get involved. As I leaned against my car, trying to gain my bearings, he yelled at the other driver, who yelled back at him. Then he was suddenly yelling at me, and then the other driver and he were both yelling at me, which didn't seem to make a lot of sense. I tried to steady myself, and spat out more blood.

The driver who had hit me wrote some kind of note on a piece of paper in Hebrew, and pushed it into my hands, trying to get me to sign it. More or less in shock, though, I couldn't decipher the scratchy Hebrew writing or understand what he was trying to get me to admit. Luckily, in spite of the shock and injury, whatever faint strains of lawyerly thinking I had picked up on my halfhearted journey through law school came to my aid, and although I signed it, I wrote a little English note beside my signature, saying that I didn't understand what he had written and giving my account of the accident.

The random interloper decided that his work, whatever that was, was done, and walked off. Taking his note with him, the other driver drove away in his relatively unharmed vehicle, and I got back in my car to gingerly drive the few feet to the curb, the crooked back wheel making strange noises as it went. Alone again, and sitting in my ruined car, I called the rental company to tell them to come pick up their car. They said that they would send a tow truck, and then take me to the hospital, if necessary, so that I didn't have to call an ambulance.

After calling Abby to tell her what had happened, I sat in the car waiting for the tow truck to arrive and looking up at the Prime Minister's Office, just a short distance away. The left side of my face ached, and my headache got worse as the minutes passed. It hurt to move my jaw, and the left side of the inside of my mouth stung. I probed around with my tongue to see how badly I had cut the inside of my cheek on my teeth. I felt nauseated and tired, and was starting to worry that I had a concussion. It seemed like I had been waiting a long time, and when I checked the clock I found that it had been over half an hour already. I called the company again, and they told me that it would just be another few minutes.

On the side of the road was a low wall made of the famous and beautiful Jerusalem stone and I stared at it for a very long time, my thoughts slow and dull. This had not been a major incident, and I knew that I was essentially fine. The car-rental company would deal with the car and give me yet another one, and my injuries would heal within a few days. I knew that I had nothing to worry about and, if anything, I should have felt relief.

But somehow it felt like, for me, the accident had repercussions beyond the moment—like it had awoken me from some kind of trance. A few years before I began working for the government, I had become deeply interested in what was happening in Israel, and, of course, once I had begun working at the U.N. Mission, events in the Middle East had become chief among my day-to-day concerns. But as the frustrations of life in Israel built up, along with the disappointments I felt about certain segments of the Israeli population and my doubts that the country's problems would ever be solved, my feeling of personal connection to it had begun to dissipate. As I looked toward a future alongside my soon-to-be wife, Israel no longer seemed relevant. And, for no concrete reason, this car accident had sealed this sad transition for me.

It was getting hot in the car, and I got out and stood on the sidewalk for a while before making my way over to the little wall to sit down. From the car, it had provided a scenic little picture: a pretty little wall in front of a hill of lush green grass. Up close, it was quite different. Between the wall and the hill, invisible from the street, there was an enormous heap of garbage: broken glass bottles, papers, boxes, food scraps, beer cans, what appeared to be a used condom. I looked at it all for moment and then got up so the trash was out of sight. I stood there looking at the wall until I had to spit out the blood building up on the left side of my mouth. I left the little splatter of blood on the sidewalk and got back in the car to continue waiting.

When I called the rental-car company again, it had been over an hour since I had first called, and they told me that the person they had sent would be another twenty minutes. By the time he finally arrived, it had been more than two hours since my first call. Although I had been waiting all that time with a bloody mouth and what had become a throbbing headache, the driver was in no way apologetic, even when he saw me spit blood. Worse: he hadn't arrived with the tow truck, but with a normal car instead, smaller even than mine.

"What's the problem?" he asked me, and I showed him the huge damage to the side and back of the car, and the way that the back wheel was now at a diagonal.

"Well, what do you want me to do?" he asked me, shaking his head. "I only have this little car."

I stared at him silently.

"What do you think we should do?" he asked.

I shook my head.

"I don't know," I told him. "I really don't know what you should do."

16

One Last Job

When I told an Israeli friend of mine about the various frustrations that I'd encountered in daily life in Israel as well as in the government, he joked, "That's why they call it the Zionist dream. Because it doesn't really exist."

Indeed, although Ehud Olmert had now assembled his coalition and officially become prime minister, the country still seemed to be spinning its wheels on the desert sand, and I myself was finding it hard to get traction. I knew it would not be right to keep Abby away from school any longer, and so for some time we had been making tentative plans for our departure. She would resume her studies, and I would try to find something to do that didn't involve working for a foreign government. I gave notice to my superiors and colleagues at the Prime Minister's Office, and all of them seemed to understand. With the situation as it was, many of them didn't even know if they would be able to keep their own jobs.

In the meantime, there were tasks still ahead of me. For one, I was still involved in preparations for the paratrooper jump. It was progressing in such a chaotic and disorganized fashion that I had trouble believing it would be safe for the paratroopers, let alone that it would prove to be the stellar publicity stunt the organizers envisioned. To succeed, they would have to coordinate hundreds of paratroopers hailing from different countries and under different commands, several huge transport planes, the use of runways and landing sites, the security of all involved, and the cooperation of the diplomatic and military branches of the participating foreign governments. I had my doubts that the people attending the planning meetings had the logistical chops needed.

But at the last meeting I attended about the jump, my problem was more awkwardness than disorganization. As usual, I showed up at the Kirya, the military headquarters, and made my way to the giant Defense Ministry. When I got to the conference room, I was surprised to find that Ra'anan was not there, and neither was anyone else from the Prime Minister's Office. Instead, there were about ten military officers, in full uniform, sitting around the conference table and waiting for the other four or so seats to be filled. Most of them recognized me as Ra'anan's aide. They greeted me as I took one of the empty seats.

"Ra'anan should be here soon," I said, with no idea if this was actually true. At these meetings, he represented the Prime Minister's Office and the government as a whole. Everyone else present at this particular meeting was from the army or air force. Most of them were men, but there were a couple women, including one of the military's most senior public relations officials, who was coordinating much of this project. As another officer came in, and I remained the only person there not from the military, I decided to call Ra'anan.

"I'm stuck in traffic coming from Jerusalem," he told me. "Tell them I'll be there in ten minutes."

I did, and they seemed only a bit annoyed. I tried to make small talk using my paltry Hebrew, convinced the army officers were thinking, *The Prime Minister's Office has really gone downhill since Olmert took over*. I listened to them as they gossiped about the doings in the army, trying to pretend that I understood all their jokes and military acronyms. After about ten minutes had passed and Ra'anan still hadn't arrived, I called him again.

"I'm downstairs," he barked. "Tell them I'm downstairs."

I hung up, and confidently announced, "He's downstairs. He'll be up here in just a couple of minutes."

Five minutes passed, and he didn't appear. I could tell the army people were getting impatient, and I called again.

"I'm downstairs," he said again.

"How long until you come *upstairs*?" I asked hopefully.

"One minute."

Another five increasingly awkward minutes passed. I looked at the middle-aged man at the head of the table who was chairing the meeting, and saw that he was watching me. I didn't really know how to tell an Israeli army officer's rank from the various little badges and insignias on his shoulders and chest, but since he was one of the older people in the room, and was chairing the meeting, I had to assume that he was fairly high ranking. As we looked at each other, he raised one bushy eyebrow questioningly, tapping a pen rhythmically on the big wooden table in front of him. The look on his face seemed to say that he was getting fed up.

I called Ra'anan again, and once more he told me that he was "downstairs" and would be up any minute. I wanted to ask which building he was "downstairs" in. All the army officers in the room were staring at me now, and I was feeling more and more uncomfortable.

After another few minutes, the officer chairing the meeting looked straight at me and asked loudly, "Can we have the government's permission to begin, please?"

So this is what it has come to, I thought, surveying the officers in the opulent Defense Ministry planning room, all staring at me expectantly. *Now I'm representing the government of Israel in meetings with the military?* Even as I was preparing to leave, every day promised a parade of new absurdities. Ra'anan, wherever he was, was making me look ridiculous.

"Yes," I answered. "You have the government's permission."

But just when I thought that my time in the government had run its course, I got a call from Olmert's foreign affairs adviser, and received my biggest speech assignment yet. Now that he was officially based in the Prime Minister's Office, Olmert was going to make his first trip abroad as Israel's new leader. He would be visiting Washington, where he would meet with President Bush and other members of the administration, and then address a joint session of the U.S. Congress, an honor only rarely bestowed on foreign dignitaries. It was also the first time an Israeli prime minister had done this in almost a decade. And coming at such an important time in the Middle East, with a new government in Israel and Olmert hoping to get American support to continue the territorial withdrawals begun by Sharon, it was a crucial speech. I was flabbergasted that they wanted me to write the first draft.

Of course, there would be many other people contributing, including the foreign affairs people from the PMO, other personal advisers of Olmert's, and even outsiders like Nobel laureate Elie Wiesel. Most important, officials from the Foreign Ministry, some of whom I knew from my time at the U.N. Mission, would have a heavy hand in crafting the final version of the speech. Even so, all of a sudden I was again under a lot of pressure.

Over the next few frantic days at my already half-emptied-out desk, in the office suite of the PMO's foreign affairs adviser, and even at home, I worked on the speech, trying to tailor it to what I believed would resonate with the congressmen and senators of the United States. I worked closely with the assistant foreign affairs adviser to Olmert and a collection of other officials, and after a long few days,

I handed in a draft that I knew would probably be changed beyond recognition. But that was the nature of speechwriting. Indeed, in the end, after so many other drafts and rewrites, only a smattering of my first draft remained recognizable in the final version, but I was flattered to hear that some of my lines had stayed in because the prime minister himself had liked them.

I sat on the couch in my apartment in Tel Aviv and watched Prime Minister Olmert give the speech to the U.S. Congress on TV. The entire Congress filed in, as well as other important members of the American leadership. Olmert appeared and was greeted by thunderous applause. The speech was very well received by the assembled U.S. lawmakers, who repeatedly interrupted it with standing ovations.

Abby, beside me on the couch, put an arm around me and said, "It's definitely a good note to leave on."

Our Israeli experiment was over.

I finished packing up my office, said good-bye to my colleagues in the Prime Minister's Office, and began making final preparations with Abby to leave the country. But shortly after Prime Minister Olmert returned from Washington, I got a call from the assistant foreign affairs adviser, telling me that the prime minister wanted me to come in one more time to see him.

The prime minister of Israel had many offices. The main one was the large, official building in Jerusalem where I worked, but there was also a smaller one inside the military headquarters in Tel Aviv, and a bunch of tiny satellite offices around the country that he rarely actually visited himself. In addition, he had a small suite inside the Knesset, the Israeli parliament, because in Israel's parliamentary system, in addition to being the head of the executive branch of government, he was also the leader of the largest faction in the legislative branch. It was to his Knesset office that I was invited.

Parking my car by the main Prime Minister's Office, I walked the short distance to the Knesset, the sun beating down on me. It was not even officially summer yet, but the desert heat was already punishing. I got to the Knesset a bit early and walked around the building a little. I had been there a few times before, but these trips had always been short and rushed, and I spent the next twenty minutes or so strolling through the busy halls. They were filled with characteristic shouting and activity. As I passed various legislators I recognized, walked through the raucous Knesset cafeteria, and bumped into an Israeli journalist I knew, I thought, with a creeping sense of early nostalgia, that in some ways I would miss all this.

I made my way to the prime minister's Knesset office. Standing outside it were a few people I knew, and a Foreign Ministry official named Michael who had been most instrumental in the congressional speech's formulation and would be joining me at the meeting with the prime minister. Together, he and I waited to be admitted to Olmert's office. I had been in the same room as Olmert quite a few times by now, and had once met him very briefly before he had become prime minister, but this would be the first time I would have a real conversation with him.

When the door swung open and we were ushered in, Olmert was standing in the center of the room. Just behind him stood Turbo, whose diminutive, bespectacled appearance belied the power he had as Olmert's closest adviser. The prime minister smiled broadly as Michael and I entered, greeting us warmly.

"I'm a pretty ambitious person," he quipped, and we all laughed, "but even I wasn't ambitious enough to try to write this speech myself. I'm very glad that we had capable speechwriters on hand to help me do it. I just hope I did your speech justice."

He spoke to Michael for a while, thanking him for his very important contribution to the speech, and then turned his attention to me.

"I heard that you're leaving us," he said, "and I want to thank you for your service to the government, and for your help on this speech."

I told him that it had been a pleasure and an honor, and added a bit lamely, "I've written speeches for a lot of Israeli diplomats and officials now, but the two who deliver them the best are you and Danny Gillerman at the U.N."

"Well," he answered, "if I'm walking around New York and someone confuses me with Danny, it would be an honor."

I didn't really know what he meant but laughed anyway. He was charming and warm, and we made small talk for a while. After he discovered that I was from Toronto, he told me that some time ago, as a regular parliamentarian, he had had an intern from Toronto. He mentioned his name and asked if I knew him.

There is a common type of conversation mockingly called "Jewish geography," in which one Jewish person gives a name or a long list of names to another to see if there is any mutual acquaintance, on the implicit theory that somewhere in the matrix of interlaced Jewish relationships, the two are connected. This little game had always aggravated me; it seemed primitive and tribal, and vaguely to confirm certain anti-Semitic clichés. I wouldn't have guessed this worldly prime minister of Israel engaged in it.

"Yeah, he was definitely from Toronto," Olmert said, nodding thoughtfully and rubbing his chin. "He got married last year?"

I think we're getting a bit off topic here, I thought. *Does absolutely EVERYBODY play this game?*

"I'm sorry," I told Prime Minister Olmert. "I don't know him."

He seemed genuinely surprised for some reason, and even a bit disappointed.

"We hope you come back to Israel soon," he said, changing tacks.

"And when you do," Turbo added from behind the prime minister, "make sure you call us. You have a pretty important friend here."

The prime minister and I both laughed at this, and thinking about the chaotic nature of Israeli politics, I restrained myself from saying to Olmert, "Just how long do you think *you're* going to be here?"

Olmert asked me to assure him that I would come back, and maybe even work for the government again, and although I complied, I didn't really think this was a promise I could keep. It had been a good run, but it was over now.

Afterward, I walked out of the building into the blinding-white sunshine. I quickly broke out into a sweat, very uncomfortable in my suit and tie. I was glad, as I made my way to my car, that I would not have to be in these clothes in the Israeli summer heat anymore. Although I knew this was probably the last time I would be in an Israeli government building, I didn't look back at the Knesset as I walked away. But as I drove off, I couldn't help but look in my rearview mirror at the Prime Minister's Office, disappearing into the chaotic patchwork of Jerusalem. I pulled out of town and headed west on the highway, and I wasn't sure if I would ever see that city again—or if that even mattered to me. I had found it only strange and depressing from my first visit until the end.

When we took off from the airport a few days later, all our belongings with us and the keys to our Tel Aviv apartment surrendered back to the landlord, Abby tried to get me to look out the window.

"Don't you want to say good-bye?" she asked, but I was starting to slip into sleep, other, more mundane dreams already replacing the "Zionist dream" in demanding my attention. And despite Israel's claims to be the homeland of Jews worldwide—and the fact that I wasn't even from New York—when our plane touched down at JFK Airport many hours later, it felt like I had finally come home.

Just a couple weeks later, Hamas kidnapped an Israeli soldier, and Israel began major military operations against the Palestinians in Gaza. Within a few days, the Hezbollah kidnapped two more soldiers in Israel's north, and a war broke out between Israel and the Lebanese paramilitary group, with Israeli soldiers and planes going deep into Lebanon, and Hezbollah missiles raining down on Israeli cities.

I watched the news on television and read the Israeli newspapers online. It felt odd, at this scary time, not to have something of an inside view on what was happening. I no longer had access to the information I would have had just a few weeks before, and with the Middle East in flames, I missed it. I spoke with a few former colleagues, both at the PMO and the U.N. Mission, to try to better understand what was happening, but it was not the same from such a far remove. I wasn't sure if I had ever really been an insider, but I was definitely just another outsider now, and although I couldn't imagine what the atmosphere was like in the PMO or the U.N. Mission, I thought it must have been utter madness. I also, of course, worried about the friends and colleagues I had in Israel, as well as the innocent Israeli, Lebanese, and Palestinian civilians who were dying, but mostly I was just relieved that Abby and I weren't there anymore.

The war eventually ground to a standstill, with hundreds of civilians killed and large swaths of Lebanon destroyed. It more or less ended in a draw, and nobody in Israel seemed to think it had gone well. There was a prolonged and agonizing period of soul-searching about the country's military and diplomatic policies, and even about its long-term prospects for survival. With the looming possibility of a nuclear Iran, as well as increasing tides of hostility in the region, Israelis were nervously aware of the fallibility of their leadership. The grandfatherly and seemingly invincible Sharon was gone, along with the confidence he bestowed on his people. The hands at the levers of government now seemed all too human.

Once the dust had settled, Israel established a commission to examine the failures of the war, and what had led to them. After some months of investigation, including testimony from many of those in the highest positions of both the government and the military, it was concluded that the ranks and operation of both were filled with rampant incompetence, negligence, and disorganization.

In the months that followed, the chief of staff of the military resigned in disgrace, the defense minister lost his post after losing an internal party primary, the justice minister was indicted on suspicion of indecent assault, the president was forced to resign because of rape allegations, advisers and aides close to Olmert, including his personal secretary, were arrested on corruption charges, and a slew of corruption allegations were leveled against the prime minister himself. As a seeming punch line to this string of embarrassments, the Israeli ambassador to El Salvador was found by the police in the yard of his residence, drunk and naked, except for some sex bondage equipment. Only after he was untied, and the ball that was gagging him removed from his mouth, was he able to identify himself as the ambassador.

In the wake of the war, Prime Minister Olmert's approval rating dropped as low as 2 percent. Because the poll had a margin of error of 3 percent, this caused commentators to wonder what the possibility of a negative approval rating could even mean, and one writer to quip that the almost unanimous sense of disapproval of how things were going represented the greatest unity of Israeli opinion since the founding of the state.

When the commission on the war began releasing its findings, efforts were launched to fix the systemic problems in both the government and the military. Watching from the other side of the world, I wholeheartedly wished Israel well. But as I waited hopefully for the promised changes to save the country from itself, I thought that maybe I finally understood the joke that had been told to me so many months before by that crazed taxi driver.

And still nothing.

Acknowledgments

It goes without saying that this book could not have been written without the help of many people. I am grateful, first of all, to Ambassador Arye Mekel, for taking a chance on someone who was, it must be admitted, just a kid off the street. I don't think either of us knew what we were getting into. I am also thankful to my other colleagues and friends in the Permanent Mission of Israel to the United Nations and in the Prime Minister's Office in Jerusalem. You gave me a ride I'll never forget.

I am profoundly grateful to Martha K. Levin and Dominick V. Anfuso, and everyone else at Free Press, for giving me the opportunity to write this book. I am deeply indebted to my generous and talented editor, Wylie O'Sullivan, who not only helped me immeasurably during the course of this endeavor, but in the process also taught me a great deal about writing. It is impossible to overstate how much I owe my agent, Mollie Glick, for her keen insights and unfailing support. Far more than just an agent, she is also a true friend. I am also thankful to Jessica Regel, Jennifer Weltz, and Marika Josephson, and everyone else at the Jean V. Naggar Literary Agency.

I am very appreciative to all my colleagues at Ryerson University, and to my student assistants, Delana McNevin and Renee Rouse. I would like to give particular thanks to Professor Susan Cody, for her constant support, encouragement, and friendship. Thank you also to my friends in the journalism world, especially Rebecca Sinderbrand, Joseph Braude, Mark Follman, and Adam B. Kushner. Without their time, guidance, and advice this project would never have come to fruition. Thank you to Mark Svartz for introducing me to Mollie, to David "That Guy" Binns for introducing me to Wylie, and to Andy Teich for providing me with a title for this book.

I feel privileged to have such a large and close-knit family: the Ipps, Dicks, Stones, Leveys, Levines, Cohens, Cooks, and Goldbergs, my sister Simone, brother Ryan, and brother-in-law Ari. I am especially indebted to my parents, Pearl and Paul, for giving me their support through one ridiculous idea after another.

But most of all, I am grateful to my wife, Abby, for both the past and the future.

Index

About the Author

GREGORY LEVEY is a regular contributor to *Salon.com* who has also written for *The New Republic, New York Post, The Globe and Mail,* and other publications. He served as a speechwriter and delegate for the Israeli government at the United Nations and as Senior Foreign Communications Coordinator for Prime Ministers Ariel Sharon and Ehud Olmert. He has appeared on television and radio as a commentator on Israel and the Middle East and is on the faculty of Ryerson University in Toronto, Canada.